Advance Praise for

Towards Post-Blackness

Towards Post-Blackness: A Critical Study of Rita Dove's Poetry is a major contribution to literary-cultural studies on the philosophy of race. In interpreting the poet's creative and liberative journey towards self-knowledge in Hegelian terms, Roy reignites the ontological questions that permeate concepts of race, identity, and the role of language in defining ideas of the Self and the Other. This book bridges the gap between poetry and visual art to define Post-Blackness as a philosophy of life for a people straining to break away from the labels that define them.
—Prof. Bijoy H. Boruah, Professor, Department of Humanities and Social Sciences, Indian Institute of Technology Jammu, India
Author of *Fiction and Emotion: A Study in Aesthetics and the Philosophy of Mind*

Towards Post-Blackness is a valuable book that reinterprets the sensibility of a significant living Black American poet, Rita Dove, from a universal point of view. Any good poet must speak to readers everywhere; they cannot be pigeonholed to a particular place, race or identity as they transcend all identity barriers to speak to the human race. Lekha Roy argues this point in her book by approaching Dove's poetry from the Hegelian view of the relationship between self and other. I recommend the book to scholars of American poetry, world literature and minority literature in South Asia and beyond.
—Prof. Mohammad A. Quayum, Professor, College of Humanities, Arts and Social Sciences, Flinders University, Adelaide, Australia
Author of *Saul Bellow and American Transcendentalism (Twentieth Century American-Jewish Writers)*

Towards Post-Blackness: A Critical Study of Rita Dove's Poetry is a much-needed revisiting of Black aesthetics in the twenty-first century. I believe that this study on Post-Blackness and on Rita Dove as a Post-Black poet will be of great use to scholars of African-American literature and race studies. I would definitely recommend it as a valuable addition to the body of critical work available on the subject.
—Dr. Ishrat Bashir, Assistant Professor, Department of English, Central University of Kashmir, Ganderbal, Kashmir
Author of *The Naked Truth and Other Stories*

Towards Post-Blackness

Studies in Criticality

Shirley R. Steinberg
General Editor

Vol. 543

Lekha Roy

Towards Post-Blackness

A Critical Study of Rita Dove's Poetry

Foreword by Amritjit Singh

PETER LANG
Lausanne • Berlin • Bruxelles • Chennai • New York • Oxford

Library of Congress Cataloging-in-Publication Control Number: 2023026868

Bibliographic information published by the **Deutsche Nationalbibliothek.**
The German National Library lists this publication in the German
National Bibliography; detailed bibliographic data is available
on the Internet at http://dnb.d-nb.de.

Cover design by Sheetal Bhola

ISSN 1058-1634 (print)
ISBN 9781636671796 (paperback)
ISBN 9781636671789 (hardback)
ISBN 9781433196102 (ebook)
ISBN 9781433196119 (epub)
DOI 10.3726/b20952

© 2023 Peter Lang Group AG, Lausanne
Published by Peter Lang Publishing Inc., New York, USA
info@peterlang.com—www.peterlang.com

All rights reserved.
All parts of this publication are protected by copyright.
Any utilization outside the strict limits of the copyright law, without the permission of the
publisher, is forbidden and liable to prosecution.
This applies in particular to reproductions, translations, microfilming, and storage and
processing in electronic retrieval systems.

This publication has been peer reviewed.

For my parents
Sunirmal and Minoti Dutta Roy

CONTENTS

Foreword		ix
Acknowledgments		xiii
Chapter 1	Introduction	1
Chapter 2	Transcultural Space in *The Yellow House on the Corner* and *Museum*	27
Chapter 3	History and Historicity in *Thomas and Beulah* and *On the Bus with Rosa Parks*	67
Chapter 4	Deconstructing Myths in *Grace Notes* and *Mother Love*	101
Chapter 5	Redefining Black Aesthetics in *American Smooth* and *Sonata Mulattica*	145
Chapter 6	*Jouissance*: The Philosopher's *Playlist for the Apocalypse*	185
Chapter 7	Conclusion	195
	Index	205

FOREWORD

I am happy to associate myself with this monograph on Rita Dove's poetry by Lekha Roy, one of the few literary scholars in India who have had a serious interest in exploring the writings of African American women writers.

Rita Frances Dove is a distinctive presence among contemporary American writers and while many readers find her poetry beautiful, they also sometimes find it hard to understand. Although primarily a poet, Dove has also published works of fiction, drama, and essays. In 1993, Dove became the youngest poet to be named the Poet Laureate of the U.S. At least two African American poets, Robert Hayden and Gwendolyn Brooks had preceded her in that role with a different title, "Poetry Consultant at the Library of Congress." Dove used her two-year appointment to generate public interest in poetry through her travels and poetry readings. Her 1986 collection *Thomas and Beulah*, which received the 1987 Pulitzer Prize in poetry, is a thinly veiled fictional treatment of her grandparents' journey during the Great Migration from the South to Akron, Ohio, from the early years of the twentieth century into the 1960s. This narrative work evokes the fragility of the couple's lives, but also the dignity and complexity of Thomas and Beulah as individuals. Their journey is narrated in two parts: the first, "Mandolin," consists of twenty-three poems giving Thomas's side, and the second, "Canary in Bloom," gives Beulah's in twenty-one poems. Like many other African American writers during the past hundred or more years, Dove chooses to tell a human story, which is at the same time a black American story. As sometimes in relation to Jean Toomer, Wallace Thurman, Melvin B. Tolson, Robert Hayden, Charles Johnson, and Toni Morrison, attempts to reduce Dove's writings—poetry, fiction, and drama—to a unidimensional racial matrix, faces the risk of missing out on their nuance and richness. In several interviews Morrison has rejected what she calls the "white gaze," the expectation that black writers of diverse backgrounds don't become "universal," until and unless they create white characters and situations in their writings. In several interviews (such as https://www.youtube.com/watch?v=15MMmgwl1V4 and https://www.youtube.com/watch?v=-Kgq3F8wbYA), Morrison makes clear that there is only one race—the human race—and that whiteness, like blackness, is a social construct.

Roy interprets Dove's creative journey in Hegelian terms, a journey in which the poet is viewed as transcending the fixity of identities to embrace "voluntary affiliations across the color-line in a changing, post-ethnic world." Dove, Roy avers, frees up the lived spaces shared by all human beings, beyond the historical, cultural, and mythic influences they might have experienced through their racialized identities. Dove's most recent volume of poems, *Playlist for the Apocalypse* (2021), notes Roy, touches upon hopes and fears that are universal. For Dwight Garner, who reviewed the volume in *New York Times*, *Playlist* is "about the weight of American history, which," Dove believes, "we are still metabolizing. It's about mortality. This book is the first time the poet has publicly acknowledged that she has—and has had for over 20 years—a form of multiple sclerosis." And still, in her poem, "The Soup," the poet prefers to think about her dinner, and not the diagnosis the doctor has given her: "Yes, soup was what I wanted: not news/but the slow courage of the lentil/as it softened, its heart splitting into wings."

While I welcome Lekha Roy's monograph, *Towards Post-Blackness: A Critical Study of Rita Dove's Poetry*, I do not expect every reader in India or elsewhere to agree fully with her readings. Like the poet's jostling of words that Rita Dove celebrates in her life and writings, the jostling of scholarly interpretations is something we should all welcome. I expect

South Asian interest in African American writers to keep growing in the years and decades to come. I believe readings of African American history and culture offer a close cousinship to the now well-established fields of Dalit and Adivasi Studies.

~Amritjit Singh
Langston Hughes Professor Emeritus,
English & African American Studies
Ohio University

ACKNOWLEDGMENTS

I would like to thank Rita Dove for inspiring this work and for generous permission to quote from her poems in my study. I would also like to thank her husband, Fred Viebahn, for allowing me to use Prof. Dove's photograph on the cover of the book. In addition, I would like to express my gratitude to the Indian Institute of Technology Ropar for the facilities to undertake the study which was later extended into this book. I am deeply indebted to my mentors, Dr. Rajyashree Khushu-Lahiri and Dr. Rano Ringo (IIT Ropar), for their insightful guidance and support during my years of study, and to Prof. Amritjit Singh (Ohio University) for his invaluable contribution in making this book a reality. I would like to especially thank Dr. Dani Green and Dr. Sheryl Steinberg at Peter Lang, New York for recommending this work for the Emerging Scholars Award in Black Studies, and for their feedback and guidance while preparing the manuscript for publication. This study was a process of becoming, and a journey of growth for me, both personal and professional, and I wish to express my deepest gratitude to Prof. Madhu Mehrotra and Prof. Nishi Pandey (University of Lucknow), Prof. T. Ravichandran (IIT Kanpur), Prof. Rana Nayar (Panjab University), Dr. Somdev Kar and Dr. Sreekumar Jayadevan (IIT Ropar), Dr. Prema Rajagopalan (IIT Madras), Dr. Bijoy Rakshit (IIM Jammu), and Dr. Ishrat Bashir (Central University of

Kashmir) for helping to build this work through insightful comments, feedback and support. I am also thankful to the Boston Public Library, the Enoch Pratt Library at Baltimore, the American Center Library at New Delhi, the Punjabi University Library at Patiala, the OUCIP Library at Hyderabad, and the library of Avadh Girls' Degree College at Lucknow, access to whose valuable collections enriched this study.

No study can be possible without people who build an invisible support system within which ideas can take root and flourish. On this journey, I wish to thank Sufia Kidwai for building in me a love for the language and for helping to smooth the rough edges as the book progressed, Sushama and Shikha Anand for sharing their rock-solid belief in life in turbulent times, Asha Rani for her prayers, Jayanti Pandey for her presence in all phases, and Sheetal Bhola for the cover design of the book, for wisdom shared during creative phases, and for her patient and unwavering support at all stages. This endeavor would not have been possible without the encouragement and incredible support given by them. Most of all, I wish to thank my mother for a childhood filled with art and colors, and my father for lessons in patience. This book owes its origin to the garden my parents built and the colors of life that filled this garden, and I dedicate this journey to them. I am grateful to all who were an intrinsic part of the structure within which this study bore fruit, and to God and to Life for being kind to me.

· 1 ·

INTRODUCTION

"Yes, I'm an African-American poet; I'm a woman poet; I'm an American poet: all those things. But I'm a poet first." (Dove interview)

It was in an interview with Thomas on 12 August 1995 that the contemporary African American author, Rita Dove, first expressed her discomfort with African Americans being stereotyped as writing in a "racially programmed" way, and her desire to distance herself from such stereotyping. This book will examine Dove's poetry in the light of this statement, identifying in it a marked shift in Black literary aesthetics from ethnocentrism to a desire to refute labels and decenter race in everyday discourse. In the attempt to discover the origins of this need to distance oneself from prescriptive labels, the book finds a startling affinity in Dove's statement with the anti-aesthetics that revealed the discomfort generated in some artists by cultural productions in the Civil Rights era that promoted a mainly Black, ethnocentric and racially prescriptive work. This gradually imprisoned artists and their work into a political domain that rejected difference, resulting in an atmosphere where individual expression was trivialized as not being "black" enough. However, it was only much later that there would be a conscious expression of the need to free Blackness from the confines of historically and culturally defined spaces that prohibited any foray into and exploration of the varied nature of Black existence. It was only at the turn of the century that the movement was given a definitive identity by Thelma Golden, curator and director of the Studio

Museum in Harlem, and Glenn Ligon, a conceptual artist whose work explores race, language, sexuality and identity for African Americans, questioning the closed nature of essential art forms. Born of the recognition that Black aesthetics was a response to the political realities of the post-Civil Rights era that needed to adjust to changing realities in the present, Post-Blackness asserts that the politicizing of art in the sixties resulted in homogenizing and restricting Black cultural representations to definitive notions of Blackness. This was the direct result of Blackness subscribing to racial binaries, much as Whiteness did. Responding to the reality of the need for a postethnic blurring of binaries in the late twentieth and early twenty-first century, the movement stresses the need to open up Blackness beyond the narrow limits of ethnocentric definitions, thus also countering its dependence on Whiteness as the Other.

Golden and Ligon first used the term "Post-Black" in 2001 to define artists who were "adamant at not being defined as 'black' artists, though their work was steeped, in fact deeply interested, in redefining complex notions of blackness" (14). Campbell quotes Golden's observation that "they coined the phrase out of necessity, sensing that terms like 'globalism' and 'multiculturalism', the then current frames of reference for talking about young artists, were no longer useful" (317). Golden, in her introductory essay in the Freestyle catalogue, notes the varied nature of influences on art and artists in the post-Civil Rights era:

> They live in a world where their particular cultural specificity is marketed to the planet and sold back to them. As a group, they exemplify the presence of art school training in that they create work that refers to multiple histories of contemporary art and culture—both non-Western and that of the Western Modernist tradition. Their influences are rich and varied. They are both post-Basquiat and post-Biggie. (14)

This was the first overt attempt to free Blackness from historical associations, allowing Post-Black artists to refute labels and celebrate heterogeneity by exploring diversity. Artists like Robert Colescott satirized popular images of black figures, filling his work with visual imagery that questioned the whole notion of a definitive idea of Blackness. In recent times, artists like Kara Walker, Adam Pendleton, Glenn Ligon, and Adler Guerrier have used visual images to juxtapose light and shadow, white and black, truth and history, questioning the archival stereotypes that make up the memory. These artists do not refute Blackness or their historical legacy, but rather interrogate the signifiers that build up the historical narrative. Remaining rooted in Blackness while rejecting it as the predominant marker of identity, Post-Black artists counter the modernist binaries particular to Western artistic tradition to initiate a reformulation of identity markers that admits of culturally porous borders. Functioning in the interspace between language and art, Dove's poetry uses the same visual imagery to delineate the process that such a reformulation of signifiers must undergo to dismantle structures in the memory that prevent a de-essentializing of racial identity. This book analyzes the techniques used by Dove to dismantle binaries and decenter race, treating memory as made up of racialized images that function as language. Positing that this racialization involves three distinctive constituents of the cultural framework—history, myths, and music—that act as signifiers to racialize culture, it traces how the poems isolate these signifiers from their cultural context to reformulate connotations. It identifies a clear pattern in the poems that moves towards a postethnic reformulation of identity—creating transcultural space, identifying history as a metanarrative of racialized images, deconstructing the racialized nature of myths, and finally, redefining black aesthetics as a juxtaposition of contraries, setting music free to become a metaphor for the post-racial "ontological expansiveness" (Shannon 10) that characterizes Post-Black identity.

Rita Frances Dove was born in Akron, Ohio, in 1952 to Ray Dove, an industrial chemist, and his wife, Elvira Hord Dove, a homemaker. Her parents' families had migrated from the South during the Great Migration, and Dove grew up to be educated in the integrated public school system. She began writing in the 1980s, when the black essentialism that had characterized the previous decade was felt by some to be limiting for artists. She experimented with different genres, publishing poetry collections *The Yellow House on the Corner* (1980), *Museum* (1983), *Thomas and Beulah* (1986), *Grace Notes* (1989), *Selected Poems* (1993), *Mother Love* (1995), *On the Bus with Rosa Parks* (1999), *American Smooth* (2004), *Sonata Mulattica: A Life in Five Movements and a Short Play* (2009), and *Playlist for the Apocalypse: Poems* (2021), a book of short stories *Fifth Sunday* (1985), a novel *Through the Ivory Gate* (1992), a collection of essays titled *The Poet's World* (1995), and a play, *The Darker Face of the Earth* (1994). *Thomas and Beulah* won Dove the Pulitzer Prize in 1987. Poet Laureate of the United States from 1993 to 1995, Dove currently resides in Charlottesville in Virginia.

Dove's poetry signals the emergence of a new aesthetics in African American literary writing in the latter part of the twentieth century, whose roots can be traced to the Post-Black in the visual arts. African American literary writing, especially poetry, has traditionally been political in nature, a product of the moment. The Black aesthetics firmly in place when Dove was growing up, as evident in the writings of Langston Hughes, Amiri Baraka, and Maya Angelou, stressed an essentialist identity that was necessary for surviving the racist policies of the time. Their poems, for example, Hughes's "The Negro Thinks of Rivers," invoked race memory, and celebrated Blackness. However, the late 1980s saw the emergence of younger writers and what Ellis defined the "New Black Aesthetic," or NBA, that explored Blackness as a heterogeneous category, even as it celebrated a nationalistic identity that was firmly Black. However, the NBA writers, too, insisted on binaries as necessary for the purpose of defining identities, with the result that those who did not subscribe to prescriptive identities were termed cosmopolitans. When Dove began writing in the 1980s, Black Nationalist protocols were still largely in place, and even as the NBA artists redefined their relation to history, the move towards cosmopolitanism was never completed as race entered the socio-cultural domain to exert a covert influence on structures that defined identity and affiliations. Dove's first two collections show traces of the New Black Aesthetic, but her later collections move towards a more empathetic and emotionally distanced analysis of the Black man's relation to the history of slavery and to the Civil Rights Movement. Moreover, there is a realization of the need to transcend binaries and initiate affiliations across the color-line. The realization that the stress on an ethnocentric identity would only result in hegemonizing identities built on difference resulted in the desire to transcend identity markers. This paralleled the developments in Post-Black art at the time.

The latter half of the twentieth century also saw a new critical interest in decentralizing race as an identity marker, and a realization that keeping modernist binaries firmly in place by stressing on Blackness was, in fact, subscribing to the project of Whiteness. In his book, *Postethnic America*, Hollinger termed race "anachronistic" (9) and proposed replacing the term "identities," which he considered a static concept that lent credence to prescriptive ethno-racial blocs, with the more dynamic term, "affiliations" (7). His theory of postethnicity visualized a voluntary crossing over across the Du Boisian "color-line" (xi) to form affiliations. This was followed by Gilroy's contention, in *Against Race*, that identity marks divisions and subsets in social lives and defines boundaries, saying that identity often "becomes a question of power and authority" (98–99). Race was one of the fundamental levels at which identity functioned, along with region, ethnicity, and nation.

This led critics to question how race remained a dominant feature of identity. Hall describes race as a "floating signifier" or "badge" whose meaning has changed over time, yet it has remained an important system of classification for "the disposition of power" (2–5). Terming race a "discursive construct" that builds on binaries of "Inside/outside. Cultured/uncivilized. Barbarous and cultivated," he contends that these differences are given meaning through the metaphors, anecdotes, and stories that culture spins for us (3–5). These binaries, reflected in cultural productions through color codes, circumscribed identities into racially defined spaces that were essentially separate. Dyer contends that the insistence on colors as racial signifiers had resulted in black people being restricted to their bodies, a prescriptive "embodiment" which he said denied them access to the white spirit, and made them "a prey to the promptings and fallibilities of the body" (23). The embodiment of black people meant that their entire identity was circumscribed by the color of their skin. Skin color as a visual and linguistic code was part of the cultural context within which race functioned. Omi and Winant called the learning of visual codes "racial etiquette" (6), which they said was part of the social learning that occurred in childhood. According to them, racial etiquette determined much of the cultural behavior that children learned, and this included the connotative meanings that were assigned to identity markers. Race was thus, learned, through the use of signifiers that evoked historical and cultural associations in the memory, making "Blackness" what Okonofua termed a "pejorative socio-political and historical referent" (5) because of its associations with the history of slavery. In fact, these associations had become so embedded in linguistic and social structures that race became an inescapable component of everyday discourse, a "metaphysical necessity" that had "assumed a metaphorical life so completely embedded in daily discourse that it is perhaps more necessary and more on display than ever before" (Morrison 63–64). Thus, although race moved from the biological to the cultural and then to the metaphysical sphere, it remained an intrinsic part of the discourse which determined identity.

Race, then, was seen to be a cultural and discursive construct which functioned as a relational system of signifiers, much like language. Dove's idea of race was that it functioned both like language and as lived space, which she also considered a Saussurean signifier. Acquiring meaning from its relation to other signifiers in the discourse, it was defined by a historically contingent system of representation. In this, Dove was much influenced by Bachelard, who, in *The Poetics of Space*, had defined the dynamics of lived space. According to Dove, lived space also functioned as language, with the result that it could be racialized through association with a racialized cultural context. The idea of language as racialized was inferred from a number of critical studies that focused on signifiers which permeated everyday discourse. In 1997, Dyer observed that Whiteness used a system of representation based on the binary of colors, wherein white as "not coloured" represented the center, the norm, "'just' human," and all that was not white was "coloured," by its very nature different, deviant, racialized, at the margins (2). In this system of representation, black found itself on the other extreme in the spectrum of colors, the binary opposite of white. In 2017, Roy and Ringo posited race as a "'perspectival' construct" that was "reinforced by socio-cultural hegemony and made real by memory," stating that "sensory stimuli function in the form of visual and linguistic codes that inform learned behaviour" (65–66). In other words, race is perpetuated through codes that inform learned behavior and form a part of cultural discourse in everyday life. In 1995, hooks considered aesthetics as shaped by lived space that in turn shapes perspectives. Stating that "aesthetics then is more than a philosophy or theory of art and beauty; it is a way of inhabiting space, a particular location, a way of looking and becoming," she concludes that "we must learn to see" (65). Imagery was more potent than language in a century where the visual played a large role in communication because of the media, and signifiers too came to be associated with images, making them both powerful tools for hegemonic purposes.

Both the Black Aesthetic and the New Black Aesthetic artists had emphasized Blackness, and till the 1980s poets subscribed to either an ethnocentric or a cosmopolitan approach to race, celebrating binaries in forming identities. However, the end of the century saw a questioning of binaries that gave signifiers meaning in a relational system, and a Post-Black emphasis on emptying signifiers of culturally constructed meanings began to push to the forefront in the visual arts. The change in representations is evident in the resistance of black artists in the eighties and nineties to an essentialist representation of Blackness. Campbell, the curator of the Studio Museum in Harlem at the time, notes that artists like David Hammons and Kara Walker "challenged notions of positive/negative with images that confronted viewers with harsh realities no matter how unpleasant for black and white alike" (329). In fact, it was felt that Blackness as a category resisted definition, with the result that Touré, in 2011, said, "We don't change the way we perform Blackness the way we change our clothes, but consciously or subconsciously we all have subtle identity choices and we adjust depending on the situation" (65).

The diversity within the category meant that it was possible to blur binaries and reformulate the signifiers that gave meaning to structures. For this purpose, Post-Black artists like Glenn Ligon, Kara Walker, and Rashid Johnson created art that deliberately avoided signifying imagery. Using light and shadow, they removed the black body from the center of the cultural frame, thus dissociating the signifier from its historical and cultural context. Having isolated it from the relational system, it then allowed the present to decipher it without the filters of the past. In 2006, Ligon created a neon light display called *Untitled* that resembled a storefront window with the words, "I sell the shadow to sustain the substance," recalling Sojourner Truth's caption to her daguerreotype portraits in the nineteenth century. However, while Truth's portraits centered the counter-image of the nineteenth century African American woman, Ligon not only removed the black body from the gaze, but also made the signifier the signified, thus making the surface image its only connotative meaning. In making the caption in the storefront window the light and the shadow, he blurs the binaries of black/white, dark/light, removing substance (or interpretation) from the surface. Dove uses the same image in her third collection of poems, *Thomas and Beulah*, Thomas's section ending with the image of Thomas dying in his car watching "the neon script leering from the shuddering asphalt" (4). The collection ends at the threshold of the Post-Black, and it would take Dove another decade to completely free the most potent of black cultural symbols, music, from its racialized associations in the memory. Her poetry is the language of art, drawing on images to effect a cultural transformation that would not be possible in any other literary form. Post-Black art and poetry empty the signifier of recorded perspective, thus leaving the imagination free to fill the space with reformulated images.

However, Post-Blackness does not mean post-racial, in the sense of color-blindness. It is, rather, a decentering of race to make possible cross-cultural affiliations. Referring to the 2012 Studio Museum exhibition, *Fore*, Crawford says: "After an understanding of post-black as post-ideological blackness, we move to a new understanding of 'black' as an emptied but full space of imagining the unimaginable" (218). This is a refuting of the concept of ethnic purity on which modernist binaries rested. This is what Touré means when he says: "If there are forty million Black people in America then there are forty million ways to be Black…what it means to be Black has grown so staggeringly broad, so unpredictable, so diffuse that Blackness itself is undefinable" (20). For Touré, Post-Blackness is a process of self-identification that is both individual and subjective. Crawford calls it a cultural "anti-name…visualizing an opening-up of space" (11). This is a Hegelian interior space "in which blackness is taken for granted to such an extent that it does not need to be a master sign" (Crawford 11). This decentralizing of racial identity would be the only way to counter the reality of Du Bois's "world which yields him no true self-consciousness" but rather insists on a persistent "double consciousness, this sense of always looking at one's self through the eyes of others" (xi). This, however, does not refer to a world bereft of meaning, but rather a reformulation of meaning as we know it through historical and cultural continuity.

Post-Blackness did not remain restricted to the visual arts but has grown as a literary and philosophical movement at the beginning of the twenty-first century. The questioning of modernist binaries that emphasized white norms, racializing black identity and centralizing race in everyday discourse, is visible in the more recent works of Toni Morrison, Ishmael Reed, and Rita Dove. Morrison argues for the recognition of the "Africanism used as a fundamental fictional technique by which to establish character" (80), that she says is an intrinsic part of the works of many American authors like Edgar Allen Poe and Ernest Hemingway. This, she argues, is proof that Blackness is an intrinsic part of American history, but the racialization of signifiers has meant that the two colors have historically remained disparate domains with their own (pure) centers and (impure) margins. Reed talks of the black man as imprisoned by history, and of positioning himself on the threshold in order to project himself on to both sides of the color-line. This corroborates Touré's definition of the Post-Black—"being rooted in but not restricted by" Blackness (37). Although Li argues that Touré's definition of Post-Blackness "threatens to become a dangerous abdication of history," stating that "black literature can never be post-black because the signifyin(g) language of black narrative affirms history," and "the tradition of African American literary expression refuses the unmooring of racial identity" (45), this study argues that the recognition of signifiers that emphasize Blackness is exactly what makes a Post-Black reformulation of these signifying affiliations possible in literature. Dove's idea of race as both language and lived space makes it possible for her to expand contours to imagine the unimaginable, using metaphors and images to reconfigure signifiers in much the same way that art does. Much as hooks states, Dove's technique involves converting the "anti-aesthetic" of owned space into the aesthetics of created space—"to re-open the creative space that much of the black aesthetic movement closed down" (hooks 65–69). In order to achieve this, Dove positions herself in a space that is liminal. Talking of the position on the threshold as being extra-sensory, she says that in this position:

...the exterior sensations filter into the interior space, taking up residence in one's storehouse of memories, becoming *recollections* of the outside. This sets up in me a peculiar state, one in which I am in two places at once and yet, curiously, not there at all. It is the moment of ultimate possibility, and of ultimate irresponsibility. Of course there is no absolute demarcation of the moment when *in* becomes *out*; indeed, one passes through a delicious sliding moment when one is *neither* in nor out but *floating*, suspended above the interior and exterior ground. (*The Poet's World* 24)

Thus, while Morrison and Hollinger state the precepts that advocate the need for a Post-Black reformulation of signifiers, Dove's poems trace the process through which this reformulation must take place.

However, repudiating race was not going to be easy, especially for a black poet. Vendler says: "Any black writer in America must confront, as an adult, the enraging truth that the inescapable social accusation of blackness becomes, too early for the child to resist it, a strong element of inner self-definition" (61). However, the reality of racial objectification escaped Dove in early life, partly because of a childhood spent in an integrated neighborhood, till her confrontation with it on her travels to Europe as a Fulbright scholar. In an interview with Taleb-Khyar, she talks of the alienation that she faced:

Suddenly, in Germany I was on display in a strange environment where some people pointed with fingers at me and others pitied me as a symbol for centuries of brutality and injustice against Blacks...serious travel can heighten the awareness a writer needs to see many sides of a story." (Ingersoll 77)

Dove's travels to Europe, like those of many African Americans like Langston Hughes and Frederick Douglass before her, gave her a new perspective on the complexity of double consciousness, making her aware of the double objectification that black women faced. It was during her travels in Europe that much of her work, especially the ones dealing with myths, was conceptualized. Her poems project themselves across the Atlantic to establish a transcultural connection that dismantles established notions of history and race as a closed category. She crafts a careful path in her collections towards a Post-Black reformulation of the signifiers that both inform and are informed by culture, and which ultimately inform identity. Towards this end, each of her collections represents an ongoing journey towards dismantling hegemonic structures. Thus, while her first collection of poems creates transcultural space by emptying signifiers of their traditional associations through a transatlantic crossing over that establishes cross-cultural frames of history, the second collection then carefully places within this trans-space a series of objects that contradicts traditional grouping. After that, each successive collection deconstructs a particular signifier as a racialized cultural construct, ending with a Post-Black reformulation of black aesthetics, and the subsequent (artistic) freedom to explore spaces unconstrained by the color-line. The recurring motif of travel and the traveler in all her poems posits Post-Blackness as a journey, in a liminal area of the reconstitution of identity that bespeaks possibilities.

However, Dove's poems are rich not just because of their understanding of the complex nature of racialized identities and their tracing of a pattern to deconstruct race as a cultural construct, but also because of their richness as lyric poems. It is interesting that she chooses poetry to explicate the nuanced variations in the process that both racializes signifiers and makes race a signifier. For Dove, poetry is the language of art, and she draws on images to effect a cultural transformation that would not be possible in any other form. In making language synonymous with lived space, she identifies in poetry a capacity to carry metaphor and allusions in a tangential manner, making it the only form she believes capable of deconstructing "gaps" or "silences"—the shadows in lived space—as active components of the linguistic structure. Dove's poetry lets the silence reverberate, informing the narrative content and imagery to a large extent. Further, to Dove, poetry is the highest floor that can be occupied by the individual. She quotes Bachelard in *The Poet's World* to define poetry's allusion to lived space:

> Words—I often imagine this—are little houses, each with its cellar and garret. Commonsense lives on the ground floor, always ready to engage in "foreign commerce," on the same level as the others, as the passers-by, who are never dreamers. To go upstairs in the word house, is to withdraw, step by step; while to go down to the cellar is to dream, it is losing oneself in the distant corridors of an obscure etymology, looking for treasures that cannot be found in words. To mount and descend in the words themselves—this is a poet's life. To mount too high or descend too low, is allowed in the case of poets, who bring earth and sky together. (qtd. in Dove 18)

Having conceptualized poetry as lived space that allows for the extremes of light and shadow, Dove then juxtaposes form and content from the lighted and the dark recesses of memory in her poems. Her use of traditional European forms and myths have caused critics like Kamionowski to call her a "cultural traveller" and to identify a "literal and metaphorical nomadism" (12) in her works, yet the careful juxtaposition of opposites contends that Dove neither borrows nor appropriates cultural material; the poems are not the journals of a cultural traveler, but are rather the deliberate bridging of black and white into a single cultural frame. This can be traced back to Du Bois's discomfort with closed intellectual spaces and the attendant denial to the black man of his share of western cultural legacy. In *The Souls of Black Folk*, he remarks on the absurdity of separate racial spaces demarcated by the color-line, whose origins are political, to effect ontological distinctions:

> I sit with Shakespeare and he winces not. Across the color-line I move arm in arm with Balzac and Dumas, where smiling men and welcoming women glide in gilded halls. From out of the caves of evening that swing between the strong-limbed earth and the tracery of stars, I summon Aristotle and Aurelius and what soul I will, and they come all graciously with no scorn or condescension. So wed with Truth, I dwell above the veil. (76)

The juxtaposition of black and white form and matter in Dove's poems has a dual purpose—first, by eschewing black forms, Dove strips her poems of any but surface meaning by a process of defamiliarization, and second, as the black subject matter strains against the boundaries imposed by the structured European forms, it emphasizes the affective. By infusing black subject matter into the traditional structure of European forms, Dove expands contours by positing the Post-Black aesthetic as a black-white domain of contradictions. By avoiding the use of free verse and black colloquialism, Dove gives her poems their narrative flight through the interspersing of words and silences, while the contradictory nature of the images calls for changed contours.

Written in the form of lyrics, sonnets, and, at one place, the villanelle, Dove's poems use enjambments and a variety of voices to achieve narrative probability. It is this interweaving of form and content—lyric and narrative—that makes the poems metaphors rich in imagery. In an interview, Dove describes the metaphorical interweaving of temporal sequences to create a pattern:

> Lyrics are discrete moments. On the other hand, a lot of narrative poems tend to bog down in the prosier transitional moments. I didn't see very many long narrative poems that really weren't smaller poems linked together. So one of the things I was trying to do was string moments as beads on a necklace. In other words, I have lyric poems which, when placed one after the other, reconstruct the sweep of time. (Ingersoll 67)

The lyrical cadence of the poems sweeps the reader along with it, and "the overall sweep of the poem threads motif to motif into an enhancing musical harmony" (Righelato 72). Music, for Dove, is the black man's language, drawing him into its stoic folds in a racialized world, and is the perfect vehicle to achieve the transition across the color-line. Although music accompanies the words in every poem, it is in *American Smooth* and *Sonata Mulattica* that Dove achieves what Gilroy termed the third stage in the progress towards self-realization, that of:

> ...liberating music from its status as mere commodity and by the associated desire to use it to demonstrate the reconciliation of art and life, that is, by exploring its pursuit of artistic and even aesthetic experience not just as a form of compensation, paid as the price of an internal exile from modernity, but as the favoured vehicle for communal self-development (*The Black Atlantic* 124).

This music draws from both black and white forms. Gilroy notes that this is the third and final stage in the project of liberation, which, as the study observes, finally frees Blackness as a signifier from its historical associations by achieving ontological expansiveness, a characteristic of Post-Black identity. The freedom to move in and out of both black and white spaces freely, which was earlier a privilege allowed only to the white man, is what Dove considers real freedom. This is especially significant in the light of her theory of lived space. Her poems stress this by showing the destruction that an incomplete psyche marred by the racialization of spaces can cause, ultimately resulting in the obliteration of artistic creativity, and also the *jouissance* that marks artistic freedom unrestricted by race. The role of art as a tool for Hegelian progression towards freedom is also analyzed in these collections, each moving the black man towards self-awareness as the ultimate aim of historical progression.

The critical study of Post-Blackness as a movement has mostly focused on the visual arts. In this sphere, where the movement originated, critics like Golden and Ligon have called Post-Black artists "adamant about not being labeled 'black' artists, though their work was steeped, in fact deeply interested, in redefining complex notions of blackness" (*Freestyle* catalogue). Ligon says, "We have to move beyond these clear binaries about where culture is imagined to reside and who has ownership of it" (qtd. in Touré 41). Campbell stresses of Post-Black artists that "they didn't reject an ethnic designation for themselves; they rejected an ethnic label for their work" (318). In the exhibition organized by Golden, the curator of the Studio Museum in Harlem in 2001, she brought together works of artists whose art was in radical opposition to the Black Aesthetic, of which Rico Gatson, Nadine Robinson, and Rashid Johnson were important ones. Other artists like Kara Walker also displayed attributes that were Post-Black. Although Walker's silhouettes ruthlessly dismantle romantic notions of slavery, for example, as portrayed in Beecher Stowe's novel, they do so by eschewing binaries of good/bad, victim/perpetrator, much as Dove's poems do. Touré says that Walker "looks at power relationships in very complex ways, she moves away from this simplistic binary between good and evil in terms of the way she recalls slavery" (35). Hers is a visual ripping apart of images to bring them together again in her silhouettes, but this time with the gaps in the narrative visible. When Walker was asked by Touré to define Post-Blackness, she said, "individualism," stating that the "racial pride" of the Black Arts Movement "felt to me a little passé maybe" (qtd. in Touré 37). Johnson says that his generation feels "less of a need to define the Black experience so aggressively" (qtd. in Touré 42). Touré says:

> ...to say "I'm a Black artist" seems to put politics and identity at the forefront of an aesthetic practice. This post-Black generation of artists saw themselves working with Black subject matter as the generations before but they were working in a world that understood that subject matter as being cultural in a general way. (42–43)

This disjunct made their works representations of a political ideology that translated into cultural life. In the sphere of the literary, Dove uses the technique used by the Post-Black artists of deconstructing images of the past to reveal gaps in the metanarrative of history. In eschewing binaries, she eschews the restriction of spaces that would otherwise adhere to racial configurations. The purpose is to delink signifiers—linguistic and visual—from the cultural contexts in which they were framed. While Walker deconstructs literary and cultural representations in her work, Dove deconstructs three constituents of culture that act as signifiers in the cultural framework of identity construction—history, myths, and music.

Although Dove's attempt to decenter race as the primary signifier of historical and cultural memory reflects much of the discomfort that some artists in the post-Civil Rights era felt, her poems manage to subvert modernist binaries through spatial revisioning. This has resulted in a variety of responses to her work, much of which centralize Blackness as the identifying lens through which any Black writer's work is to be studied. The critical study of Dove's works has ranged from studies that take into account her general outlook as well as those that deal with specific features of Blackness that are evident in her work. Righelato terms her "a much-traveled cosmopolitan figure" (1), saying that "there is a Rilkean intensity in the condensing of her symbolist poems, mythic, culturally questing, ironic, yet with an ardor tamped in their meticulous craftings" (5). Dove herself had stated in the Foreword to *Mother*

Love that the poems in the collection, mostly sonnets, were "in homage and as counterpoint to Rilke's *Sonnets to Orpheus*" (1). In contrast, Vendler studies the difficulties Dove must have faced as a Black poet, and states that "no black poet has blackness as sole identity; and in lyric poems, poems of self-definition, one risks serious self-curtailment by adopting only a single identity-marker" (63). Thus, she concludes that Dove does not stress on Blackness as solely defining her poetry, but does not escape it either. She chooses as part of her œuvre, men and women who are black *and* intellectual, with the purpose that "these historical personae, taken one by one, female and male, represent Dove's steps, characteristically objective ones, toward the representation of her own identity as a black" (65). This quest for her own place in the history of Blackness often refers to associations that symbols in the present evoke in the memory. For Dove, the lyric is not an idyllic form devoid of the political; it is, rather, a form that is best suited to explore a reformulation of these symbolic associations.

Much of Dove's work is seen as her own inward journey towards understanding what Blackness means for the present generation. Identifying Dove's anxieties about miscegenation and incest, both biological and cultural, in many of her poems, Pereira classifies Dove as "an elder sister/sister of the NBA, the first major African American artist to articulate New Black Aesthetic poetics" (2), tracing in her work "mulatto imagery and symbolism" (5). Kamionowski, however, talks of a nomadic restlessness that takes Dove on cultural travels, yet he traces in her work a tendency to return home, that is, to a celebration of Blackness. Saying that "Dove's literal and metaphorical *nomadism* allows her to borrow and assemble her poetic material across seemingly rigid categories," he classifies her as a "cultural mulatto," which Ellis had not in his essay, "The New Black Aesthetic," stating: "Dove can be perceived as Trey Ellis' 'cultural mulatto'—a black artist 'educated by a multi-racial mix of cultures' who can 'navigate easily in the white world'" (Ellis 235 qtd. in Kamionowski 12). Ellis had earlier refrained from including Dove among the NBA artists, probably because of the complex nature of her transatlantic crossing.

Dove's poetry reflects the complexity of the transatlantic crossing by defying labels. Steffen analyzes Dove's aesthetics as bridging the political and the aesthetic to explore issues of Blackness. She studies "her aesthetic and thematic departure" from the Black Arts Movement, saying that "she picks up the political impetus, a sense of politics as the given starting point...but refuses and ironizes the clichéd political discourse and aesthetic dilettantism" (7). She also studies her macro- and micro-poetics of space, observing her delineation of the dialectics of inside and outside with reference to cultural space, coming closest to identifying her work as Post-Black when she talks of her celebration of Blackness as "black *jouissance* beyond sociocultural concepts, affirmative action, and the like," saying that "it simply and uniquely *is* a celebration of black nature in its beauty, humanity, and joy of life" (149). She sets out to explore what color means to Dove in her book, *Crossing Color*, comparing her celebration of the impure in her refuting of labels to Said's:

> No one, today is purely one thing. Labels like Indian, or woman, or Muslim, or American are not more than starting-points, which if followed into actual experience for only a moment are quickly left behind. Imperialism consolidated the mixture of cultures and identities on a global scale. But its worst and most paradoxical gift was to allow people to believe that they were only, mainly, exclusively, white, or Black, or Western, or Oriental. (Said 336 qtd. in Steffen ix)

Steffen's comments about Dove's relation to the history of Blackness and the Black aesthetic are similar to Rampersad's observation that "in many ways, her poems are exactly the opposite of those that have come to be considered quintessentially black verse in recent years." Rampersad says:

> Instead of looseness of structure, one finds in her poems remarkably tight control; instead of a reliance on reckless exploration, one recognizes discipline and practice, and long, taxing hours in competitive university poetry workshops and in her study; instead of a range of reference limited to personal confession, one finds personal reference disciplined by a measuring of distance and a prizing of objectivity; instead of an obsession with the theme of race, one finds an eagerness, perhaps even an anxiety to transcend—if not actually to repudiate—black cultural nationalism in the name of a more inclusive sensibility. (53)

Both, though, stop just short of identifying her work as Post-Black, or tracing in her work a continuation of the discomfort with closed spaces that Du Bois had talked about. Thus, though a number of critics have identified Dove's work with reference to the Black man's relation to the Civil Rights Movement and to Blackness, or her aesthetics with reference to her position in a diachronous chain of African American women poets like Gwendolyn Brooks, Audre Lorde, Nikki Giovanni, and Sonia Sanchez, Dove's poems trace their ancestry to the visual arts, both in terms of aesthetics and content, indicating the emergence of Post-Blackness as a literary and philosophical movement, paralleling Post-Black art in its refutation of binaries and its refusal to adhere to prescriptive definitions of Blackness. Stressing individuality, her poems foreground the personal against the backdrop of the political, deconstructing the cultural as a racialized structure of signifiers that have gained meaning through discourse.

Post-Blackness itself is a movement that is just beginning to be visible in the literary sphere. Crawford calls it an "anti-name" (11), explaining its relation with Blackness and its own emergence as a hyphenated category that identifies itself with the Black Arts Movement yet moves on from it:

> The black post-blackness of the BAM was most nuanced when it understood movement itself as the ethos of black style; the black post-blackness of the twenty-first century is the most nuanced when it troubles blackness without worrying about its loss of blackness. (6)

Calling it "a state of suspension," Crawford says that "in this state of suspension, black consciousness-raising and black experimentation are inseparable; being and becoming cannot be separated" (2). Gilroy had also talked of "the problems of racialised ontology and identity—the tension between being and becoming black" (*The Black Atlantic* 116) that earlier writers like Du Bois had found difficult to escape in the racialized South.

Post-Blackness does not, thus, institute a separate category and a complete break from the Black Arts Movement; it is, rather, a process of becoming, where the answers to the quest are in the journey. This reveals itself in the recurring motif of the traveler in Dove's poems, as well as the titles of most of the poems being mostly linguistic metaphors for transition. The vertical drop of some of her poems as well as her use of enjambment parallel the use of light and shadow, and the deliberately visible gaps, in Post-Black art. Li's contention that the techniques of Post-Black art cannot be equally applied to literary forms resists the effective use of imagery to signify the relational. She says that "the expansive nature of post-blackness poses critical problems to the notion of a coherent racialized identity and consequently to the development of a recognizable literary tradition," cautioning that "in understanding a literary tradition, we must bear in mind the formal qualities that shape language and narrative. There is a crucial gap here between individuals who are black and literature that is black" (47). However, it is precisely in the separation of the poet and his art, through an eschewing of labels and an opening up of the Self to the Other, that the literary is able to encompass what is essentially a visual transformation of the links between signifiers and their historical and cultural contexts.

In order to study Dove's movement towards the Post-Black Aesthetic, deconstructing racialized representations that define history as a metanarrative and give meaning to race as a language, the book has been divided into seven chapters, each tracing the pattern of deconstructing the various facets that make race a cultural construct. While the Introduction sets out the arguments for positing Post-Blackness as a literary aesthetic that developed from the visual arts, and Dove as a Post-Black poet, Chapter 2 presents Post-Blackness as a liminal area of existence, outlining the creation of a transcultural space that functions as a Foucauldian heterotopia by emptying signifiers of their traditional associations in Dove's first collection of poems, *The Yellow House on the Corner*, published in 1980, and then filling this space with objects that contradict the objects in the traditional European museum in *Museum*, published in 1983. Titled "Transcultural Space in *The Yellow House on the Corner* and *Museum*," the chapter explores Dove's poetry as an attempt to subvert the politics of consciousness of the self, built through racialized imagery. In the first collection, *The Yellow House on the Corner*, the individual is imagined as standing on the threshold, in a liminal area of existence. The title of the collection is significant. Pereira says that "a corner offers an urban parallel to the idea of a crossroads, symbolic of identity choices, destiny, and change" (54). This presents the idea of choice as individual. This collection introduces each of the contexts that give signifiers meaning as markers of identity, identifying three such associations that Dove's next collections will deconstruct—history, myth, and the aesthetics of music. The collection is divided into five sections, each a juxtaposition of the past and the present, of memory and experience. Rooted in Blackness, historical memory and the legacy of slavery occupy central place in each visitation. Tracing Dove's concept of race as both that of a language and a spatial domain, the chapter studies how the liminal space allows for an opening up of contours in the memory to transform occupied space into created space by the process of delinking signifiers from their cultural contexts. Creating what Steffen terms "artistic enspacement" (28) to initiate a crossing over into the psycho-spatial domain of the Other, the new space enables postethnic affiliations and a reformulation of Blackness.

Dove's second collection of poems, *Museum*, is an exploring of the cultural artifacts that fill the transcultural space that the first collection created. Recognizing the museum as the place where most cultural myths originate, Dove incorporates the characteristic features of both the BAM and the NBA, as well as the recognition of (rooted) universalism as a feature of contemporary identity. Dusting the cobwebs from the newly created transcultural space in the memory, the poems in the collection subject the gaps in the memory, the metaphorical fossils, to intense scrutiny. In its exploration, the collection includes trauma from both sides of the Atlantic, the masculine nature of the Civil Rights Movement, and a revisiting of the Haitian massacre. It also places art and the artist in the museum, subjecting both to scrutiny, and making the creator reflect on his own part in the narrative. The collection explores how the choice of artifacts decides the narrative, aiming to dismantle myths that originate in the closed spaces of the traditional museum that treats history as a racially disjointed narrative.

Chapter 3, titled "History and Historicity in *Thomas and Beulah* and *On the Bus with Rosa Parks*," explores the underside of history in these two collections, foregrounding individual lives against the backdrop of important historical events. Dove's theory of history is that of a Hegelian dialectics of historical progression towards absolute knowledge or freedom, a freedom that Dove defines as the achievement of ontological expansiveness for black people. This builds on Post-Blackness's insistence on freeing Blackness as a signifier from the constrictions of its historical associations. In treating history as individual experience, Dove reveals the gaps that belie the metanarrative of officially recorded history. Describing each event as historically contingent, the poet insists that no moment exists by itself, but necessarily contains within itself a *trace* of moments that lead up to it as well as an anticipation of future events. Further, it is individual lives that constitute history. History, Dove seems to say, is a metanarrative of images that are often suppressed beneath linguistic structures that preclude "the union of erudite knowledge and local memories which allows us to establish a historical knowledge of struggles" (Foucault 71). When the focus is turned on individual experiences, the self builds on its own interpretation of what is happening at the moment; history becomes a collection of individual interpretations or micro-narratives that often exist as gaps in the official version. In foregrounding the individual, Dove's treatment of history foreshadows and references Post-Blackness and postethnicity.

Thomas and Beulah, written in 1986, revisits the Great Migration that occurred between 1916 and 1970 as lived experience. The Great Migration was one of the defining events of the twentieth century, shaping black lives in as definitive a way as slavery had in the earlier century, signaling not just an economic, but a cultural demographic shift as well. Dove captures the event from two different perspectives, that of Thomas, loosely structured around the life of her grandfather, and of Beulah, representing her grandmother, Georgianna. For Dove, history is lived apart from official records; it is in the everyday lived experience of common men and women that history is to be found. Here, the personal is political, and reality is metaphorical. The poems in the collection are Dove's use of the African practice of weaving memory into facts. The rejection of temporal linearity reconstitutes the teleology of history, placing the individual at the center of a perspectival circle, each part of which is vital to the whole narrative.

Dove's sixth collection of poems, *On the Bus with Rosa Parks*, is a more explicit outlining of the process that defines a great historical moment. The collection was published in 1999 and retains Dove's signature as a feminist outlining of the Civil Rights movement. Rosa Parks, whose refusal to give up her seat in the bus to a white fellow passenger in 1955 started the historic Montgomery Bus Boycott against racial segregation in an act of defiance that would become one of the defining moments in the movement, has been overshadowed in official history by male Civil Rights leaders whose role in the movement received greater prominence. The collection itself was published thirteen years after *Thomas and Beulah*, with four more volumes of poetry, a novel and a play having been published by Dove in the interim, yet it begins where *Thomas and Beulah* left off. It is divided into five sections, the first describing the sequence of an ordinary life—birth, graduation, job, marriage, children—before the next four sections discuss the importance of freedom in that ordinary life. Implying that history is actually a process, the volume explores how the ancestors of people who played an active role in the Civil Rights Movement were people whose lives lead up to the historically defining moment, which carried forward to post-Civil Rights cultural and social life as well. *On the Bus with Rosa Parks* utilizes the changing contours of lived space delineated in Dove's first collection to facilitate the intellectual exploration that prepares the African American for the idea of freedom. She concludes that only when the black-white becomes a constituent unit in history does the black man achieve freedom from restrictive (racialized) spaces, and only then can he appreciate Lady Freedom.

Chapter 4, titled "Deconstructing Myths in *Grace Notes* and *Mother Love*," studies Dove's deconstruction of myths by presenting them as narrative bridges across concepts of race, space, and time. This chapter is a Post-Black exploration of how myths function as racialized signifiers that inform cultural discourse. This follows Hall's theory of race as a "discursive practice," given meaning through the metaphors, anecdotes, and stories that culture spins for us (Hall 2). Myths, as a form of story that endures over time, are part of the culture. Race, according to Hall, acquires meaning in the cultural system as a "floating signifier" or "badge" (6–7) that perpetuates itself through discursive practice. The chapter studies how Dove deconstructs the discursive practices that have given race, a socio-cultural construct that functions much like language, meaning. Taking as a framework the theories of Hall, Lévi-Strauss, and Barthes, it deconstructs the racialized nature of myths in Dove's fourth and fifth collections of poems, *Grace Notes* (1989) and *Mother Love* (1995). Stating that myths function like language, it studies how Dove's poems analyze them as signifiers that acquire meaning through their relation to other, racially informed signifiers in a cultural continuum. By taking a myth out of this system, she isolates it from its cultural context to prove the fallacy of its racially informed nature. Myths are also deconstructed as delusionary filters that prevent an acceptance of present reality. This realization initiates a Post-Black reformulation of the components that inform discourse, crossing over into the psycho-spatial domain of the Other in the poems to explore the cultural contexts that inform both literary associations and reality through a bridging of myth and reality, ancient and contemporary, black and white.

Much like Dove's perspective, the allusions to the mythic in *Grace Notes* are tangential, more an obtuse comparison than a bold transposing as in her next collection. Like similes, they serve to open up the contours of the image to a wide range of references. Referring to the Biblical myth of Eden and the great Fall, and, having proved in the first section that one association leads to another, Dove posits the idea of the Edenic within oneself. The struggle to retreat from the Symbolic is visible in the poems, bringing together race memory and Biblical imagery in a search for the self that is significant. The journey down the Mississippi river is significant in that it invokes Hughes's "The Negro speaks of Rivers." The "slippage" associated with rivers associates Biblical genesis with the Negro's soul, thus tracing his ancestry back to the beginning of the world. It is also the linguistic slippage that allows the journey down the river to mark the fluidity of racial identity. Presenting the specifics of the mythical Eden as a utopia of images that precludes the acceptance of reality, the collection posits that it is only in acceptance that the individual is able to enter the Edenic within, ending on a hard questioning of the reality of contemporary life in America.

In *Mother Love*, Dove makes the Greek myth of Persephone and Demeter a metaphorical revisitation of the black mother-daughter relationship in the twentieth century. The collection builds itself around the myth of Demeter, the Greek goddess of the earth, and her daughter Persephone, the Greek goddess of fertility, to weave a tale about the grief of a mother separated from her daughter, a common feature of slave life, and the myth of black natal isolation.

This collection is a significant example of postethnic affiliation across the color-line, pain a connecting factor between the races. It is a transition from the ethnocentric to the postethnic, the acceptance of a cultural affiliation between the victim and the perpetrator for a shared future, a Post-Black acceptance of the state of in-betweenness and of trauma as part of identity. As the motif of the traveler recurs towards the end, it emphasizes the journey being an individual one. This journey posits the acceptance of a reality that must both converge on the mythical and finally diverge from it.

Chapter 5 outlines how Black aesthetics has metamorphosed into the Post-Black, analyzing African American literary aesthetics as it moved from a specifically Black aesthetic in the 1960s and 1970s to an avant-garde New Black Aesthetic in the 1980s, and is at the threshold of a Post-Black aesthetic that shaped itself towards the end of the twentieth century and the beginning of the twenty-first. The chapter studies two of Dove's latest collections of poems as the movement towards a crescendo of freedom for the black man from the shackles of identifiers that bind him to the color of his skin. Rich in metaphor and imagery, the collections trace music as the vehicle for moving towards the realization of the destructive nature of modernist binaries both on the human psyche and on artistic creativity.

American Smooth and *Sonata Mulattica*, published in 2004 and 2009 respectively, exemplify most clearly the Post-Black aesthetic. In making music the tenor for change, Dove follows the Black tradition, but deviates from it in including *all* music, not just black music, as free for the African American to inherit. Hers is not a cultural borrowing; it is, rather, an extending of cultural borders to admit the Other. Further, in making music not just the vehicle, but the tenor, for change, Dove's poems follow Gilroy's identification of the stages towards self-realization in black cultural representations to indicate a shift in the status of music as an independent cultural variant in the politics of representation. This tenor for change is political as well as personal, and even as *American Smooth* takes the reader through the metaphorical twists and turns of ballroom dancing, *Sonata Mulattica* is a culmination of musical cadence that confronts the core of the problem of identity resolution for African Americans at the end of the twentieth century—miscegenation, and the politics of silence surrounding it. *American Smooth* sets the rules of the dance as a partnership where each sets the other free to dance individually, initiating the metaphorical journey that is Post-Black in its stress on individual freedom as the condition for a confrontation with trauma. This confrontation, outlined in *Sonata Mulattica*, will allow for the ontological expansiveness that Post-Blackness posits as the essential nature of a Black identity freed from the trauma of the past. The destruction that marks continued adherence to ontologically confined spaces that are racially defined could not be clearer.

Dove's seventh collection of poems, *American Smooth*, is divided into five sections, three of which comprise poems on dance. The sections are an exercise in grace and rhythmic movement, an experiment in balancing community and freedom. The poems, much like the form they represent, liberate the spirit with the individuality of the rhythmic self, carrying the self into a Paradise of Hegelian withdrawal. Music here is a language in itself. The rhythm mimics the beats of the heart, expressing desires that cannot be fulfilled without accepting the contraries that complete the person. In an interview, Dove says:

> The way that a chord will resolve itself, is something that applies to my poems—the way that, if it works, the last line of the poem, or the last word, will resolve something that has been hanging for a while. (Ingersoll 154)

This journey from the outward worldly activity to inwardness is what the poems trace. Towards the end of the collection, the objective contemplation of nature moves to a contemplative internalizing of nature. In this collection, Dove likens creativity to life, admitting that the journey cannot be easy. Despite the advances made by science, phenomenological questions remain the same. The musings of the creative mind are also a metaphorical quest for identity in the real world, and the deferred nature of the quest is a feature of the postmodern celebration of inconclusiveness.

Dove's next collection, titled *Sonata Mulattica*, written in 2009, is a specifically Post-Black quest for identity in a postethnic world. The collection tells the story of George Augustus Polgreen Bridgetower (1778–1860), the biracial violinist who is best remembered for being the first performer of Beethoven's "Kreutzer" Sonata. Born of a Polish woman and an African prince, Bridgetower was a talented violinist who made his debut in Paris at the age of nine. In 1803, he traveled to Vienna to meet Ludwig van Beethoven, performing with him on stage on 24 May at the Augarten Theatre, Beethoven on the piano and Bridgetower on the violin. Beethoven, impressed by Bridgetower's talent, dedicated his Violin Sonata no. 9 to him, with the dedication "*Sonata per un mulattico lunatico.*" Undoubtedly, Dove's use of the term "mulattica" in the title of her collection is an ironic reference to Beethoven's calling Bridgetower a "lunatic and a mulatto." It is also a tangential reference to the ironic reality that *both* Bridgetower and Beethoven were mulattoes, in the sense of each being incomplete without the other, their different skin colors notwithstanding. Race is a subtle force in the spectacle involving the two, and Bridgetower's exoticism is always at the forefront of his persona as a musician. However, in spite of being equals in artistic talent, the naturalization of the dichotomy of the normal/exotic is clearly evident in the image of the two figures on stage, both equally talented, distinguishable only by the color of their skin. The downfall of both after their separation points to the necessity of the acceptance of the miscegenated psyche for creative genius to function as a whole.

Chapter 6 describes the post-racial worldview of a free man, firmly rooted in his black ancestry, yet unconstrained by the contours of predefined Blackness. Dove's latest collection, *Playlist for the Apocalypse: Poems* (2021), published after a gap of twelve years, is the lived experience of the artist freed of the label and the associated connotations of Blackness. The poems are the impressions of a black person who has lived through her own complex history and who revisits sites of history to explore what freedom means to people around the world. It is a world that is perfect in its imperfection; it is Steffen's concept of "black *jouissance*" (149) that marks the post-racial experience of the black man having achieved ontological expansiveness. As in all of Dove's earlier collections, the motif of the traveler is a recurrent one.

The study concludes with a summing up of the various facets of Post-Blackness that Dove's work exemplifies. Stating that the Post-Black movement is still in its nascent stage in the literary sphere, it argues that much of Post-Black literature functions like the visual arts, through imagery. It also makes it clear that Post-Black does not mean post-racial in any but the Hegelian sense, and should not be confused with color blindness. Admitting that the need to decenter race in cultural discourse would need an understanding of the way Whiteness hegemonized identities, it identifies Dove's delineating of the process through which a reformulation of spatial contours and linguistic associations was necessary to admit of new meanings. This requires a reformulation of the cultural context that gives meaning to language. The study ends on a note of hope for race relations and trauma resolution, but does not propose that the present movement suggests a utopian solution to issues concerning race in the United States. As the title suggests, Post-Blackness is both a dynamic process and an individual one.

Works Cited

Bachelard, Gaston. *The Poetics of Space*. Translated by Maria Jolas. Beacon P, 1994.
Campbell, Mary Schmidt. "African American Art in a Post-Black Era." *Women & Performance: A Journal of Feminist Theory* 17.3 (2007): 317–30.
Crawford, Margo Natalie. *Black Post-Blackness*. U of Illinois P, 2017.
Dove, Rita. *American Smooth*. W. W. Norton, 2004.
———. *Grace Notes*. W. W. Norton, 1989.
———. "An Interview with Rita Dove." By M. Wynn Thomas. *The Swansea Review*, 1995, www.english.illinois.edu/maps/poets/a_f/dove/mwthomas.htm. Accessed August 1, 2015.
———. *Mother Love*. 1995. W. W. Norton, 1996.
———. *Museum*. Carnegie Mellon UP, 1983.
———. *On the Bus with Rosa Parks*. W. W. Norton, 1999.
———. *Playlist for the Apocalypse: Poems*. W. W. Norton, 2021.
———. *The Poet's World*. Library of Congress, 1995.
———. *Sonata Mulattica: A Life in Five Movements and a Short Play*. W. W. Norton, 2009.
———. *Thomas and Beulah*. Carnegie Mellon UP, 1986.
———. *The Yellow House on the Corner*. Carnegie Mellon UP, 1989.
Du Bois, W. E. B. *The Souls of Black Folk*. Dover, 1994.
Dyer, Richard. *White: Essays on Race and Culture*. Routledge, 1997.
Ellis, Trey. "The New Black Aesthetic." *Callaloo* 12.1 (1989): 233–51.
Fanon, Frantz. *Black Skin, White Masks*. 1952. Translated by Charles Lam. Pluto P, 1986.
Foucault, Michel. "Of Other Spaces: Utopias and Heterotopias." *Architecture/Mouvement/Continuité*, Oct., 1984, www.web.mit.edu/allanmc/www/foucault1.pdf. Accessed June 8, 2014.
———. *Power/Knowledge: Selected Interviews and Other Writings 1972–1977*, edited by Colin Gordon. Translated by Gordon, Colin et al., Pantheon, 1980.
Gilroy, Paul. *Against Race: Imagining Political Culture Beyond the Color Line*. The Belknap P of Harvard UP, 2000.
———. *The Black Atlantic: Modernity and Double Consciousness*. Harvard UP, 1993.
Golden, Thelma. *Freestyle*, exhibition catalogue, April 28–June 24, 2001, Studio Museum, Harlem, New York.
Hall, Stuart. "Race, the Floating Signifier: Featuring Stuart Hall." *Media Education Foundation*, 1996, www.mediaed.org/transcripts/Stuart-Hall-Race-the-Floating-Signifier-Transcript.pdf. Accessed July 5, 2015.
Hollinger, David A. *Postethnic America: Beyond Multiculturalism*. Basic, 1995.
hooks, bell. "An Aesthetic of Blackness—Strange and Oppositional." *Lenox Avenue: A Journal of Interarts Inquiry* 1 (1995): 65–72.
Hughes, Langston. "The Negro speaks of Rivers." *The Collected Poems of Langston Hughes*. Ed. Arnold Rampersad and David Roessel. Vintage, 1995. 23.
Ingersoll, Earl G., ed. *Conversations with Rita Dove*. UP of Mississippi, 2003.

Kamionowski, Jerzy. "Homeward Dove: Nomadism, "World"-Travelling, and Rita Dove's Homecoming(s)." *Crossroads. A Journal of English Studies* 3 (2013): 12–21.

Li, Stephanie. "Black Literary Writers and Post-Blackness." *The Trouble with Post-Blackness*. Ed. Houston A. Baker Jr. and K. Merinda Simmons. Columbia UP, 2015. 44–59.

Morrison, Toni. *Playing in the Dark: Whiteness and the Literary Imagination*. Vintage, 1993.

Okonofua, Benjamin Aigbe. "'I am Blacker Than You': Theorizing Conflict Between African Immigrants and African Americans in the United States." *SAGE Open* 3.3 (July–September 2013): 1–14. doi: 10.1177/2158244013499162.

Omi, Michael, and Howard Winant, eds. *Racial Formation in the United States: From the 1960s to the 1990s*. Routledge, 1994.

Pereira, Malin. *Rita Dove's Cosmopolitanism*. U of Illinois P, 2003.

Rampersad, Arnold. "The Poems of Rita Dove." *Callaloo* 26 (Winter 1986): 52–60. doi: 10.2307/2931043.

Righelato, Pat. *Understanding Rita Dove*. U of South Carolina P, 2006.

Roy, Lekha, and Rano Ringo. "Interrogating Racialized Perceptions in Toni Morrison's *The Bluest Eye* and *God Help the Child*." *Dialog* 29 (Spring 2016): 65–78.

Said, Edward W. *Culture and Imperialism*. Vintage, 1994.

Shannon, Susan. *Revealing Whiteness: The Unconscious Habits of Racial Privilege*. Indiana UP, 2006.

Steffen, Therese. *Crossing Color: Transcultural Space and Place in Rita Dove's Poetry, Fiction, and Drama*. Oxford UP, 2001.

Touré. *Who's Afraid of Post-Blackness? What It Means to Be Black Now*. Free P, 2011.

Vendler, Helen. *The Given and the Made: Strategies of Poetic Redefinition*. Harvard UP, 1995.

· 2 ·

TRANSCULTURAL SPACE IN *THE YELLOW HOUSE ON THE CORNER* AND *MUSEUM*[*]

This chapter studies Dove's first two collections of poems, *The Yellow House on the Corner* and *Museum*, as initiating a transatlantic journey to revisit history, race and the role of imagery in constructing narratives. This follows Hall's contention that race is a "floating signifier" or "badge" whose meaning is informed through its cultural context, building on binaries of "Inside/outside. Cultured/uncivilized. Barbarous and cultivated" (2–5). Asserting that Dove's first two collections aim at delinking knowledge from cultural signifiers, the chapter traces the method followed to examine the relationship between race, a cultural construct, and the signifiers used to represent identity. Positing that stressing Blackness as an identity marker has precluded interracial "affiliations" (Hollinger 7) in a postethnic world, the study follows Dove as she charts a path towards a refuting of labels to initiate in literature an aesthetics that would be termed "Post-Black" in 2001. Dove's poems foreshadow a Post-Black rejection of modernist binaries in a space that is liminal, deconstructing race as a dynamic construct encoded in visual and linguistic codes that turned the ethnocentrism of the 1960s into a hegemonic tool. Towards this purpose, her first collection of poems, *The Yellow House on the Corner* (1980),

---

[*] Part of this chapter includes a study first published in *Transnational Literature* Vol. 11 no. 1, Dec. 2018.

introduces the themes to be deconstructed in her later collections, creating transcultural space wherein black and white frames of memory are juxtaposed to isolate signifiers from their traditional (racialized) meanings. The second collection, *Museum* (1983), then reformulates the cultural contexts within which the signifiers gain meaning, juxtaposing black and white in a single cultural frame of reference. The transcultural space that is created is both literal and metaphorical.

The process of creating transcultural space devoid of cultural markers with their attendant historical associations was born of the need to rethink identity in terms of closed ethnocentric spaces that were no longer viable. The first stirrings of this desire to refute labels was visible in Harlem in the 1960s, in the work of artists like Raymond Saunders, who in his 1967 pamphlet, titled *Black is a color*, rejected the idea of Blackness as an aesthetic. The Civil Rights Movement and the Black Arts Movement, seen as male-centric, also alienated and marginalized many women activists and artists, and as Harlem became the center of political and cultural revolution, and the Studio Museum a representative of black art in the public sphere, a homogeneous identity centered on Blackness gained strength as a counter to Whiteness. hooks says of the Black Aesthetic Movement: "The black aesthetic movement was fundamentally essentialist. Characterized by an inversion of the 'us' and 'them' dichotomy, it inverted conventional ways of thinking about otherness in ways that suggested that everything black was good and everything white bad" (68). In other words, the Black Aesthetic Movement simply inverted the conventions of Whiteness without dismantling the racialized center. Race still occupied prime place in this inverted structure, with the result that Blackness remained a racialized category cut off from white spaces.

This dichotomy would, however, be challenged by the 1990s, when the next generation of artists like Kara Walker confronted complex notions of Blackness and cultural heritage in their works. According to hooks, this need "to re-open the creative space that much of the black aesthetic movement closed down," called for "a radical aesthetic" that "acknowledges that we are constantly changing positions, locations, that our needs and concerns vary, that these diverse directions must correspond with shifts in critical thinking," stating that "narrow limiting aesthetics within black communities tend to place innovative black artistry on the margins" (69–70). Campbell, the executive director of the Studio Museum in Harlem from 1977 to 1987, talks of how the new generation of artists challenged the ethnocentrism of the previous decades, feeling that centering race as the main identity marker denied them an opportunity to explore the complexities of the African American experience. She says of these artists:

> They challenged notions of positive/ negative with images that confronted viewers with harsh realities no matter how unpleasant for black and white alike. What these dialectics emphatically demonstrate is that perhaps the most important function of a black fine arts museum has been as a site where contested paradigms of "blackness" can engage (329).

This role of the museum was recognized by Dove as a vital sphere of cultural and artistic revolution, but she also realized that the revolution would not be a sudden one. The dialectics of inside/outside could only be changed through a revolutionary reformulation of the dialectics of space, and this would need a positioning on the threshold to avoid being trapped in racially configured spaces. Only from a position that was liminal would the artist be able to create a transcultural space that would make it possible to reconfigure the mythical artifacts in the museum that were signifiers of the historical metanarrative. In an earlier study, Roy and Ringo say that this position allows for a "recognition of the gaps between fixed notions of truth and the historicity of modes of representation," stating that:

> ...existing in a liminal space that still carried traces of the past, the need to separate from the white normative was complicated by an unconscious appropriation of white ideals, including a negation of miscegenation, both historical and cultural. Born of the idea that racial identity must adhere to the binary of pure/impure, it turned African American ethnocentrism into a hegemonic subscription to white ideals. ("Liminality" 2–3)

Dove's first collection of poems, *The Yellow House on the Corner*, was written during a time when essentialism and pride in Blackness characterized most African American writing and art. It was, however, also a time when the political efficacy of the emphasis on Blackness had begun to translate into artistic restriction. Individual expressions of Blackness that diverged from the homogeneous, male-dominated norm sought forms to locate their art and identity. The title of Dove's first collection is a significant positioning of the house—a symbol of lived space—at the corner, presenting choice as individual. Inhabiting this house would enable Dove to position herself on the metaphorical threshold between both worlds, both an insider and an outsider, eschewing binaries from her vantage position as an onlooker to juxtapose racially demarcated cultural frames into a single frame that would fill in the gaps in each to make a whole. Her concept of race as a spatial category enclosing identity within prescriptive domains enables her to visualize signifiers as "occupied space" (*The Poet's World* 15), whose specific contours need to change, and this change can be effected only from a liminal position. The creation of the liminal space in her first two collections helps to initiate a postmodern reformulation of complex notions of ethnic identity and racial memory, countering modernist binaries and "the representation of history as a racialised domain in collective memory" by "initiating a crossing over into the psycho-spatial domain of the Other to explore objectification and identity in a transatlantic journey that is both real and metaphorical" (Roy and Ringo, "Liminality" 1).

The Yellow House on the Corner begins with a transatlantic crossing. Dove's transatlantic travels, like those of Langston Hughes and Frederick Douglass before her, allowed her to imagine herself on the metaphorical threshold between both worlds. The first section takes the reader on a journey to the world of Japanese mythology, post-war Europe, and the life of a famous German musician, before talking of "sightseeing," and moving back across the Atlantic to talk of meeting a famous Civil Rights leader. In the very first section, Dove places herself on the threshold in the poem titled "Small House." This, significantly, establishes her position as both insider and outsider, her own identity in the shadows, looking out and looking in, herself unobserved. This liminal space is the vantage position from where all her poems will speak. In this position, she is able to juxtapose cultural frames from both sides as an individual whose vantage position allows her to eschew the binaries of inside/outside.

At the beginning of the twentieth century, Du Bois talked of race as a "social construct," saying that "the problem of the twentieth century is the problem of the color-line" (*The Souls* 9). The post-Civil Rights era emphasized intense pride in Black cultural heritage and history. However, Roy and Ringo observe that "placing the trauma of slavery and post-Emancipation discrimination at the centre of a teleological narrative of Blackness…only succeeded in a double marginalisation, paradoxically defining African Americans as outsiders to American history and culture" ("Liminality" 3). Thus rose the need for a transcultural space that would locate the African American as being both inside and outside history. In this liminal space that is neither inside nor outside, the individual can project himself into either space. This is especially so in the use of signifiers with historical associations. Historically, black and white have signified the power paradigms manifest in the institution of slavery. Hall has argued that because of this, Blackness was no longer a category associated with just the color of the skin but carries with it connotations of a "long history of political and historical oppression" (4). This limits frames of the past to a particular narrative determined (and signified) by the dichotomous binaries of black/white, us/them, center/margin. This essentialist domain encloses identity within its borders. Before the 1980s, this "strategic essentialism" (Spivak 214) was a tool to resist discrimination. However, emphasizing pride in Blackness could at best be temporary, a closing of boundaries in response to racist policies in place at that particular time. Eide studies Spivak's theory to conclude that strategic essentialism:

> ...entails that members of groups, while being highly differentiated internally, may engage in an essentializing and to some extent a standardizing of their public image, thus advancing their group identity in a simplified, collectivized way to achieve certain objectives. The risk is that, by doing so, they may be playing into the hands of those whose essentialism is more powerful than their own. (76)

In other words, closed boundaries may, over time, further disadvantage the marginalized group by turning into a hegemonic identifier of difference.

The 1980s saw a realization of the hegemonic nature of signifiers that stressed essentialist identities, and this brought to the fore the need to dismantle boundaries. For this purpose, blurring the dichotomy of the binaries that asserted racial identification was needed. This builds on the contention that it is now unrealistic to expect two parallel frames of identities in a system where they were not culturally sealed off from each other, and also shared a history. Race itself needed to be decentered in everyday discourse. Winant says that the acceptance of race as "a central signifier" legitimizes binaries that build on difference. He says:

> Race generates an "inside" and an "outside" of society, and mediates the unclear border between these zones; all social space, from the territory of the intrapsychic to that of the U.S. "national character" is fair game for racial dilemmas, doubts, fears, and desires. (30)

This was because of the historical connotations that the signifier carried within itself. In fact, the concept of identity itself came to be seen as hegemonic, so that in the 1990s, Hollinger stressed the need to replace "identity," which was static, implying what he called "fixity and givenness," with the fluidity of voluntary "affiliations" (7) across the color-line that would take into account the changing connotations of race as well as the reality of postmodern fluidity.

In *Against Race*, Gilroy also called for the dismantling of identities which he felt gave rise to power structures (98–99). Ashcroft termed the "naming" of marginalized groups synonymous with "knowing" (163), leading to a call for a Post-Black "un-naming" (Crawford 11) at the beginning of the twenty-first century. However, this un-naming would need a reformulation of the racial and ethnic borders that defined spatial domains. These critics stressed the need to rethink modernity (and its representations) in terms of hybridity of culture and ethnicity.

Growing up in a period characterized by the struggle for civil rights, Dove had as early examples Paul Lawrence Dunbar and Langston Hughes's representations of African American life. However, she realizes that the celebration of Blackness had turned African American identity into a closed domain wherein the celebration of difference—of "ancient, dusky rivers" (Hughes)—reconnects the black man to the land from which he was taken into slavery, without a trace of historicity. This made race a fixed entity with connotations leading back to Africa, in every age. A rejection of modernist binaries and a formulation of postethnic affiliations demanded the recognition of gaps between fixed notions of truth and the historicity of modes of representation. Dove achieves this through an expansion of the metaphorical spatial contours of race.

Dove's poems begin the journey in her first collection towards the expansion of spatial contours through a metaphorical displacement of race. In *The Poet's World*, she talks of the "poetic consciousness of occupied space—of the space we inhabit, of the shape of thought and the pressure of absence" (15), stressing that "language is a house we inhabit" (17). For this purpose, she juxtaposes racial frames of memory by creating what Steffen terms "artistic enspacement" (28) in the first collection, celebrating the fluid nature of identity construction, and deconstructing race through a transatlantic crossing over into the domain of the white to reclaim its share in history. The collection introduces the idea of the transatlantic crossing as the origin of miscegenation, each myth a metaphorical extension of racial space, occupying both the inside and the outside. This has caused critics like Kamionowski to identify in Dove's works a "literal and metaphorical nomadism" (12); others like Vendler emphasize that this metaphorical inclusiveness in no way detracts from her rootedness in Blackness, saying, "Dove shows blackness as an ever-present, unsheddable first skin of consciousness" ("Identity Markers" 395). Using history, myth, and language, Dove bridges the two seemingly incompatible strains in her poems to define the emergence of the Post-Black.

In *The Yellow House on the Corner*, Dove experiments with a theory of racial positioning that is in a liminal space, strongly connected to its roots yet inclusive in its rejection of binaries. Relating the title of the collection to Dove's idea of race as occupied space, Pereira says that the corner was a metaphorical crossroads (54). At this historical crossroads, the poems choose to repudiate ethnocentrism in favor of a Post-Black inclusiveness, positing modernist binaries as untenable in a postmodern world. Giving method to this precept, the collection provides for a reconstitution of the space within which a reformulation of identity shall take place in the later collections. Quoting Bachelard in *The Poet's World*, Dove stresses existence within "definable space" (15), tracing a direct line back to images in the memory that define the contours of habitable space for African Americans. Vendler calls her lyric poems "poems of self-definition," noting that "the problem of the representation of blackness in lyric is present from the beginning in her work" (*The Given* 63). Each poem in the collection is part of a reconstituted framework of images, both looking in at history (and African American selfhood) from the outside and looking out, as it were, at history (and African American selfhood) from the inside. The poet positions herself on the threshold to effect a Post-Black liminality. This positioning allows her to reformulate spatial dimensions that enclose images in the memory without being accused of prejudice. The collection is divided into five sections, each a juxtaposition of the past and the present, of memory and experience, tracing race as it moves from the sphere of the overt to the symbolic, exploring what it means to be African American in the contemporary world. History and the legacy of slavery occupy central place in the memory in each visitation.

The first section in the collection initiates a literal and metaphorical transatlantic crossing over as Dove begins her long journey towards Post-Blackness, transposing Japanese and European myths on to black reality in the first poem to prove the fallacy of racially segregated spaces in cultural narratives. In *Against Race*, Gilroy states that "ancient, prescientific racial myths, fears, and typologies were mobilized around the modern racial sciences of the nineteenth century" (286). In her first collection, Dove strikes at the structural unit of learned behavior—socially sanctioned myths with the covert intent of regulating beliefs and behavior as mythically ordained. The first poem in this section, titled "This Life," portrays miscegenation as the natural outcome of the transatlantic crossing. On her travels through Germany, Dove became increasingly aware of her own alienation, her identity circumscribed by the color of her skin, making her the representative of the suffering of slaves—"the object of cultural stereotyping" (Righelato 7). In striking at myths in this section, Dove is striking at the myth of Blackness that limits identity to black skin, centralizing race and interpreting experiences through racialized filters. In including a Japanese myth in her first poem, Dove defines the cultural basis of ideals that originate in childhood images. The poem juxtaposes myth and reality in a frame where the two converge to expose memory as constructed through imagery, tracing how images that live in the mind as reality filter experiences in adulthood. The child, unaware of racial differences, identifies with a Japanese girl:

> As a child, I fell in love
> with a Japanese woodcut
> of a girl gazing at the moon.
> I waited with her for her lover. ("This Life")

In this transcultural space, the poem posits racial identification as constructed through social learning. The black child, unaware of race, identifies with the Japanese wooden figure of a girl gazing at the moon, waiting for her lover. However, the traveler who says, "the possibilities/are golden dresses in a nutshell," soon comes face to face with racial objectification, saying of herself, "and I a stranger/in this desert,/nursing the tough skins of figs." Righelato, referring to Dove's experiences of stereotyped objectification on her travels in Europe, says: "As a writer she turns her own estrangement to account" (8). In the poem, white and black converge to imply that miscegenation provides a difficult alternative to both:

> Our lives will be the same—
> your lips, swollen from whistling
> at danger,
> and I a stranger
> in this desert,
> nursing the tough skins of figs.

Exploring colors as cultural motifs, the poem traces the complex nature of the transatlantic crossing that defies labeling; black and white, myth and reality come together in an image of cultural miscegenation—"he had // your face, though I didn't know it."

This awareness of the racialization of cultural symbols leads Dove to deconstruct both European and African American history to expose trauma as a common area for both. Roy and Ringo observe that the racialization of symbols occurs as part of social learning to filter all stimuli: "In the case of characteristics attributed to race, sensory stimuli function in the form of visual and linguistic codes that inform learned behaviour" ("Interrogating" 66). Gilroy terms this "the ethnocidal energy released in the conjunction of raciology and culture" (*Against* 287). By invoking historical trauma as universal, Dove's poems deconstruct racialized frames of memory on the basis of what Gilroy terms the "central Manichean dynamic—black and white" ("The Black Atlantic" 1–2), which gives rise to a "cultural insiderism" that "typically construct the nation as a homogeneous object and invoke ethnicity a second time in the hermeneutic procedures deployed to make sense of its distinctive cultural content" (3). In her exploration of the cultural insiderism that informs official history, Dove deconstructs images that subscribe to the hermeneutics of disjointed racialized frames as social codes that both inform and are informed by cultural discourse.

The poems in Dove's first collection portray history as a symbolic spatio-temporal domain wherein trauma is neither black nor white, but a series of images. The images that inform memory at this point are devoid of color, trauma a connecting factor on both sides of the Atlantic. In the poem titled "The Bird Frau," the image of the old lady "still at war" emphasizes the perpetuation of the images of World War II that live on in the memory of those who lived through it. The old lady, wild with grief at the loss of her son, in her traumatic state "went inside, fed the parakeet,/broke its neck." Here, Dove touches upon the effects of trauma, which live on in the victim to turn her into a perpetrator of violence. Righelato says of the lady, "Her wildness marks her as ideologically still at war yet as having regressed to an asocial existence," terming "the ambiguity of tenses" a "poignant" exercise in blurring the borders between imagination and reality (9). She exists in what Roy and Ringo term "a trans-temporal zone where past and present are indistinguishable" ("Liminality" 5), a significant effect of trauma. This poem is significant in that it conjoins man and Nature as witness to history, an important idea in Dove's poems. It also explores the psychology of the perpetrator of violence, tracing the cycle of violence to its origins. Dove uses this idea again in her next collection to explore the reasons for the Dominican dictator, Rafael Trujillo's massacre of Haitian workers in 1937 in the poem "Parsley." In this exploration, she deconstructs the affective through an emotional distancing that allows her to access the psyche of the Other. This distanced empathy, however paradoxical, is an important feature of the Post-Black intellectual's revisiting of the past.

The next poem clearly introduces the idea of the liminal position that is the Post-Black, both looking in and looking out, the body portrayed as indistinct to counter racial signification. The idea of the body in shadow is an important concept used by Post-Black artists like Kara Walker. Dove's poem, "Small Town," builds on the unseen gaze that makes visible only "the woman, indistinct, in the doorway," while "the man in the chestnut tree/who wields the binoculars" leaves the person inside the house without an identity. "Someone is sitting in the red house./There is no way of telling who it is," says Dove, and the image names neither the subject nor the object, their indistinct, liminal positioning allowing for a reversal of roles:

> The man,
> whose form appears clearly among the leaves,
> is not looking at her
> so much as she at him.

The advantage of being on the threshold is portrayed by the indistinct form of the woman in the doorway, and whether her presence serves to hide the person within or to lend credence to the gaze without is a question that remains unanswered. The identity of both is masked, blurring the subject/object dichotomy. Finally, it is the one on the threshold who is in a position to look both in and out, and it is this position that lends her subjectivity. The chestnut tree, symbolizing rural idyll, is transformed in this poem into an image that serves to both hide and reveal these changes. The poem posits the image of the poet in a position of knowledge, her vantage position allowing her to know both the form within as well as observe the form of the man outside with the binoculars. In *The Poet's World*, Dove speaks of being in this position:

> This sets up in me a peculiar state, one in which I am in two places at once and yet, curiously, not there at all. It is a moment of ultimate possibility, and of ultimate irresponsibility. Of course there is no absolute demarcation of the moment when *in* becomes *out*; indeed, one passes through a delicious sliding moment when one is *neither* in nor out but *floating*, suspended above the interior and exterior ground. (24)

This is the position of the Post-Black artist who accepts the threshold as being the position of knowledge, allowing emotional distancing—"floating," the poet is in a trans-region where binaries are suspended and she can look down on both worlds. She herself is unobserved, free of the gaze that both the insider and the outsider are subject to.

From her liminal position, Dove delves into the semiotics of historical configurations even as she deconstructs the underside of war. In a reconstitution of memory in the transcultural space created by an abandoning of racialized filters, Dove states that Whiteness as an independent entity cannot sustain itself for long. She posits that Whiteness is itself dependent on the Other for its existence, and once the slave is free of the master, the master will dissolve in his own isolated world. The poem, titled "The Snow King," talks of "white spaces" in "a far far land" where "lime filled spaces" are empty, bereft of "the night as soft as antelope's eyes." It is a world of destruction, where the white psyche of the perpetrator of violence "cracked…a slow fire, a garnet." In an image resonating of the burning fires of Hell, the poem reaffirms Morrison's assertion of the "Africanism" (65) that permeates white experience—even as the violence inflicted on the slave destroyed the white man's heart, it gave him his pure identity. Separate black and white frames are posited as untenable.

The next poem in the section, ironically titled "Sightseeing," explores trauma as symbolized in myths, tracing its epistemic and linguistic origins to images in the memory. Sightseeing demands emotional distancing, making it a precondition for revisiting sites of trauma with the purpose of deconstructing history. Visiting a church destroyed after the Allies bombed it, Dove talks about the impossibility of viewing history devoid of symbols; however, the symbols that lend credence to the narrative and the myths connected to it change meaning with the temporal distancing of the present from the past. She says:

> Let's look
> at the facts. Forget they are children of angels
>
> and they become childish monsters.
> Remember, and an arm gracefully upraised
>
> is raised not in anger but a mockery of gesture.

Inferring that meanings are conferred upon symbols to perpetuate the narrative, Dove raises the possibility of symbolic interpretation being open to change as a result of emotional distancing brought about by a lapse of time. The present generation, who did not experience the trauma of war firsthand, will be less likely to have a reverential attitude towards the symbols that construct the historical metanarrative. For most, history will be akin to "sightseeing," and wandering the labyrinths of memory in a different time and space will construct its own relationship with the past.

This reconstituted vision of history as a narrative constructed through symbols opens up space whence the shadows or gaps are lighted up. Reverence gives way to a clear vision of how real-life figures have attained a larger-than-life stature. Having understood this on the transatlantic crossing, Dove returns to revisit the black man's frame. She moves back to America to shift the focus on political leaders who dominate the frame of African American history. The next poem in the collection, titled "Upon Meeting Don L. Lee, In a Dream," portrays the prominent poet of the Black Arts Movement as an ordinary, even ridiculous, figure whose stature diminishes as the myth surrounding him disintegrates. Dove's description of Lee appears as a feminist response across time to Lee's "Blackwoman." In the poem, she describes her meeting with the poet in a dream:

> I can see caviar
> Imbedded like buckshot between his teeth.
> His hair falls out in clumps of burned-out wire.
> The music grows like branches in the wind.

As the mythic is reduced to human form, music, a potent symbol of Black culture, grows as it is set free of the past. The poem not only deconstructs the myths that sustained the Black Arts Movement, but also seems to indicate the need to question the relevance of the ideals that sustained both the movement and black identity at the time. In critiquing these, Dove's poem proves that myths are aimed at imprisoning the black man in the past:

> "Seven years ago..." he begins; but
> I cut him off: "Those years are gone—
> What is there now?" He starts to cry; his eyeballs
>
> Burst into flame.

It is in this poem that Dove adopts satire as a tool to emotionally distance herself from the past for a more objective view. Righelato terms this "a significant artistic positioning for Dove as a young poet coming up against the established black ideology. In this early poem, Dove is separating herself from the exclusive celebration of blackness" (13). Vendler explains this distancing as a poetic strategy, saying that a black poet needs to move beyond a single identity marker (*The Given* 63). However, Dove does not repudiate Blackness, instead refusing merely to be curtailed by the myths that restrict it. Her use of satire is only to dismantle the myths that prevent an objective view of the past.

The section ends with a poem that moves to the present to celebrate freedom, albeit a poverty-ridden one. Neither the past nor the present can be romanticized in this revisiting of Blackness:

> We six pile in, the engine churning ink:
> We ride into the night.
> Past factories, past graveyards
> And the broken eyes of windows, we ride
> Into the gray-green nigger night.
> ....
> In the nigger night, thick with the smell of cabbages,
> Nothing can catch us.
> Laughter spills like gin from glasses,
> And "yeah" we whisper, "yeah"
> We croon, "yeah." ("Nigger Song: An Odyssey")

The blackness of the life portrayed is intentionally unapologetic, celebratory, free of all but the joy of being alive and free. This is a deliberate stance, a necessary prelude to initiating the push to expand space to celebrate Blackness in all its dimensions. The bravado is characteristic of youth, the music taking them past neighborhoods that are unmistakably urban pockets of poverty, the exact opposite of images of racial pride evoked by earlier poets. Campbell says of Post-Black artists: "They challenged notions of positive/ negative with images that confronted viewers with harsh realities no matter how unpleasant for black and white alike" (328–29). For Dove, the poet's canvas performs the same function.

Having deconstructed the racialized nature of historical frames and dismantled images of racial pride, Dove begins the second section of the collection by examining memory as a closed domain conforming to racialized dimensions of experience. The first poem in the section, titled "Five Elephants," talks of the restrictive nature of the images that construct memory, circumscribing the space that should be open to all, but is not for the "split // pod of quartz and lemon":

> Five umbrellas, five
> willows, five bridges and their shadows!
> They lift their trunks, hooking the sky
> I would rush into, split

> pod of quartz and lemon. I could say
> they are five memories, but
> that would be unfair.
> Rather pebbles seeking refuge in the heart.
> They move past me. I turn and follow,
>
> and for hours we meet no one else.

Stressing that the realization of the racialization of identity is the first step toward transcending it, the poet delineates the constructed nature of race in the image of the process by which a colorless gem is transformed into a colored stone. Limiting the experiential transcending of barriers, the metaphorical trunks of elephants "hooking the sky" are the memories (of historical trauma) that close in lived space for African Americans, living like "pebbles seeking refuge in the heart." It is significant that the journey portrayed here is an individual one, wherein the choice to follow these memories or unhook the sky from their influence is the traveler's. This (constructed) restrictive space then lodges in the heart the images that prevent its escape, acting as experiential filters that lead the black man on a lonely journey: "for hours we meet no one else."

Following her theory of race as "occupied space" which includes "the shape of thought and the pressure of absence" (*The Poet's World* 15), and having established a transatlantic connection in the first section, Dove outlines the process by which this space can be expanded to include the reality of biological and cultural miscegenation, an inescapable part of the black man's legacy. The poem "Geometry" traces the process by which the contours of the metaphorical room expand to reveal the sky. Vendler considers this poem to be an innocent realization of "the coherence and beauty of the logical principles of spatial form," one which "has not a word to say about the fraught subject of blackness" (*The Given* 67). Yet, this poem is one of the most important in Dove's œuvre, outlining both the precept and the method for a Post-Black reformulation of identity. For Dove, spatial specificity is imbued with racial subjectivity. In a meticulous and exact description of the mathematics of comprehension, she contends that the mere realization of the presence of systemically structured norms that inform images which in turn construe memory as distinct frames opens up a transcultural space that is heterotopic in nature. She says:

> I prove a theorem and the house expands:
> the windows jerk free to hover near the ceiling,

> the ceiling floats away with a sigh.
>
> As the walls clear themselves of everything
> but transparency, the scent of carnations
> leaves with them. I am out in the open.

What is noticeable is that Dove's characters do not break free of the old mould; rather, the mould itself expands, metamorphosing, as it were, to include the changing contours of reality. This follows Roy and Ringo's contention that a Post-Black "decentering of race would necessitate a dismantling of the images that make up memory, a process that would need the dimensions of the mind itself to expand to incorporate the inside-outside, the black-white" ("Liminality" 8). Crawford claims that Post-Blackness "is a way of visualizing an opening up of space," where the changed contours allow for an "unnaming" which then allows for "an interior space in which blackness is taken for granted to such an extent that it does not need to be a master sign" (11). Dove's first collection creates this space which, though admitting race as an occupant, is not racialized. The concluding lines of the poem "Geometry" effect a metaphorical dismantling of the ceiling to effect this change in spatial contours, symbolized by the "windows" which then turn into winged butterflies:

> I am out in the open
>
> and above the windows have hinged into butterflies,
> sunlight glinting where they've intersected.
> They are going to some point true and unproven.

In this lived space, the individual pushes against prescriptive barriers, the metaphorical windows expanding, representing memory freeing itself of racialized filters that wall in perception. Like the space created, the journey too is free of prescribed paths, the destination "true" yet "unproven."

A change in perception to effect spatial expansion would need a realization of the historicity of images and an individual perception *sans* the filters imposed by those images. Hollinger, in proposing postethnicity as a way to build affiliations across the color-line, talks of the growing acceptance of historicity, that is, "the contingent, temporally, and socially situated character of our beliefs and values, of our institutions and practices" (60). Roy and Ringo state that "Dove's poems act as the praxis to Hollinger's theory, examining closely the myths and beliefs that live on as larger-than-life truths in the memory, preventing emotional distancing" ("Liminality" 9). In her first collection of poems, Dove posits traveling as a way towards this distancing. As "the ceiling floats away" in the memory, Dove then revisits slavery and historical trauma without racialized filters in the next section.

Each poem in the third section of the collection deals with individual lives affected by slavery. The use of excessively formal language in "Belinda's Petition" emphasizes the irony and the pathos of the plea made in the white man's language. "Belinda's Petition" is a plaintive cry for emancipation, following the Declaration of Independence, couched in the genteel language of the white man:

> Lately your Countrymen have severed
> the Binds of Tyranny. I would hope
> you would consider the Same for me,
> pure Air being the sole Advantage
> of which I can boast in my present Condition.

Belinda's request is doomed, and the pathos of the request is brought out in the next poem, "The House Slave," where the house slave sheds futile tears as she looks out on the hardships faced by the field slaves:

> The first horn lifts its arm over the dew-lit grass
> and in the slave quarters there is a rustling—
> children are bundled into aprons, cornbread
>
> and water gourds grabbed, a salt pork breakfast taken.
> I watch them driven into the vague before-dawn
> while their mistress sleeps like an ivory toothpick
>
> and Massa dreams of asses, rum and slave-funk.

The drudgery of the slaves is contrasted with the freedom in which the white master and mistress luxuriate: "and as the fields unfold to whiteness,/and they spill like bees among the fat flowers,/I weep. It is not yet daylight." The stark imagery continues in the next poem, "David Walker (1785–1830)." Based on the moment when the abolitionist David Walker published *An Appeal to the Coloured Citizens of the World*, the poem describes the outrage, the fear and the accolades that followed the distribution of his bold pamphlets:

> Men of colour, who are also of sense.
> Outrage. Incredulity. Uproar in state legislatures.

> *We are the most wretched, degraded and abject set*
> *of beings that ever lived since the world began.*
> The jewelled canaries in the lecture halls tittered,
> pressed his dark hand between their gloves.

Continuing with the description of men who are not at the forefront of history but without whom the narrative would be incomplete, Dove's next poem, titled "The Abduction," is the tale of the abduction of Solomon Northrup, a free man with papers who was nevertheless drugged and sold into slavery:

> I remember how the windows rattled with each report.
> Then the wine, like a pink lake, tipped.
> I was lifted—the sky swivelled, clicked into place.
>
> I floated on water I could not drink. Though the pillow
> was stone, I climbed no ladders in that sleep.
>
> I woke and found myself alone, in darkness and in chains.

Slavery as an economic enterprise that dehumanized both the white man and the black is a feature that has only recently been explored. Northrup was betrayed by two people he considered his friends, and subsequently spent twelve years as a slave. Slavery also very often fostered moral conflicts, and indiscriminate racial affiliations often benefitted the white man. The poem, "The Transport of Slaves from Maryland to Mississippi," talks of an incident in 1839 when a wagonload of slaves would have escaped after killing two white men had not one of the slave women helped the injured black driver to ride for assistance. The hegemonizing nature of racial affiliation brings to the fore individual consciousnesses that work towards their own destruction in an incident where such affiliation works towards the detriment of escaped slaves. The poem traces the slave woman's justification for her act:

> *I don't know if I helped him up*
> *because I thought he was our salvation*
> *or not.* Left for dead in the middle
> of the road, dust hovering around the body
> like a screen of mosquitoes
> shimmering in the hushed light.
> ....
> *Death and salvation*—one accommodates the other.
> *I am no brute. I got feelings.*
> *He might have been a son of mine.*

The next dot on the pattern outlining the narrative is "Pamela." Alternating between prose and verse, Pamela's escape and subsequent capture is witnessed by Nature which records the courage it took for that first step:

> At two, the barnyard settled
> into fierce silence—anvil,
> water pump glinted
> as though everything waited
> for the first step.

Pamela's stepping out is all the braver because she is not presented as a bold creature of the hills, but rather one who escapes as a last resort to save her spirit. Bringing to mind Richardson's virtuous Pamela, the slave girl finds communion in Nature as she moves North, towards freedom. However, the friendly shadows soon turn ominous, for she is recaptured, the poem ending on the terrifying note of men with rifles coming for her.

Moral conflicts and human dilemmas resurface in the poem, "Someone's Blood," making the myth of black natal isolation a realistic event. The mother, who leaves her child all alone on the wharf at Missouri so that she can escape into freedom is fraught with emotion, and here the image of the rising sun as blood from a needle becomes the objective correlative for the pain of separation:

> As the sun broke the water into a thousand needles
> tipped with the blood from someone's finger,
>
> the boat came gently apart from the wharf.
> I watched till her face could not distinguish itself
> from that shadow floated on broken sunlight.

Dove maps the last point on the slave's existence in the poem "Cholera." The pandemic, which in 1849, swept the Mississippi river system, killing many and resulting in slaves being sold down the river to be transported to the deep South, reveals the superstitions prevalent at the time: "Who could say but that it wasn't anger/had to come out somehow?"

The deconstruction of the historical metanarrative in the third section delves into the recesses of the memory, the poems positing a frank acceptance of an enslaved past *sans* bitterness or denial. Dove does, however, bring to the fore the hegemonizing forces that kept the black man in chains. Critiquing nineteenth century Reason as directed towards justifying slavery in the poem,

"The Slave's Critique of Practical Reason," she depicts the slave pondering his reasons for running away. Ironically, he finds none:

> Ain't got a reason
> to run away—
> leastways, not one
> would save my life.
> So I scoop speculation
> into a hopsack.

In critiquing Reason, Dove revisits the original Black Aesthetic that concluded with Josiah Henson's (un)reasoning: "I had never dreamed of running away. I had a sentiment of honor on the subject" (166). Dove's use of black colloquial language along with a word like "speculation," denoting the black man as a thinking individual, deconstructs the hegemonizing nature of Whiteness that reduces the black man to naught but "the Owl/of the Broken Spirit." Arguing that the Enlightenment project used Reason and religion to hegemonize the enterprise of slavery emphasizes the need to revisit racial definitions.

These poems, like dots on paper, trace the path back in memory to the site of historical trauma. What Dove is aiming for in this newly opened up space is the ability to look, to wander through sites in the memory with a conscious awareness of how the black perspective has been systemically fettered into a closed sphere of existence. Campbell points out that Post-Black art aims for the same unfettering of perspective:

> The rebelliousness of a phrase like "post-black art", in part, is resistance to habits of mind that inhibit the ability of viewers to have an opportunity to see and experience the work of black artists unmediated by a predisposition of one kind or another. (321)

They follow the New Black Aesthetic's unflinching examination of the warts and fissures that mark Blackness as a historical category, but the purpose is to counter hegemonic systems by establishing a trans-space for bringing in the Other. Vendler talks of Dove's "willingness to make her readers uneasy," yet ascribes to her poetry a "wish to achieve historical linguistic probability" ("Identity Markers" 66). In terming her poetry "relatively unsuccessful historical excursions in a lyric time-machine" ("Identity Markers" 66), however, she misses the pattern that does not aim for historical accuracy or lyrical perfection, but uses both to light up memory built through images that are perspectival. In the space opened up by the ceiling having floated away, history is deconstructed as a hegemonizing narrative perpetuated by imagery. The poems in the second section of the collection serve as guiding lights to the heterogeneous nature of black life.

The third section of the collection stresses this heterogeneity, tracing the process of entering womanhood as a black woman. This is womanhood seen not through the lens of the male black poet or the white man, but the black woman herself outlining personal details of growing up. Countering objectification, this is a section that celebrates the awareness of female sexuality. "Adolescence—I" traces how a visiting cousin enlightens her adolescent cousins on details about the opposite sex:

> In water-heavy nights behind grandmother's porch
> We knelt in the tickling grasses and whispered:
> Linda's face hung before us, pale as a pecan,
> And it grew wise as she said:
>   "A boy's lips are soft,
>   As soft as baby's skin."

Adolescence is a time of idealism and dreams. As the adolescent's body grows, so do the dreams. The vulnerability in "Adolescence—III" is a rare insight into a black woman's longing for love:

> Looking out at the rows of clay
> And chicken manure, I dreamed how it would happen:
> He would meet me by the blue spruce,
> A carnation over his heart, saying,
> "I have come for you, Madam;
> I have loved you in my dreams."
> At his touch, the scabs would fall away.

There is always a hint of trauma lurking behind the dreams in Dove's poems, and it is perhaps a feature of the trans-space that allows both to co-exist. The reality of poverty is ever present, and an acceptance and compromise are devised in "The Kadava Kumbis Devise a Way to Marry for Love":

> There is no comfort in poverty.
> "Better," they say, "to give yourself
>
> to the soil under your feet
> than to a man without jewels.
>
> Who can feast off wind?"

This is an acceptance of the realities of love. In the next two poems, the ephemeral nature of adolescent love in a world filled with poverty is outlined. In "First Kiss," the vulnerability of giving in to unrealistic dreams in a harsh world is portrayed:

> And it was almost a boy who undid
> the double sadness I'd sealed away.
> He built a house in a meadow
> No one stopped to admire,
>
> And wore wrong clothes.

The next poem, "Then Came Flowers," talks of the heartbreak left behind, the chrysanthemums an ironic symbol of the optimism and joy that never lasted:

> If I begged you to stay, what good would it do me?
> In the bed, you would lay the flowers between us.
> I will pick them up later, arrange them with pincers.
> All night from the bureau they'll watch me, their
> Plumage as proud, as cocky as firecrackers.

The irresolvable conflict between happiness and reality contends with riches that do not, however, compensate for absence. In "Pearls," the poet reverses the pearls' symbolism to term them "white eyes,/a noose of guileless tears." The section ends with the classification of the poet as "a brontosaurus," compared to the mantis just outside the window. The black woman is the most vulnerable in this entire structure, the metaphorical oneness with Nature blocked by the glass window. As the recollections of adolescence draw to a close, the poet retreats into the natural world in this trans-space, where inside is outside, and the extinct is the present reality.

The last section in this collection completes the creation of the trans-space by positing travel as the journey towards knowledge. It is through travel that it suggests the Post-Black union of the abstract and the sensuous. Travel also heightens awareness of a world beyond prescriptive domains of existence. Moving from Tunisia to the Sahara, the images in Dove's poems are sensual and exotic, alluring the reader to *look*, making the poems an artist's canvas. Righelato says that "the sense of color and taste connect the exotic and the local, the birds and lemons in the desert and the yellow neighborhood house," stating that "the heightened awareness of the whole section, the sense of magical transformations, of revelatory salience, is because these poems seem *shared*. They are all, in a sense, love poems" (28). Thus, the eroticism in the landscape of the first two poems in the section, "Notes from a Tunisian Journal" and "The Sahara Bus Trip," translate into the more specific erotic exoticism of "For Kazuko": "The bolero, silk-tassled, the fuchsia/scarf come off: all that black hair // for the asking!" In this section, Nature unifies with sensuous apprehension to trace the carnal in "Beauty and the Beast" and "His Shirt." While the former insinuates that "gray animals are circling under the windows," waiting to snatch their prey, the latter deciphers the colors of desire as incomprehensible to the man himself. Implying that the erotic is a journey towards knowledge, the poet traces how its colors change through the day. Its shifting contours suggest a fluidity of experience that differs from the earlier dichotomy of the Self into the beauty and the beast.

Dove's final aim in this journey is "to define the power of linguistic forces where racialized formulations extend beyond the epistemic domain in which they were realised" (Roy and Ringo, "Liminality" 10). Morrison says, "Literature redistributes and mutates in figurative language the social conventions of Africanism" (66). The final poem in Dove's collection, titled "Ö," the Swedish word for island, speaks of language as a metaphorical journey that constructs reality as it progresses:

> Sometimes
>
> a word is found so right it trembles
> at the slightest explanation.
> You start out with one thing, end
> up with another, and nothing's
> like it used to be, not even the future.

Thus, the poem and the collection deconstruct language, positing meaning as uncertain and never devoid of contextual associations. As the associations change, it changes interpretation, and that, Dove seems to imply, could change the entire narrative. Vendler's observation of Dove's "sure way with images, which are always, in her poems, surrogates for argument" (*The Given* 68) places the poems on the same canvas as art. While offering the possibility of linguistic accuracy, the images stress the constructed nature of narratives, and their contextualized rendering of the past. The individual must forge his way through this linguistic (im)probability of a rendering of identity in a postethnic world through decontextualizing word and image, image and memory. In the quest for meaning, the collection stresses the recurring motif of the traveler, on a metaphorical journey to sites in memory to reformulate the relationship between the semantics of race and images in the memory, the poems revealing the roots wherein an epistemic reformulation will take place.

Dove's second collection of poems, *Museum*, was published in 1983. As the title suggests, the collection explores the cultural artifacts that the poet places in the transcultural space that the first collection created. The relics in this specially created museum are then subjected to careful scrutiny. The relics introduced here are associated with the three signifiers that Dove attempts to reformulate as Post-Black constituents of cultural identity in her later collections—history, myth, and music. Campbell stresses that the role of the Post-Black museum is "as a site where contested paradigms of 'blackness' can engage" (329). Dove's *Museum* attests to this, subverting the traditional closed spaces of the museum to reveal it as a place where artifacts from both sides of the color-line find place. As a place where the greatest myths—historical and cultural—originate, the reformulation of the museum is perhaps an attempt to dismantle the myths that lend credence to the historical metanarrative.

In *The Poet's World*, Dove says: "*Museum* evokes that specially prepared space for contemplation of significant achievements of the past" (15). The contemplation in this collection, however, distances itself from both the retrospective reverence of the Black Aesthetic Movement as well as the satirical irreverence of the New Black Aesthetic, instead assuming a Post-Black willingness to objectively explore the past *sans* the filters imposed by both the white gaze and black cultural protocols. As the site where cultural and historical myths originate, the museum was the best place for this change. This corroborates Crawford's statement that the Post-Black "exhibit" would need an "opening up of space" to accept the change in depth necessitated from "a transnational motion" that moves on from "a spatial and temporal strategy of resistance that insisted on blackness as the past, present and future" (12–13). In an interview with Rubin and Kitchen, Dove says:

> I suppose what I was trying to do in *Museum* was to deal with certain artifacts that we have in life, not the ordinary artifacts, the ones that you'd expect to find in a museum, but anything that becomes frozen by memory, or by circumstance, or by history. (Ingersoll 6)

In the poems, she outlines the process of revisiting the artifacts specially selected for scrutiny in this collection.

Museum begins its journey by dusting the cobwebs from the newly created transcultural space in the memory. Aptly titled "Dusting," the prologue to the collection stands in a separate space by itself, introducing Beulah to the readers, following her:

> her gray cloth brings
> dark wood to life.
>
> Under her hand scrolls
> and crests gleam
> darker still.

Using stream of consciousness as a literary device, Dove traces the path in the memory back to the site of the event, "each dust/stroke a deep breath." As "wavery memory" clears a path through the dust that has settled across untouched areas, images arise to form associations that eventually give the person an identity—"Maurice." In an interview with Davis, Dove refers to an incident recounted to her by an actress she had met in Berlin. The actress, incidentally named Maurice, told her of how the goldfish in their apartment had frozen after the windows had been left open, and was then slowly warmed back to life on the stove (Ingersoll 43). This incident started the poem which works itself back into the memory from the last word in the poem, Maurice. After a path has been cleared, Dove urges the reader to activate the senses to perceive what had remained buried in the memory. Having established the oneness of man and Nature in the first collection, the first section in this collection, titled "The Hill Has Something to Say," establishes Nature as the only true witness to history. It introduces itself with a quote from a "tombstone near Weimar, Texas," positing that the journey starts from the in-between space, a space where no affiliations are needed: "Heathen./No chance of Heaven,/No fear of Hell."

It is from this in-between space that the poem subjects the images in the memory, the metaphorical fossils, to intense scrutiny, lighting up the shadows or the gaps in the memory. The first poem in the section, "The Fish in the Stone," outlines, in the image of the fossilized fish, the irreconcilability of the gaze with the reality of the present, entrapping identity in a distant past. The metaphorical fish in the stone is frozen into its fossilized form by time and space, uncomfortable at the scientific scrutiny it is subjected to, yet unable to escape objectification, to escape to its homeland, back into the life it knows.

Neither does it know how to stop itself from being seen as a frozen relic of the past:

> The fish in the stone
> would like to fall
> back into the sea.
>
> He is weary
> of analysis, the small
> predictable truths.
> He is weary of waiting
> in the open,
> his profile stamped
> by a white light.

The poem deconstructs the fossilizing for ever of the identity of the creature into a fixed image that results from the white gaze—"his profile stamped/by a white light." This is the reason the transcultural space needed to be created; to allow the fish its natural existence, it would need the heterotopic domain to allow it to free itself of the gaze while at the same time transcend the "impossible mourning" (Mishra 9) that marks its yearning for its old home, the sea. This would need a (sensory) reconstitution of filters that marked images of the past as well as of belonging, preventing a postethnic acceptance of the racial fluidity of the present. Vendler talks of Dove's "willingness to make her readers uneasy" (*The Given* 66), and Righelato notes her insistence in *Museum* on "meditations on the two-way exchange between past and present, and explorations of the gaps in ideology and belief that the long fall through time has created" (35). She further notes that the recreation of artifacts can never recreate the original, stating that "if the past is a collection of artifacts, it is also the stories about them that succeeding generations reshape" (35). This has the potential to introduce new cultural contexts to signifiers with historical associations, thus de-contextualizing the signifier to reformulate its meanings. In the case of racialized significations, it would effectively decenter race, thus effecting a Post-Black transformation of history as a metanarrative of signifiers. In the poems that follow, Dove takes her readers on a journey through the ruins of Europe, asking them to search for history in the antiquities before finally concluding that real history needs to be discerned in the gaps (recorded by Nature). In each of the poems, Nature is witness to history.

The poem, "The Ants of Argos," begins with a tourist-like visitation of the ruins of the Greek city of Argos. "We stood at the citadel—nothing left," says the opening line of the poem, indicating the vacuum that surrounds the glorious past of this ancient city. Implying that Nature is the only real witness to catastrophic events, Dove contrasts the emptiness and wilderness that surrounds the human visitor with the ability of ants to detect the earthquake that destroyed the city of Corinth in 1858, ending the poem with this ultra-sensory revisitation of the event: "Even the ants,/marching skyward, had been in Corinth." Likening the human body to a metaphorical container which has the ability to isolate the person from external sorrows, the next poem, "Pithos," speaks of the binaries of lived space, evoking the sensibility of history in the cool interiors of the Greek pithos. The pithos symbolizes the inside of enclosed space and the perception of being within, which might be very different from that of the spectator without. Steffen identifies the metaphorical collusions present in Dove's identification of spatial categories as repertoires of history, saying that "opposites such as open-closed, private-public, near-distant, above-below, one's own-foreign, past-present, here-there, allowed-forbidden are always already inscribed" (35) in her revisitations. Tracing existence in the cool interiors of the pithos, Dove records the insider's view of lived space:

Chill earth.
No stars
in this stone
sky.

You have ceased
to ache.

Your spine is
a flower.

Dove follows Morrison and Walker in her insistence on revisiting sites of trauma, additionally calling upon Nature as a witness to history. Nature's records, however, exist in a realm beyond language, one which can be accessed only through sensory perception in the expanded space. In the poem, "The Hill Has Something to Say," Europe's hills speak its history, Dove says, and we would know the entire truth but for our inability to access its sensory messages, possible only "if we would listen":

(For all we know
the wind's inside us, pacing

our lungs. For all we know
it's spring and the ground
moistens as raped maids break
to blossom. What's invisible
sings, and we bear witness.)

In the poem, Dove conveys a sense of the dialectic between history and the individual. We can't escape history, even as we construct it—for it is "inside us, pacing/our lungs." In Dove's enspacement of time, the silent hill represents a wilderness above the busy valley. The poet must realize that "what's invisible/sings, and we bear witness." This poem is a significant example of Dove's revisiting of the past, in a journey where man and nature unite to explore and expose trauma fossilized in Nature. Righelato observes:

> The act of climbing the hill initiates the process of taking in the past. ... The poem echoes with human and atmospheric exchanges: the wind "groans," its breath "pacing/our lungs." The hill is nature, yet the shape of the land is human, referred to as if a human figure. (38)

The conjoining of man and Nature initiates the quest for truth—in accepting the veracity of Nature as witness to history, man is able to transcend the power-knowledge nexus that characterizes official history. The hills, according to Dove, contain layers of time. She says:

> Every hill contains things which make it a hill, speaking specifically of Europe where practically every hill has ruins underneath it. So it has its history, if we would just listen, if we could look at what is very obvious—a hill—and imagine the layers of time. (Ingersoll 7)

Steffen calls this poem a "spatialization of time" (85). In *The Poet's World*, Dove speaks of the binaries of space as metaphor: "The larger world, then, becomes synonymous with collapsed time, while the illusion of real time occurs in carefully scripted dialogues within the sanctum of our residential cubicles" (38). The hills, in this context, symbolize a shift in the occupied space recorded in historical archives. They also indicate open spaces that transcend the moment, a break from the spatio-temporal realities that separate past and present.

Functioning within the reformulated spatial dimensions, the next few poems are voices that speak from the past. Righelato calls these poems "narrative vignettes" (38), and Dove herself uses a metaphorical term, "living architecture," in the poem "The Copper Beech." The poems are female voices from the past describing their experience of events; using the stream of consciousness technique in a compressed poetic structure characterized by enjambment, Dove experiments with recounting history in individual events. In "The Copper Beech," there is an ironic reference to the European Rococo or baroque style that originated in France in the early eighteenth century. The copper beech, itself an artificially mutated version of the European beech, is initially termed an "aristocrat among patriarchs,/this noble mutation." The tree is an exhibit exemplifying the (cultural) mutations that accompany uprooting, transforming the "best/specimen of Rococo" into "…their // melancholy individualist,/the park philosopher." This change mutates into an aesthetic principle, leading to a baroque display of the tree's wounds:

> The aesthetic principles
> of the period: branches
>
> pruned late to heal
> into knots, proud flesh ascending
> the trunk:
>
> living architecture.

Although the poem speaks of architectural form, the subtle hint at miscegenation and its accompanying trauma is visible in the image of the mutation that results in the tree's "copper" variant.

The idea of the baroque as a feature of tragedy is carried over into the next poem, "Tou Wan Speaks to her Husband, Liu Sheng." The wife of the princely ruler of Chung-Shan uses the legend of Liu Sheng to give voice to the Chinese custom of burying the dead with everything needed for the journey. However, her words are also a satirical comment on the extravagances of the ruler, and the image resonates in the memory with the parallel image of the white master's riches and the poor slave's servitude:

> In the south room all
> you will need for the journey
> —a chariot, a
> dozen horses—
> opposite,
>
> a figurine household
> poised in servitude
> and two bronze jugs, worth more

> than a family pays in taxes
> for the privilege to stay
> alive, a year, together…
>
> but you're bored.

The riches that accompany the deceased prince in his tomb include not just a suit made of "two thousand jade wafers/with gold thread," but also an ironic reminder of lifeless existence in the form of "a statue/of the palace girl you most/frequently coveted." The reference to the white master's coveting a favorite black slave girl, a situation which the white mistress was powerless to resist, is not lost on the reader. In an interview, Dove says that since legends from the past cannot speak for themselves, it is up to us to recreate the time when they lived: "They can't speak to us anymore. We have to go through what they've left behind and fashion it" (Ingersoll 7). The poem resonates with a narrative that individual perspective weaves into the evidence found in the form of artifacts.

The next two poems, "Catherine of Alexandria" and "Catherine of Sienna," talk of two female saints distanced from their iconic images. According to legend, Saint Catherine of Alexandria was a princess and a scholar in the early fourth century, converting hundreds of people to Christianity before she was martyred by the pagan emperor, Maxentius. Highly venerated by the Eastern Orthodox Church and the Roman Catholic Church, her persona is made human by Dove's poem, which focuses on her reply to Maxentius's proposal of marriage. When the pagan king could not win her over through argument, he proposed marriage, but Catherine refused him, saying that her spouse was Jesus Christ to whom she had consecrated her virginity. The poem resonates with Freudian images of intellectual repression being projected onto an intense religious dedication:

> Deprived of learning and
>   the chance to travel,
> no wonder sainthood
>   came as a voice
>
> in your bed—
>   and what went on
> each night was fit
>   for nobody's ears
>
> but Jesus'.

Unlike Catherine of Alexandria, Saint Catherine of Sienna was a Scholastic philosopher, theologian and writer who had great influence on the Catholic Church in the fourteenth century, and is one of four women to be declared a Doctor by the Church. However, Dove's poem narrates the hardships Catherine faced as she lived in her home in silence and solitude as a tertiary:

> You walked the length of Italy
> to find someone to talk to.
> ....
> Under the star-washed dome
> of heaven, warm and dark
> ....
> you prayed
> until tears streaked the sky.
> No one stumbled across your path.
> No one unpried your fists as you slept.

Deconstructing sainthood as the lofty achievement of a life of deprivation, Dove explores the irony of posthumous veneration, contrasting the image with the reality. Stating that much of the fame associated with saints is a result of the images that are allowed to dominate the narrative, she deconstructs sainthood as a myth. Implying that the lives of saints have parallels in black slave life as well, she compares it to the suffering caused by the intellectual repression of slaves. The cultural context creates the narrative; however, once this context separates from the images, what is left is the isolated nature of existence for the literate slave. Revered by his own community, he nevertheless leads an isolated existence, tortured by the reality of the existential dilemma of the philosopher trapped in his skin. Both these poems deconstruct sainthood, yet the tone is compassionate rather than irreverent. Dove separates herself from the NBA artists in two ways—firstly, in her readiness to accept white saints as paralleling black life, and secondly, in translating irreverence towards history's icons into a compassionate understanding of the structures that framed the lives of these personages.

Museum, however, is much more than a feminist deconstruction of history's icons. Once saintly figures are seen as constructed through social structures, religion itself is deconstructed as a system of constructed beliefs. The next poem in the collection, titled "Receiving the Stigmata," analyzes the role of the stigmata in relieving pain. Symbolizing the wounds inflicted on Jesus during his crucifixion, the stigmata was an inexplicable phenomenon that lent credence to the Faith. This poem is essentially a reflection on a tapestry in a hall in Munich, and seems to reflect on the concept of Paradise as succor for the tortures the slaves, not unlike Jesus, were subjected to: "Back when people died for/the smallest reasons, there was/always a field to walk into." Religion could be used to enslave, propagating itself as both a relief for the exploited of the earth and as a power for absolution:

> Simple men fell to their knees
> below the radiant crucifix
> and held out their palms
>
> in relief. Go into the field
> and it will reward. Grace
>
> is a string growing straight
> from the hand. Is
> the hatchet's shadow on the
> rippling green.

The sudden transformation to the chilling image of "the hatchet's shadow on the rippling green" contrasts with the "fields" that religion offered to the suffering.

While there was extensive use of Biblical myths in early slave narratives, it was after the Black Arts Movement of the 1960s that the use of Biblical myths by African American writers began to explore the relationship between these myths and the individual. Sonia Sanchez's "Summer Words of a Sistuh Addict" describes a character who uses drugs to alter her feelings immediately after attending a church service. Likewise, Carolyn Rogers's poem, "Jesus was Crucified," favors individual expression over Biblical teachings. Writers like Morrison, Angelou, and Walker allude to Biblical myths in their works, but they do so in relation to their effect on black lives. However, Dove's poems deconstruct the myths themselves as formed of the struggle by (white) women in a repressive social structure, their lives mythologized to lend credence to exploitation as the suffering needed to enter Paradise. This has the function of deconstructing the Christian narrative of the white man's supremacy. In drawing parallels between the lives of white saints and black slaves, it posits religion as a tool for the hierarchical structuring of power that exploits the marginalized.

The second section, "In the Bulrush," talks of memory as a reservoir of images from the past. The section intertwines man and nature, endowing nature with human qualities and man with nature's disposition. With Nature as witness and companion, Dove revisits sites of slavery in the memory. The poem, "Three Days of Forest, A River, Free," describes the terrifying feeling of running for freedom, where the river symbolizes escape:

> The terror of walking is a trust
> drawn out unbearably
> until nothing, not even love,
> makes it easier, and yet
> I love this life:
>
> three days of forest,
> the mute riot of leaves.
>
> Who can point out a smell
> but a dog? The way is free
> to the river.

The poem evokes the acute terror which the trees, the leaves underneath, and the river ahead stand witness to, as the fugitive slave runs towards the river to escape the dogs that would sniff him out and tear him to pieces. The poem brings to mind Hughes's poem, "A Negro Speaks of Rivers," to mark rivers as witnesses to history. Like Hughes's poem, Dove's imagining of the river is suffused with death and, at the same time, life. Dove's poem is also reminiscent of Richter's 1953 novel, *The Light in the Forest*, which draws on a real incident during the American Revolutionary War in the eighteenth century, when a white boy who was taken captive by the Native Lenape tribe as a child refuses to accept his white lineage when he is rescued and spends three days crossing rivers and mountains to return to his adopted family. The idea of identity being socially constructed, not natural, is visible in these images. There is also an indication of the need to allow voluntary "affiliations" (Hollinger 7) instead of definitive prescriptive identities that fix belonging into a sealed ethnoracial category that negates all intercultural influences as insignificant.

This leads Dove to the racialization of identity for African Americans, wherein identity is circumscribed by the color of the skin. The next poem, "Bannekar," describes the obscurity that is the lot of the African American astronomer, mathematician, and architect, Benjamin Bannekar, who helped to plan the city of Washington, D.C., and is presented by Dove as equal to Benjamin Franklin and Thomas Jefferson, iconic figures and signatories of the Declaration of Independence. Bannekar's eccentric public image is contrasted with his intellectual and creative brilliance as he conceptualizes the city. The poem implies the racism inherent in society's treatment of the genius:

> But who would want him! Neither
> Ethiopian nor English, neither
> lucky nor crazy, a capacious bird
> humming as he penned in his mind
> another enflamed letter
> to President Jefferson—

Bannekar is a black intellectual, an antithetical contradiction of the assumption of the inferiority of the black race. This makes him an oddity, and an outsider. Steffen says of him: "Bannekar, neither this nor that, fills a pioneering liminal gap of creative activity beyond firm inner and outer associations or conventional behavior" (68). Righelato notes that unconventionality of behavior often translates into racial isolation, saying, "Dove is also aware of the negative aspects of unconventionality in any form, the fate of people who are culturally defined as hardly human but also as exotic oddities, like museum exhibits" (43). Bannekar is an exhibit, his eccentricities magnified to make him seem a strange and exotic creature different from (and for) both the black and white races. He occupies the transcultural space created by Dove, and it is here that he can finally visualize his idea of the city of Washington.

The poem, "Agosta the Winged Man and Rasha the Black Dove," uses *ekphrasis* to juxtapose black and white, subject and object, art and artist, creativity and creation. This poem can be said to be a Hegelian examination of art's role in historical progression, and a movement towards its freedom from historical forces. This is signified by the use of *ekphrasis* in a quest for self-knowledge. The inclusion of this poem is a significant pointer towards Post-Blackness being a Hegelian philosophy of individual and historical progression towards freedom. This includes freeing art from its role in pushing history forward, and subject and object become one in the poem as art is left free to reflect on itself. The poem is based on a painting of the same name created in 1929 by the German painter, Christian Schad. Like Dove, Schad chose as his subjects people who were usually not the subject matter of art. In Dove's poem, the painting turns its gaze on itself as imagined by the painter. So while Schad's gaze paints Agosta and Rasha, Dove's gaze paints Schad. Agosta and Rasha were sideshows at a circus in Berlin, on the fringes, one black and the other white. Schad captures them both on the same canvas, juxtaposing differences to make a complete whole where each complements the other. Ironically, both Dove's poem and Schad's painting equate black skin and deformed (winged) ribs as deformities. Thus, while the painting deals with the objectification of the two artistes at the fair, the poem deals with the objectification of the artistes in the painting, art reflecting on itself, and the artist becoming an object in the creative process:

> Schad paced the length of his studio
> and stopped at the wall,
>   staring
> at a blank space.
> ....
>   The canvas,
> not his eye, was merciless.
>
>   Agosta in
> classical drapery, then,
> and Rasha at his feet.
> Without passion. Not
> the canvas
>   but their gaze,
>   so calm,
> was merciless.

The poem ends with the word "merciless," emphasizing the objectifying nature of the gaze, and the power of art freed from its role in history. As subject, art is merciless in examining itself and its role in framing the narrative. Taylor examines this role of present-day art through the Hegelian lens:

> Art began to evolve by working out different ideas about what it was, and eventually found an answer that closed the cognitive-historical circle: just as world history is the history of Geist's journey to self-awareness, and of Geist positing increasingly adequate worldly embodiments along the way, art history is the history of art's continual reflection on its own nature—of artists producing objects that correspond to their various stages of progress toward true self-consciousness. (637)

Dove's attempt to free art by placing the artist in her "museum" turns art into a subject that becomes one with the object. In an interview with Schwartz, Dove says:

> What I was interested in poetically was less the final product—what's already been done and done beautifully—and more of what was behind it, the whole process. For me that poem is not the description of the portrait; it is about an artist seeking

common ground with his subject as well as a meditation on being "exotic," being thought of as "other." (Dove interview)

Dove's poem denies the artist mastery over his objects, and in objectifying the artist, she subverts the power of the gaze by blurring the subject-object dichotomy. Vendler notes that "it is *what* is rendered through eye and generic convention—the socially-marked persons of Agosta and Rasha in 1929 Berlin—that mercilessly indicts German culture" (*The Given* 76–77). However, what is significant in Dove's rendering is the juxtaposition of black and white in a structure that allows them to direct their collective gaze at the world that had objectified them. It is an unmistakable image of cultural miscegenation, both parts deformed, yet beautiful, powerful as black *ekphrasis* that exists in the interplay of word and image. It is also a Hegelian progression towards freedom.

Having carefully selected its artifacts from Europe and deconstructed them in a transcultural space, *Museum* selects as its last exhibit a momentous event in Black resistance. The last poem in the collection, "Parsley," revisits the Dominican Republic of 1937 to understand the psychology of a racist executor. Divided into two parts, the poem juxtaposes frames from the perspective of the victims and the perpetrator. Both are rife with images as Dove traces the moments before the Dominican dictator, Rafael Trujillo, orders the execution of more than twenty thousand Haitian workers who had crossed the border. This poem is a renunciation of the satire of NBA poetry, instead choosing a genuinely empathetic desire to understand the workings of a racist mind. This empathetic crossing over, according to Dove, is necessary in order to understand the gaps that suppress trauma beneath the surface. Eschewing the absolutist binaries of good/ bad, she enters the dictator's mind as he searches for a reason to kill, finding it in a simple linguistic device for deciding Otherness—all workers will be asked to pronounce the word "*perejil*," Spanish for parsley—those unable to pronounce the "*r*" will be killed. In an interview with Schwartz about writing the poem, Dove says:

> Instead of thinking of evil as a force just blazing through, destroying things, I began to understand that evil could be creative, devious—that evil is human and, therefore, part of us. This is what was haunting me. This is what I needed to get behind. So, I opened myself up to possibility. And, in that realm, I was completely free to imagine a scenario which humanizes evil, but also would explain why Trujillo chose that particular word, *perejil*, for his shibboleth. (Dove interview)

In revisiting the workings of the dictator's mind, Dove constructs the poem to reflect the intensity of trauma. The structural rigor of the sestina in the second part contrasts with the more flexible villanelle in the first. Dove calls this choosing of form "time signature" (Ingersoll 155), emphasizing the "acoustic imagery in the repetition of *r* in words such as 'parrot' so that the sounds become symbolic of the fixated mindset of the dictator and the predicament of the victims" (Righelato 65). As the intensity of violence increases, the frenetic workings of the mind are reflected in the tautness of construction. Language becomes a tool for power in this chilling sequence.

The first part of the poem, titled "The Cane Fields," follows the screams of the Haitian workers in the cane fields as they are shot, the image of the parrot recurring throughout:

> Like a parrot imitating spring,
>
> we lie down screaming as rain punches through
> and we come up green. We cannot speak an R—
> out of the swamp, the cane appears
>
> and then the mountain we call in whispers *Katalina*.
> The children gnaw their teeth to arrowheads.
> There is a parrot imitating spring.

As the poem progresses, the images increase in hideousness to accord with the nature of events. Nature seems once again to unite with man, both distorted by the cruelty of events. This is one of Dove's most powerful renderings of the Post-Black consciousness of history—the images are perspectival, and color and sound unite to form a startling visual reality with the gaps lighted up. Righelato says: "Whether as color or sound, parsley is a mocking emanation of evil erupting from within the familiar and of destruction as a hideous parody of the renewal of spring" (65–66). The first section relives the horrors of the massacre in a visual and acoustic redefining of language intertwining with the sensory. Yet this is only one part of the narrative.

The second part of "Parsley" crosses over into the psychic domain of the perpetrator to understand the workings of a racist mind. This is a postethnic reframing of black identity which does not restrict itself to black experiential reality. The Post-Black artist, according to Golden, was interested in "redefining complex notions of blackness" (14). Dove extends this notion of Blackness to incorporate an understating of what drove people to a racist ideology. In this part of the poem, she studies the workings of Trujillo's mind as he paces the room:

> It is fall, when thoughts turn
> to love and death; the general thinks
> of his mother, how she died in the fall
> and he planted her walking cane at the grave
> and it flowered, each spring stolidly forming
> four-star blossoms. The general
> pulls on his boots, he stomps to
> her room in the palace, the one without
> curtains, the one with a parrot
> in a brass ring. As he paces he wonders
> Who can I kill today.

Positing that trauma causes a person to inflict further trauma, Dove delves into the psychic depths of racist violence. Trujillo is shown to be in the grip of intense mourning at the loss of his mother, and transfers his reverence for her to her pet parrot, coupled with an intense hatred of all that differs from her: "his mother was no stupid woman; she/could roll an R like a queen. Even/a parrot can roll an R!" His frenzied mind making comparisons, the Enlightenment notion of the racial inferiority of black people finds reason in the linguistic anomaly of the Haitian workers' inability to pronounce the Spanish *r*. Concluding that this is enough reason to shoot them dead, he chooses a word that would act as a password to life— *perejil*. Those who say it, live; those who cannot, must necessarily die: "He will/order many, this time, to be killed // for a single, beautiful word." The cycle of violence increases in intensity at each stop.

"Parsley" is Dove's most forceful deconstruction of the abnormalities of racist reasoning, as well as an example of the necessity of revisiting racist encounters in history without preconceived notions of good/ bad. Extreme racist encounters, Dove seems to say, are the result of a mind grown sick from past trauma. Righelato commends the intensity of the imagined monologue, stating: "The inexorability and absurdity of this crazed progression is finely dramatized. The general is both a child again sobbing for his mother and a practiced dictator with a childish self-importance" (66). Yet the narrative can be fully understood only when both frames of experience are juxtaposed. The massacre of more than twenty thousand Haitian workers from across the border by Trujillo led to the first significant movement of black resistance, and is an important event on the path leading back to the historical trauma of slavery in the memory. In closing her second collection with a revisiting of this incident, Dove opens the gateway for memory to revisit the trauma. It is only after this revisiting of Blackness that the other collections will move on to deconstruct it as a signifier whose historical associations make it difficult to dissociate it from its cultural context. This emphasizes the resolution of trauma for the emotional distancing that will make possible an objective reconstitution of the past.

Both *The Yellow House on the Corner* and *Museum* are Post-Black deconstructions of race as a spatio-temporal category, representing a "dialectical synthesis" (Steffen 70) rather than a complete break between past and present. The collections seem to suggest a postmodern reformulation of the present through a revisiting of the past in the memory. Dove does not, however, restrain herself to events in the lives of slaves in America. Her poetry insists on a wide range of global and historical reference, challenging the black essentialism of the Black Arts Movement. Steffen says that the poems:

> ...illustrate the extraordinary power of threshold figures, migrants, exiles, visitors in different cultural contexts who not only gain a home in art through Dove's lyrical enspacement but who also fuse various cultural backgrounds or cut out their own pluricultural identity and niche in an unprecedented way. (87)

They envision a postethnic fluidity that is liminal in its cultural positioning. Dove—like Audre Lorde and Adrienne Rich—adopts a retrospective and reconstructive method that places her squarely against the conventional essentialism of the Black Arts movement. Both the collections introduce issues that need to be dealt with to initiate a postethnic reformulation of racial affiliations. A recurring theme in Dove's poetry is biological and cultural miscegenation, and her later works revisit it in detail.

Works Cited

Ashcroft, Bill, et al. *Post-Colonial Studies: The Key Concepts*. Routledge, 2003.
Bachelard, Gaston. *The Poetics of Space*. Translated by Maria Jolas. Beacon P, 1994.
Campbell, Mary Schmidt. "African American Art in a Post-Black Era." *Women & Performance: A Journal of Feminist Theory* 17.3 (2007): 317–30. doi: 10.1080/07407700701621541.
Crawford, Margo Natalie. *Black Post-Blackness*. U of Illinois P, 2017.
Dove, Rita. "An Interview with Rita Dove." By Claire Schwartz. *VQR: A National Journal of Literature and Discussion* 94.2 (Winter 2016), www.vqronline.org/interviews-articles/2016/01/interview-rita-dove. Accessed August 22, 2018.

———. *Museum*. Carnegie Mellon U P, 1983.

———. *The Poet's World*. Library of Congress, 1995.

———. *The Yellow House on the Corner*. Carnegie Mellon U P, 1980.

Du Bois, W. E. B. *The Souls of Black Folk*. Dover, 1994.

———. "Strivings of the Negro People." *The Atlantic Monthly* 80.478 (1897): 194–98.

Eide, Elisabeth. "Strategic Essentialism and Ethnification: Hand in Glove?" *Nordicom Review* 31.2 (2010): 63–78.

Gilroy, Paul. *Against Race: Imagining Political Culture Beyond the Color Line*. The Belknap P of Harvard UP, 2000.

———. "The Black Atlantic as a Counterculture of Modernity." *The Black Atlantic: Modernity and Double Consciousness*. Harvard UP, 1993.

Golden, Thelma. *Freestyle*, exhibition catalogue, April 28–June 24, 2001, Studio Museum, Harlem, New York.

Hall, Stuart. "Race, the Floating Signifier: Featuring Stuart Hall." *Media Education Foundation*, 1996, www.mediaed.org/transcripts/Stuart-Hall-Race-the-Floating-Signifier-Transcript.pdf. Accessed July 5, 2015.

Henson, Josiah. "Truth Stranger than Fiction." *Early Negro American Writers*. Ed. Benjamin Brawly. Dover, 1970. 166–67.

Hollinger, David A. *Postethnic America: Beyond Multiculturalism*. Basic, 1995.

hooks, bell. "An Aesthetic of Blackness: Strange and Oppositional." *Lenox Avenue: A Journal of Interarts Inquiry* 1 (1995): 65–72.

Hughes, Langston. "The Negro speaks of Rivers." *The Collected Poems of Langston Hughes*. Ed. Arnold Rampersad and David Roessel. Vintage, 1995. 23.

Ingersoll, Earl G., ed. *Conversations with Rita Dove*. UP of Mississippi, 2003.

Kamionowski, Jerzy. "Homeward Dove: Nomadism, "World"—Travelling, and Rita Dove's Homecoming(s)." *Crossroads. A Journal of English Studies* 3 (2013): 12–21.

Mishra, Vijay. *The Literature of the Indian Diaspora: Theorizing the Diasporic Imaginary*. Routledge, 2007.

Morrison, Toni. *Playing in the Dark: Whiteness and the Literary Imagination*. Vintage, 1993.

Pereira, Malin. *Rita Dove's Cosmopolitanism*. U of Illinois P, 2003.

Rampersad, Arnold. *The Life of Langston Hughes—Volume II: 1941–1967—I Dream a World*. 2 vols., 2nd ed. Oxford UP, 2002.

Reed, Ishmael. "Dualism: In Ralph Ellison's Invisible Man." *The Norton Anthology of African American Literature*. Ed. Henry Louis Gates and Nellie Y. McKay. W. W. Norton, 1972. 2292.

Righelato, Pat. *Understanding Rita Dove*. U of South Carolina P, 2006.

Roy, Lekha, and Rano Ringo. "Interrogating Racialized Perceptions in Toni Morrison's *The Bluest Eye* and *God Help the Child*." *Dialog* 29 (Spring 2016): 65–78.

———. "Liminality and Otherness: Exploring Transcultural Space in Rita Dove's *The Yellow House on the Corner*." *Transnational Literature* 11.1 (2018): 1–12, www.https://fhrc.flinders.edu.au/transnational/home.html.

Saunders, Raymond. *Black Is a Color*. 1967.

Spivak, Gayatri Chakravorty. "Subaltern Studies: Deconstructing Historiography." In *Other Worlds*. 1987. Routledge, 1988. 197–221.
Steffen, Therese. *Crossing Color: Transcultural Space and Place in Rita Dove's Poetry, Fiction, and Drama*. Oxford UP, 2001.
Taylor, Paul C. "Post-Black, Old Black." *African American Review* 41.4 (Winter 2007): 625–40.
Vendler, Helen. "Rita Dove: Identity Markers." *Callaloo* 17.2 (1994): 381–98.
Walker, Alice. *The Given and the Made: Strategies of Poetic Redefinition*. Harvard UP, 1995.
———. *The Way Forward Is with a Broken Heart*. Ballantine, 2000.
Winant, Howard. *Racial Conditions: Politics, Theory, Comparisons*. U of Minnesota P, 2002.

· 3 ·

HISTORY AND HISTORICITY IN *THOMAS AND BEULAH* AND *ON THE BUS WITH ROSA PARKS*

> Well, it really begins with two feelings I had as a child: first, that *I* wasn't represented in History—I'm talking of History with a capital H—neither as a female nor as a Black person. And second, the nagging sense that ordinary people were not represented in history, that history gives you the tales of heroes, basically—and not what happens to "ordinary" people who live through the events. (Ingersoll 103)

In an interview with Ratiner in 1992, Dove expressed her dissatisfaction with history as an impersonal narrative disconnected from individual experience. Positing that history with a capital "H" is a universal or totalizing view of the past as recorded from the center, which excludes the experiences of the subjugated, or marginalized, she underscores the need to revisit history. Traditionally, history has remained a closed racial domain for blacks and whites in America with separate narratives, heroes, and perspectives of what essentially is shared time-space for both races. Realizing that this disjunct has inevitably resulted in "gaps" in the metanarrative, Dove uses her vantage position on the threshold to look both in and out of prescribed living spaces, lighting up shadows to deconstruct the gaps in a Post-Black reformulation of the past. Taking as examples two of her collections of poems, *Thomas and Beulah* (1986) and *On the Bus with Rosa Parks* (1999), the chapter traces Dove's reformulation of images through an inverted perspective that foregrounds individual experiences against the background of momentous historical events, presenting history as lived space. While recent postmodern writers like Toni Morrison, Alice Walker, and Octavia Butler have centralized race in a revisiting of history and memory in their writings, Dove's revisiting of history aims to decenter race on each visitation, deconstructing the signifiers that racialize historical contexts. Further, treating history as a Hegelian progression towards absolute knowledge or freedom, Dove makes the Post-Black reformulation of the past part of a strategy of resistance against the totalizing nature of the historical narrative.

The history of Blackness is a complex one, the signifier itself connoting a long history of oppression and trauma. Recent Post-Black artists have questioned the truth and reliability of history in their art, and the historical archive remains a predominant issue for concern among artists like Glenn Ligon, Adler Guerrier, and Kara Walker. Even though their work is not predominantly preoccupied with issues of Black identity, these artists explore history as a complex system of signifiers that filter Blackness. Slavery and its attendant horrors make Blackness a central signifier in the historical archive, thus making every black person a representative of the historical trauma suffered by the race. Circumscribed by this (racialized) frame of the past, the contemporary African American is unable to transcend the binaries that determine his identity in the present. While Blackness and Black history were celebrated during the 1960s and 1970s as markers of pride in an ethnocentric identity, there was a rethinking of the role of modernist binaries as hegemonic tools towards the end of the century. Walker stated that she was tired "of being a role model" and "of being a featured member of my racial group and/or gender niche" (R. Smith), a feature that Dove described as requiring "one to erect certain walls or obey certain rules," all of which is "anathema to the artist" (Steffen 169).

The decentering of race as a central identity marker would require the blurring of binaries that set Black and White as opposites in the system of signifiers. In the 1990s, Hollinger stated that the blurring of binaries would facilitate voluntary "affiliations" (7) across the Du Boisian "color-line" (xi). Gilroy claimed that the transcending of binaries would need a contradictory turning away from the past—referring here to official historical archives—to reconfigure the associations between past and present. He says that these binaries precluded healing from historical trauma and prevented an engaging with the present:

> Whether it was read primarily as heroic, noble, wise, and regal or abject, brutalized, de-humanized, and enchained, their transnational and intercultural history had now to be set aside. Its claims upon the present had been rendered illegitimate by the demands of autonomy and self-possession. (336)

However, setting aside history would first need a decentering of race as a signifier, the two being inextricably linked in memory, and this could only be done through an epistemological reconfiguration of images that informed its sociocultural contexts. Paradoxically, this would need a revisiting of the sites in memory where the contexts originated. In an interview with S. Smith, Dove reiterates that her aim is to arrive at "that moment where a historical event intersects with an ordinary person's daily trot" (Dove interview).

In order to achieve a reconfiguration of the image in relation to its social and cultural contexts, Dove would need to reconfigure the lens through which history was viewed. In *The Poet's World*, she talks about "occupied space" (15), of being sealed into enclosures that define clear boundaries between inside and outside, saying: "Each comfortable little home shelters a comfortable little soul—and a wall at the back shuts out completely any communication with the world beyond" (56). Having created a transcultural space of liminal existence in her first collection, *The Yellow House on the Corner*, Dove uses her position in the liminal space to reconfigure the lens, her vantage position on the threshold allowing her to invert the perspective that governed linearity, so that the image that was closer is relegated to the background, while the image that was farther off appears larger as it is foregrounded. This would reveal gaps in the historical metanarrative as interstices that remain suppressed in the dominant linguistic structure.

The use of the inverted perspective in her poems allows Dove to foreground the lives of individuals who form a minimal detail in historical archives, while relegating to the background details that dominate the narrative. She effects this change by (re)structuring lived space in her collections to transform the linearity of the lens into a perspective that inverts the relative size of the image. Arguing that history is a metanarrative of images that live in the memory, she first creates space in her first collection for the inversion. In order to study the African American's existence within hegemonic structures, she visualizes the "opening" of space that blurs the barrier between exterior and interior to create a "nearly illusory, a gray space" (*The Poet's World* 23). The altered state of consciousness in such a space would allow for a postethnic reformulation of memory as a storehouse of sensory, visual, and linguistic signifiers that act as experiential filters defining recollections of the past. In this metaphorical "sliding moment" (24) that defines the postethnic, the individual is able to blur the binary of inside/outside and revisit history in the gray space where hegemonic structures remain suspended. This is a necessary creation to allow for an impartial "witnessing" of history. Dove says, "Witnessing is very powerful; in a way, each poet does exactly that every time he or she writes a poem—witnessing a little piece of life" (Ingersoll 105). This defines history as a collection of flashes of disjointed points, allowing a reformulation of the narrative through a personal revisiting. These flashes are also what Post-Black artists like Kara Walker use in the form of silhouettes, leaving gaps clearly visible for the viewer to interpret.

In rejecting the totalization of history, Dove adheres to Foucault's theory of history as discontinuity rather than continuity. As racial domination moved from the external domain of the body in the nineteenth century to be internalized within the self in the twentieth, the subject as agent gave way to a hegemonic network of racialized configurations that permeated everyday discourse. This is what Morrison refers to when she states that race has become a "metaphysical necessity" (64) in the twentieth century. Poster says: "Domination today takes the form of a combination or structure of knowledge and power which is not external to the subject but still unintelligible from his or her perspective" (123). He concludes that "the early modern period is separated from the nineteenth century and its unique structure of knowledge/power by a dramatic discontinuity" that has metamorphosed into what he terms "an extraordinary 'microphysics of power,' extending throughout the social landscape" (125). This is characterized by a Foucauldian "*insurrection of subjugated knowledges*" (Foucault 81), which refer to "those blocs of historical knowledge which were present but disguised within the body of functionalist and systematising theory" (82). What was subjugated in this overarching narrative, states Foucault, was "a *historical knowledge of struggles*" (83). White assigns to history the fallacies of narrative constructivism, stating that "the dominant tropological mode and its attendant linguistic protocol comprise the irreducibly 'metahistorical' basis of every historical work" (*Metahistory* xxxi). In an earlier study, he had observed:

> A simply true account of the world based on what the documentary record permits one to talk about what happened in it at particular times, and places can provide knowledge of only a very small portion that "reality" consists of. ("Introduction" 147)

Admitting of possibilities that had been suppressed in official records, Dove looks to images that reside in individual memory. In an interview with Pereira, she says:

> I think that because I was acutely aware, even at a young age, that my perception of an "official" historical event was very different from that "official" version, I thought

that that must be the same for every person, if they stopped to think about it...in the end, unless you have a writer, or artist, or an oral history, the only version left is the one that is the official version, and I really resist that. I feel that all of us cannot ever forget that the official version is merely a construct that we may need to order our time line, but there are human beings, all sorts of individual human beings, to punctuate it. (Ingersoll 152)

History, Dove seems to say, is a narrative of images that is often suppressed beneath linguistic structures that preclude "the union of erudite knowledge and local memories which allows us to establish a historical knowledge of struggles" (Foucault 71). When the focus is turned on individual experiences, the self, as a *"sensory and emotional entity* encapsulating individual experiences" (Hook 141) builds on its own perspectives of what is happening at the moment; history becomes a collection of individual perspectives that often exist as gaps in the official version.

In foregrounding the individual to reveal and light up shadows in the narrative, Dove's treatment of history foreshadows and references Post-Black art and Hollinger's theory of postethnicity. In the 1990s, Hollinger posited postethnicity as a way to accept the realities of a multicultural society made more complex by the legacy of slavery and miscegenation, and stated that "identity," which was static, needed to be replaced by voluntary "affiliations" (7), which would take into account both the legacy of the past as well as the postmodern fluidity of existence. This would also counter the hegemonic nature of ethno-racial blocs which prescribed identities and consequently regulated the position of the individual as inside/outside. Anderson states that the "systematic *quantification"* of these ethno-racial classifications "put down deep social and institutional roots" that perpetuated "the principle of ethno-racial hierarchies which were, however, always understood in terms of parallel series" (168–69). Thus, these blocs became one of the agencies through which racial and ethnic identities became a closed domain. Historical frames too subscribed to these domains, ensuring that disparate frames of historical reference meant that non-whites would always be at the fringes of the dominant narrative in collective memory. Dove foreshadows Hollinger's theory in her poetry, formulating a new collective memory by countering the metanarrative of history as a racialized domain built on binaries. The Post-Black aesthetic allows Dove to situate Black life against the backdrop of important historical events, significantly claiming both white and black space as ancestral. Incorporating images as defining and dominating the historical narrative, the aesthetic resists historically defined linguistic categories.

Till the 1980s, the binaries of black/white, us/them, center/margin, were built through the belief that identity could subscribe to only one side of the Du Boisian color-line. This consciousness of the racialized self constructed the historical narrative through the dichotomy of colored/white. Whiteness used linguistic tools to construct history with the white man at the center of a "pure" category that relegated all other narratives to the domain of subjugated knowledges, so that "history is seen through the lens placed at the centre and invariably lights up the margins as 'different'" (Roy 185). Critics in the twentieth century realized the need to bring the images suppressed beneath oppressive linguistic structures to the surface. Foucault stresses this when he says, "In the specialised areas of erudition as in the disqualified popular knowledge there lay the memory of hostile encounters which even up to this day have been confined to the margins of knowledge" (71). In a study that focuses on imagery as constructing and racializing reality, Dyer states that images organize the modern world, observing that "since race in itself—insofar as it is anything in itself—refers to some intrinsically insignificant geographical/physical differences between people, it is the imagery of race that is in play" (1). Historically, the color of the skin became the sole identifier for African Americans, and the term "black" a pejorative signifier that carried undeniable associations with slavery, wherein links between past and present were forged through the color of the skin. These codes that defined identity separated history into black/white, and affiliations on either side of the color-line subscribed to these codes in the first half of the twentieth century.

In an effort to dismantle binaries, Dove's poems eschew both ethnocentric singularity and an assimilationist outlook, exploring the possibilities of a postmodern juxtaposition of frames of existence to revisit historical narratives. Building on the precept that race is an "anachronistic term" (Hollinger 9) that nevertheless gained the force of reality through segregation of domains in the psyche reinforced through racial memory, Dove seeks a Foucauldian break with the politics of the dichotomous framing of the past. The way to this Post-Black reformulation would be through the individual, where cultural experience would realistically not subscribe to strict segregation. Dove's poetry seeks to counter the linearity of traditional historical frames through metaphor and imagery, making black and white collaborators in an attempt to juxtapose parallel frames of memory. Through an appropriation of popular stereotypes, her poetry brings to the fore the heterogeneous nature of individual lives. It also analyzes what history means for individuals who live through these moments, rather than the other way around. In all these representations, the individual is placed in the "gray space" which is both inside and outside, allowing a revisiting of the past *sans* racialized filters. In *Thomas and Beulah*, Dove qualifies this space with black subjectivity, allowing for a changing of contours to effect it. Thus, even as *Thomas and Beulah* foregrounds individual lives against the backdrop of slavery, it eschews the celebration of Blackness as a counter to the ethnocentric, essentialist norms of identity construction for African Americans. *On the Bus with Rosa Parks* places one of the defining moments of the Civil Rights Movement, led by a woman, in a personal frame. Through a revisiting of the psycho-spatial domain of the memory, the poems in both these collections reformulate the framework which defines historicity and the epistemology of race. In this epistemic reformulation of history, Dove emphasizes how cultures carry their antecedents and memory perpetrates itself through signification. Even as the language of the poems retreats into the symbolic, it emphasizes the role of perspective in framing ideologies which then become learned truth. The poems transcend space and time in attempting to explore what it means to be African American; in the quest, slavery remains a recurring motif, and color a potent symbol of identification.

Positing that history plays an important role in the construction of images that then live on as truth, Dove's liminal positioning reveals how the construction of dichotomous identities on either side of the color-line excludes the important role played by the Other in the narrative. White analyzes historical consciousness in the nineteenth and twentieth centuries to conclude that it is nothing more than the theoretical basis of the ideological position that defines the synchronous and diachronous relationship of the West with other cultures. "It is possible," he says, "to view historical consciousness as a specifically Western prejudice by which the presumed superiority of modern, industrial society can be retroactively substantiated" (2). Post-Blackness recognizes this, with most Post-Black artists refraining from the center/margin conflict of space in their art. Dove's awareness of the constructed nature of double consciousness leads her to explore difference as a myth.

Thus, the juxtaposition of racial frames of history builds on the growing realization towards the end of the twentieth century that true art need not separate the personal and the political into disjunctive frames of experience. The African American poets who rose to prominence during the 1980s employed stylistic traditions that stretched back to Langston Hughes and other Harlem Renaissance writers. Though the themes of survival and freedom remained pronounced in their works, the major difference was that they confronted the effects of time and history on the individual, and stressed on the personal as opposed to the political. Audre Lorde, in an interview with Tate, spoke against the Black Arts Movement's stress on the representation of the global experience of blacks and the oppressed. Rejecting the notion that African American art is political at its core, she saw poetry as a reflection of the personal:

> Black men have come to believe to their detriment that you have no validity unless you're "global," as opposed to personal. Yet our *real power* comes from the personal; our real insights about living come from the deep knowledge within us that arises from our feelings. (Hall 91)

Dove too perceives history as an integral part of the individual. According to her, history is within us, and we cannot escape it. History is part of every man's story. This is visible even in later collections like *Mother Love* where Persephone looks at the embryo in her womb as proof that history grows inside an individual. Dove's assertion that social conditioning limits the experiential transcending of barriers, visible in the image of the metaphorical trunks of elephants "hooking the sky" (9) in her first collection, *The Yellow House on the Corner*, permeates her sense of African American identity being limited by cultural and social norms structuring identity construction. She contends that the mere realization of the presence of systemically structured norms that inform images that in turn construe memory as distinct frames opens up a transcultural space that is heterotopic in nature. She says, "I prove a theorem and the house expands" ("Geometry"). The deconstruction of memory as a frame built through (racialized) imagery lends credence to the concept of contingent historicity. As the contours of occupied space change, Dove says, "I am out in the open" ("Geometry").

Hollinger, in proposing postethnicity as a way to build affiliations across the color-line, talks of the growing acceptance of historicity, that is, "the contingent, temporally, and socially situated character of our beliefs and values, of our institutions and practices" (60). Dove's poems examine closely the myths and beliefs that live on as larger-than-life truths in the memory, preventing emotional distancing. As "the ceiling floats away" in the memory, the poet revisits slavery and the sites of historical trauma, bringing to the fore individual consciousnesses buried in the metanarrative of disjunctive frames of memory. The use of the lyric makes this imagery more effective, and the resultant interweaving of lyric and narrative makes the poems metaphors rich in imagery. In an interview, Dove describes the metaphoric interweaving of temporal sequences to achieve lyrical and narrative probability: "So one of the things

I was trying to do was string moments as beads on a necklace. In other words, I have lyric poems which, when placed one after the other, reconstruct the sweep of time" (Ingersoll 67).

Having woven music into a narrative of the black man struggling to achieve the American Dream, Dove then presents history as individual, rather than as part of a collective memory. This aims at reconstituting the entire framework that constitutes memory. Her third collection of poems, titled *Thomas and Beulah*, revisits the Great Migration that occurred between 1916 and 1970 as lived experience. Righelato says that Dove "wanted to capture the lives of ordinary people caught up in the migration of African Americans from the rural South to the industrialized towns of the North in the early years of the twentieth century" (70). But Dove's portrayal of an individual life caught up in a defining moment in time gives that moment a startling reality and an immediacy that transcends intervening periods. The Great Migration was one of the defining events of the century, shaping black lives and signaling an economic and cultural demographic shift. Dove captures the event from two different perspectives, that of Thomas, loosely structured around the life of her grandfather, and of Beulah, representing her grandmother, Georgianna. In an interview with Moyers, she says: "I think we understand history through the family around the table, and those who aren't there anymore but who are called in through the past…How we act in our lives is how we memorize ourselves in the past" (Moyers 124). The poems follow Thomas as he leaves Tennessee in 1919, arrives in Akron, Ohio, in 1921, and marries Beulah. The collection traces their lives through the Depression of the thirties, the Second World War, and the Civil Rights movement, till Thomas's death in 1963, and Beulah's in 1969, following the experiences and emotions of both separately as they live through these moments in history; the foregrounding of ordinary individual lives—"these nobodies in the course of history" (Ingersoll 10)— bringing to life moments that would otherwise be mere points of reference in the chronology of the struggle for survival after Emancipation. Here, the personal is political, and reality is metaphorical. In an interview, Dove says of the collection:

> I was after the essence of my grandparents' existence and their survival, not necessarily the facts of their survival. That's the distinction I'm trying to make. …One appropriates certain gestures from the factual life to reinforce a larger sense of truth that is not, strictly speaking, reality. (Ingersoll 66)

Steffen quotes Bellin's definition of History with a capital "H" to understand Dove's interpretation of it as a process made up of moments:

> History with a small *h* consists of a billion stories. History with a capital *H* is a construct, a grid you have to fit over the significant events in ordinary lives. Great historians, those who can make history "come alive," realize that all the battles lost or won are only a kind of net, and we are caught in that net. Because there are other interstices in that large web. (Bellin qtd. in Steffen 96)

It is these interstices that consist of subjugated and personal knowledges that must be brought to the surface for a coherent narrative. In interpreting these gaps, Dove's collection bespeaks possibilities, rather than factual accuracy. As a historicizing procedure, this is the Foucauldian "genealogy" that entertains "the claim to attention of local, discontinuous, disqualified, illegitimate knowledges against the claims of a unitary body of theory which would filter, hierarchise, and order them in the name of some true knowledge" (71). The poems in the collection, using the African practice of weaving memory into facts, reject temporal linearity to reconstitute the teleology of history, placing the individual at the center of a perspectival circle, each part vital to the narrative.

Thomas and Beulah is divided into two sections, the first, titled "Mandolin," tracing the life of Thomas, and the second, titled "Canary in Bloom," tracing the life of Beulah. The poems portray the struggle of the protagonists as each aspires to the American Dream, examining closely what it means to be black in postbellum America. Eschewing both the formal lyrical mode and black colloquial language, they incorporate a rich sequence of metaphor and imagery. Righelato observes that "both sequences include free, indirect discourse or quoted monologue to register the protagonists' sense of identity, which is woven into omniscient narrative comment" (71). Both genders occupy equal space in the historical frame as the lives of both Thomas and Beulah play themselves out against the backdrop of historical events, indicating the social and cultural significance of these events for individual lives. If "Mandolin" emphasizes the significance of music and of traveling to Thomas's story, "Canary in Bloom" is a metaphor for the more restricted domesticity of Beulah's. Lived space becomes a metaphor for dreams in this collection. In *The Poet's World*, Dove talks of the mind as analogous to lived space:

> Our minds, all of our minds, are like dull little houses, built more or less alike—a dull little city with rows of little detached villas, and here and there a more pretentious

house, set apart from the rest, but in essentials, seen from a distance, one with the rest, all drab, all grey. (56)

In pointing out the heterogeneity in the dwellings that all appear the same from a distance, Dove emphasizes the need to view each life in isolation, yet as part of a community of souls, alike when viewed from afar, but each distinct from the others.

The first poem in Thomas's section, titled "The Event," marks the beginning of his journey from Tennessee in 1919 as part of the Great Migration. Recording the metaphorical importance of this migration, Morrison says: "The flight from the Old World to the New is generally seen to be a flight from oppression and limitation to freedom and possibility" (34). Music accompanies Thomas to the land of hope, the mandolin recording his hopes and sadnesses. The lyrical cadence of the poems sweeps the reader along with it, and "the overall sweep of the poem threads motif to motif into an enhancing musical harmony" (Righelato 72). Music, for Dove, was the black man's language, drawing him into its stoic folds in a racialized world. Accompanied by music and filled with hope, Thomas and Lem leave Tennessee for Ohio. The "event," however, becomes one of personal tragedy as Lem drowns, leaving Thomas only the "half-shell mandolin" and the wheel, an ironic symbol which will recur at the end of his life. Unacknowledged now and a forceful presence later, the wheel symbolizes the force of individual destiny: "Where the wheel turned the water // gently stirred." Man's powerlessness even when at the wheel is outlined at the start of the journey, and the difference in paths marking individual destinies underlines the transition to the next poem.

The second poem, titled "Variation on Pain," initiates Thomas's journey as the metaphorically reductive "two strings, one pierced cry." Personal grief takes the shape of the mandolin as Lem struggles for air. Pain connects the dead man and the living, but the healing from trauma will carry the fissures: "Two greased strings/For each pierced lobe:/So is the past forgiven." The third poem, titled "Jiving," carrying the ironic ecstasy at having migrated to the North, sees Thomas arrive in Akron, alone and full of dreams. The memory of trauma, however, marks his struggle in the new city: "Since what he'd been through/he was always jiving."

The stereotypical image of the jiving black man is humanized in an awareness of trauma. As the poems trace Thomas's life in Ohio, they deconstruct the American Dream and what it meant for African Americans who had migrated from the South. Righelato says: "Thomas's peacock colors and frenetic strumming are compensatory, overcompensatory" (75). The transition is both physical and metaphorical, as the old identity is pushed away, back "into another's life," and Thomas, with his "straw hat/cocked on the back of his head, // tight curls gleaming" becomes the symbol of the glittering, exotic image of the American Dream. However, the pain is carried over from poem to poem like the French *liaison*, alternating with Thomas's work like the notes on the mandolin: "To him, work is a narrow grief."

The mourning that dominates Thomas's frame can only be relieved by an object to fill the space left empty by Lem's death. This takes the form of Beulah, who, though unnamed, appears in the next poem, titled "Courtship." Dove indicates the meaninglessness of freedom and material struggles without human succor to relieve the hardships, as Thomas, in "his yellow scarf" finally finds fulfillment as he shares his success: "…so he wraps the yellow silk/ still warm from his throat/around her shoulders." Beulah accepts his gift, and Thomas is ecstatic. Healing takes place as love blossoms in his heart, melting the harshness of his existence. The American Dream is translated as personal fulfillment in love, contradicting its image as just the material glitter that deludes the eye. As each day is lived out, Dove stresses on the universality of experiences and the ordinariness that makes up individual lives through all time.

The mandolin, Thomas's companion on his journey, reasserts its musical presence in the next poem. Titled "Refrain," the poem alternates between the ordinary and the sublime, the poetic and the mundane. Carrying over the metaphor of the festooned ship from the earlier poem, the lover is portrayed as "sailing/past the bedroom window." Yet the metaphorical sailor carries within his heart traces of the painful past, which live in the memory inseparable from the music: "Now he's raised a mast/and tied himself to it/with rags." The image of Thomas taking the rags at his feet and anchoring himself with them is a poignant revisiting of the site of trauma to allow for healing. Rather than push grief back into the recesses of his mind as he had tried to do till now, he allows its symbolic remnants to resurface at a happier moment, making them symbols of his fortitude. The Post-Black insists on opening up the wound to healing, stressing on the impossibility of escaping the constrictions imposed by trauma till a resolution takes place.

The next poem in the section, titled "Variation in Guilt," is once again a revisiting of the traumatic "event." However, love has expanded the contours of the heart, and it merges with loss to ameliorate its effects. Time and space have also caused emotional distancing. Waiting anxiously for news outside the room where his wife is confined, Thomas muses:

> Wretched
> little difference, he thinks,
> between enduring pain and
> waiting for pain
> to work on others.
>
> The doors fly apart—no,
> He wouldn't run away!

The metaphorical doors open to news that he both dreads and awaits, but this time, Thomas is ready to face it. As he hears of his daughter's birth, he realizes that hardship has numbed him: "But he doesn't feel a thing."

The variations in emotion follow the cadences of the mandolin's notes, reasserting themselves at each significant event in Thomas's life. The next time it appears is when his daughter gets married. Titled "Variation on Gaining a Son," the poem marks the completion of the process of healing as Thomas experiences a tender bond of comradeship with his son-in-law: "For the first time Thomas felt like/calling him *Son*." The suppressed rage in his heart reaches a peak in the poems just preceding his final reconciliation with his past and his transition to the status of a family man. In delineating this aspect of his character, Dove strikes at the stereotype of the absent black father and husband and the myth of natal isolation as characteristic of the dysfunctional black family structure. Nurturing, she seems to say, is a reciprocal experience.

One of the most important poems in Thomas's section is "Aurora Borealis." Ironically, the "Aurora Borealis" in this section refers not to the bright northern lights but the "crippling radiance" of Hiroshima. The year is 1943 and as tired and bewildered people spill out on to the streets, Thomas feels himself drowning in the guilt of having survived life's tragedies (which Lem has not). Filled with guilt and rage, despair engulfs him as he tries to find a beacon in the form of a thought. Dove is at her metaphorical best in this poem as she juxtaposes the personal and the political in the flash in a movie theater:

> Thomas walks out of the movie house
> And forgets where he is.
> He is drowning and
> The darkness above him
> Spits and churns.

> What shines is a thought
> Which has lost its way. Helpless
> It hangs and shivers
> Like a veil.

Here, Thomas's despair is the common worker's sense of insufficiency during World War II; the rage at being alive is crippling. Righelato observes: "The psychic blight of war, the failure of the follow-through from spirit to action, is evident in the negativizing of the imagery of light in the poems" (84). The darkness is both literal and metaphorical.

The memory of Lem's death never leaves Thomas as he lives out his life in the North. Noting the contrary nature of the Migration, Dove says in an interview with Schneider, "It's the first time that Blacks in this country had rooting and displacement. It's the first time that Blacks in this country had any chance, however stifled, of pursuing 'the American Dream'" (Ingersoll 67). While Thomas is part of a city filled with lights, he has never really been the one in control of his life. The poem, "The Stroke," indicates the stressful lifestyle that success in America demands. Existing as a gap in the glittering image of the Dream, the illness assumes the form of the metaphorical Lem, the carefree part of himself that Thomas lost on the journey up North:

> Later he'll say Death stepped right up
> to shake his hand, then squeezed
> until he sank to his knees. *(Get up,*
> *nigger. Get up and try again.)*
> ....
> He knows it was Lem all along:
> Lem's knuckles tapping his chest in passing,
> Lem's heart, for safekeeping,
> he shores up in his arms.

Resilience marks Thomas's character, and the cold days are painted with a positivity that has been the hallmark of his life: "They were poor then but everyone had been poor" ("The Satisfaction Coal Company"). The image, however, is of a changed world, and Thomas looks back on the familiar old ways of doing things with wistfulness, comparing it to the present emptiness—"What to do with a day."

As Thomas lives out his life in a mechanized world where the individual is in danger of being negated by all the comforts, death approaches him. The title of the last poem in his section, "Thomas at the Wheel," indicates that life has come full circle for him. Ironically, although he is at the wheel, Thomas has never been in complete control of his life. He has lived through two World Wars and has spent his life trying to assert his identity in a world marked by economic hardship and racial inequality, the end of his journey marked by the image of water wherein it had begun:

> This, then, the river he had to swim.
> Through the wipers the drugstore
> shouted, lit up like a casino,
> neon script leering from the shuddering asphalt.

The journey down the river merges with the neon script as surface signifier. In projecting the neon script, Dove portrays the first truly Post-Black image in the collection. Much later, in 2006, the same image would be used by Ligon at an exhibition at the Studio Museum in Harlem to portray the Post-Black emptying of signifiers as the black body is removed from the gaze. In Dove's poem, the focus moves away from Thomas to a description of the drugstore lit up before him at the moment of closure. It is significant that Thomas, who has lived through all of the century's most momentous historical events, struggling to be part of the mainstream, should die at the very moment that Post-Blackness initiates a decentering of race.

The next section in the collection portrays history as lived space for the black woman. Beulah's life is marked by color. Her section of the collection is titled "Canary in Bloom," the image of the caged canary in direct contradiction to the image symbolizing Thomas's freedom, water. The first poem of the section, titled "Taking in Wash," shows the child's awareness of her Blackness: "She was Papa's girl,/black though she was." The hint of violence within the family unit marks many of Dove's poems, albeit touching upon it in a tangential manner. The poem emphasizes the mother as the strong moral center of the family, protective of her daughter and firm in the face of her husband's vagaries: "*Touch that child // and I'll cut you down/just like the cedar of Lebanon.*" The danger of violence in the home is reminiscent of Angelou's "caged bird" (*I Know Why the Caged Bird Sings*). Dove portrays the female spirit encaged as it seeks solace in "wavery memory" ("Dusting"). Memory for Beulah acts as a protector who helps her weather hardships during the war. For Beulah, reality is much like a dream, and memory takes on the shape of reality. In a poem titled "Weathering Out," she describes herself as "large and placid, a lake," even as "outside/everything shivered in tinfoil." In this caged world, stereotypes retain their shape and the traditional binaries of gender and race play themselves out in the images. Beulah becomes a calm center of refuge in the disturbed outer world, much like the image of the strong black Mammy, helping both herself and her family to weather storms. In "Daystar," Beulah wishes she had time for herself, but domestic chores are waiting for her: "She wanted a little room for thinking:/but she saw diapers steaming on the line,/a doll slumped behind the door."

However, domestic constrictions do not restrict Beulah's mind. The Post-Black individual is a thinking, analytical person, and this is reflected in Beulah's observations as she notices the hypocritical attitudes of the French women she serves. Color as a racial identifier reiterates its presence in the poem titled "The Great Palaces of Versailles" as Beulah contemplates the difference between myth and reality: "*Nothing nastier than a white person!*" This decentering of European grandeur dismantles the projection of greatness vested on the white man in history, making his palaces but symbols of the evils which fostered them. Versailles, close to Paris, projects itself as a racist world marked by a deceptive façade in the poems, and the fashionable evenings are marked by hypocrisy:

> Beulah remembers how
> even Autumn could lean into a settee
> with her ankles crossed, sighing
> *I need a man who'll protect me*
> while smoking her cigarette down to the very end.

Beulah's observations are quick and realistic, and are not colored by racial hatred or reverence. Following the stream of consciousness, they are, rather, perceptive observations of social mores.

The section on Beulah acknowledges the past and changes in the present in a more direct manner than the one on Thomas. Even as Beulah reiterates the importance of history, saying, "Where she came from/was the past" ("Wingfoot Lake"), she expresses no understanding of the yearning back to roots in Africa, saying, "What did she know about Africa?" History for Beulah is personal, and the past is "12 miles into town/where nobody had locked their back door." The past for her transcends events as they live on in public memory to result in a weaving together of bits of personal memory. This new fabric woven out of bits of individual lives forms the new "collective memory" that Dove believes is necessary for a postethnic transcending of ethno-racial borders. Beulah's stance can be likened to that of the Post-Black artist, Glenn

Ligon, whose piece, "Nobody Knew Me," expresses the same lack of connectedness with Africa that Beulah shows.

Beulah is also portrayed as strong, despite the limitations that her situation in life impose on her. In an interview with Schneider, Dove says of her:

> I think of Beulah as being a very strong woman, who still has no way of showing how strong she could be. She is the one who really wants to travel, to see the world. She is curious, she is intelligent, and her situation in life does not allow her to pursue her curiosity. If there is anything I want to honor in her, it is that spirit. (Ingersoll 70)

Beulah's spirit finds release only in dreams, her constrictive domestic space not allowing for much freedom. She experiences the restraints imposed by gender in the 1920s, yet, within this restricted space, her story is as much part of the history of the times, according to Dove, as Thomas's, or the monumental events against which both lives are foregrounded. This collection explores the personal and the political as inseparable parts interwoven into a narrative that builds on individual experiences. It also grants the black man and the black woman equal space in the historical frame.

Thomas and Beulah is also an introspective reflection on her own identity by Dove, a descendant of the protagonists. Vendler asserts that "*Thomas and Beulah* represents Dove's rethinking of the lyric poet's relation to the history of blackness" (82). In asserting heterogeneity of experience, it reasserts the Post-Black quest for identity as an individual journey. Thus, even though the protagonists of the collection are unmistakably black, Dove eschews both racial pride and focus on trauma, lighting up instead the whole process of living life in the post-Emancipation era. The collection presents the protagonists in a realistic frame, every observation recorded within that frame. Vendler says:

> Dove no longer looks to the "picturesque" antebellum slave record, nor to an exotic collective massacre in the Dominic Republic, nor to interwar Berlin, to revive history; she records instead the history, living vividly in contemporary memory, of the industrial and domestic servitude of two ordinary American people in the earlier twentieth century. (78)

It is a rethinking of the lyric poet's own position in relation to the history of Blackness. Race as identifier and as lived space presents itself most wilfully in these poems. In this collection, says Steffen, "Text meets countertext" (96). As Dove incorporates a portrayal of black life in this defined and confined space that neither shies away from admitting of the existence of the Other nor vilifies it, her poetry foreshadows the processes that would be needed for co-existence as racial equals in postethnic America.

Dove's next collection, *On the Bus with Rosa Parks*, is a more explicit outlining of the process that defines a great historical moment. It is in this collection that we see more clearly a movement from the New Black Aesthetic to the Post-Black Aesthetic. Using the inverted perspective, Dove foregrounds the ordinary people, especially women, who lay the foundation of great enterprise in history. Moving on from the satirical irreverence expressed in images of male Civil Rights leaders characteristic of NBA artists, Dove presents a feminist alternative to the quest for icons. Rosa Parks, whose refusal to give up her seat in the bus to a white fellow passenger in 1955 started the historic Montgomery Bus Boycott against racial segregation in an act of defiance that would become one of the defining moments in the movement, has been overshadowed in official history by male civil rights leaders whose role in the movement has received greater prominence. Parks's arrest triggered widespread protests and 42,000 African Americans boycotted Montgomery buses for 381 days till The United States Supreme Court ruled on 13 November 1956 that the Montgomery segregation law was unconstitutional. On 20 December 1956, officials in Montgomery were ordered to desegregate buses. This was the beginning of the Civil Rights Movement which would lead to the Civil Rights Act of 1964, making *de jure* equality a reality for African Americans, and any form of discrimination, including segregation in public facilities, illegal. However, Parks's quiet dignity meant that her act was soon overshadowed by the male leaders of the resistance, notably Martin Luther King Jr., A. Philip Randolph, Bayard Rustin, John Lewis, Roy Wilkins, and Whitney M. Young, and the movement soon became known for its masculine leadership. Women like Rosa Parks, Dorothy Height, and Gloria Richardson had an equally important role to play in the movement, and Dove's collection on Parks marks an important crossroads in African American resistance to racial discrimination in the post-Emancipation struggle for equal rights, bringing to the forefront of public memory the image of the quiet, inconspicuous woman who formed the base of that resistance.

On the Bus with Rosa Parks spans a period of seventy-four years, from 1925 to 1999. The collection itself was published in 1999, thirteen years after *Thomas and Beulah*, yet it begins where *Thomas and Beulah* left off. Following Dove's theory of history as a process, the volume "expresses not only the civil rights journey (still in process) but also the life journey, the movement forward, the panorama glimpsed as it recedes, already, from view" (Righelato 175). The collection is divided into five sections, the first describing the sequence of an ordinary life—birth, graduation, job, marriage, children—before the next four sections discuss the importance of freedom in that ordinary life. Righelato says that the description of ordinary lives in the first section, titled "Cameos," "serves as a prelude to the poems that express how these same kind of ordinary people became politically active" (174). She quotes Dove's "fascination with the underside of history" (Dove, *The Poet's World* 85), stating that "closure invites recall and return" (Righelato 175). Implying that the movement towards Post-Blackness could never be completed without an unearthing of all of history's light and shade, the collection explores not just the moment, but the preceding moments from which it constitutes a break.

Perception and the American way of life play a major role in defining lived space in the collection. Reiterating Dove's realization of the importance of lost spaces, which remain suppressed in the memory yet shape consciousness, the poems in the first section trace the domesticity that drives lives unaware of the fact that they are the predecessors of a great moment in American history. Righelato says: "History is preoccupied with units of time and the volume has its share of end-of-century and end-of-millennium thoughts" (175). This involves creating a communality of interwoven lives in the midst of the individualism that defined life in twentieth-century America. This is reflected in the titles of the poems in the first section, which are either dates, or events, significant in the life of the individual. Thus, the first poem, titled "July, 1925," traces Lucille's movements as she lies down in the shade to await childbirth, waiting for Joe, who has abandoned her:

> Lucille lies down
> between tomatoes
> and the pole beans: heavenly shade.
> From here everything looks
> reptilian. The tomato plops
> in her outstretched palm. *Now*
> *he'll come*, she thinks,
> *and it will be a son.*

Lucille's yearning for domesticity is comparable to the older Beulah's dreams in *Thomas and Beulah*. In the next poem, titled "Night," Joe thinks of the father he has never known, and his stout mother. Yearning for freedom, Joe wishes he could find the space to think:

> Joe
> thinks, half
> dreaming, if he ever finds
> a place where he can think,
> he'd stop clowning
> and drinking and then that wife
> of his would quit
> sending prayers through the chimney.

The collection commences on a familiar note, reinforcing the stereotypical dysfunctional nature of the African American family. Righelato observes, "The narrative progression of Joe's altogether standard behavior (for a man whose absentee father was the model of the masculine role), succinctly balances self interest and contrition" (177). Both Lucille and Joe alternate to recreate cultural patterns, and the comparison with Thomas and Beulah's lives is inevitable.

The image of natal isolation is carried over into the next poem—"no reception but/accumulated time" ("Birth"), outlining the ordinary nature of the event. Yet the change is in the birth of the black intellectual. In the Introduction to her collection, *Selected Poems*, Dove deliberates ontological questions that punctuate material dreams:

> The mystery of destiny boils down to the ultimate—and ultimately unanswerable—questions: How does where I come from determine where I've ended up? Why am I what I am and not what I thought I'd be? What did I think I'd be? Where do I reside most completely? (xxi)

As Joe and Lucille's children grow up, the gradual metamorphosis of the black man into an intellectual being takes place. Joe and Lucille existed on a level of physicality that is marked by the stereotypical irresponsibility of the male towards his family. Joe's son, in contrast, is an analytical being who goes to college and is shown to deliberate on the sciences and the arts. Dove traces the changes that mark each generation as they move further away from mere essentialist survival strategies to explore choices. The availability of choices gives birth to dreams, and as Joe's son turns away from the song celebrating Negritude as a place of belonging, the movement signals the end of strategic essentialism as the only identity available to African Americans; a more cosmopolitan choice of astronomy as a course of study is also a counter to Booker T. Washington's advice to all African Americans to master a trade for survival. Joe's son is a *thinking* man, an intellectual, one who hates music, and displays resistance:

> Shit,
> he'll take Science, most
> Exacting Art.
> In school when the teacher
> makes him lead
> the class in song,
> he'll cough straight through.
> Better
> columns of figures, the thing
> dissected to the bone.
> Better
> the clear and incurious *drip*
> of fluid from pipet
> to reassuring beaker. ("Homework")

This, and the other poems in the first section of *On the Bus with Rosa Parks*, begin a process of intellectual and artistic growth that moves beyond essentialist minimalism. Steffen calls this collection "an ongoing Bildungsroman in verse for African Americans both personally and collectively" (144). This is the initiation of the Post-Black, which implies not a negation of Blackness or black history, but a refusal to be circumscribed by them. Though steeped in Black life, it refuses to make Blackness, and its connotative associations with historical trauma, a central identifier for the individual. In fact, the black man here refuses to be seen as a representative of the race, choosing instead to transcend race lines to excel intellectually. This is the Post-Black male, a person with a complex combination of traits who refuses to abide by prescriptive ideas of what Blackness should mean. Though not named, the scientist son might be the ancestor of the poet daughter in Dove herself—seen in this light, the collection is a postmodern self-reflexive analysis of the artistic process of creation and of the African American literary tradition. It is also a positioning of the poet as Post-Black, treating the transition as a response to the choices available. The poet is at the crossroads that marked the first collection—at this moment, the intervening years have resulted in her refusal to be prisoner to the past. The past, however, views this transition with distrust:

> Joe
> sees his son
> flicker. Although

>   the air is not a glass,
>   watches as he puts his lips to
>   the brim—then turns away, bored.
>   *He is not mine, this son,*
>   *who ripens, quiet*
>   *poison on a*
>   *shelf.* ("Graduation, Grammar School")

The need to separate from the crowd, growing serious and thoughtful, not attracted to drinking like most black men of the previous generation, makes Joe's son an aberration in the eyes of his father. He views his evolving philosophical musings and criticism of Black homogeneity as poisonous for the mind. Yet, this is the beginning of the Post-Black questioning of essentialist identities and the assertion of ontological freedom.

The next section, titled "Freedom: Bird's-Eye View," moves to the present. The title suggests emotional distancing (from past trauma) as the mind progresses from scientific analysis to ontological questioning. This is also the experience of unrestricted skies after the windows have floated away, an expansion of space effected by Dove in her first collection. The first poem in the section, titled "Singsong," contrasts the ageing world with youthful innocence. Dealing with the existential nature of being, it talks of a time of innocence: "When I was young, the moon spoke in riddles," and goes on to conclude: "And the world was already old./And I was older than I am today." Having established an ontological connection between the self and the world, the poems that follow explore the meaning of freedom for African Americans in the twentieth century. Existential questions about life and death dominate the train of thoughts. The poem "Freedom: Bird's-Eye View" follows a sequence of poems on death, shadows, and the role of books in deciphering the meaning of existence. The first of these, titled "Parlor," likens the mind to a house, where memories were like rooms, some entered, some left undiscovered. Dove says: "We passed through/on the way to anywhere else./No one lived there."

In "passing through," Dove once again stresses the fundamental positioning of the poet as neither inside nor outside. As the poet explores the uninhabited parlor filled with silence, lived space becomes a metaphor for the liminal. This is especially significant for an African American, for the parlor was reserved in earlier times for receiving white people, while black people would normally enter and leave the house through the kitchen. It is a black person examining white space. In *The Poet's World*, Dove asks a rhetorical question: "Do we, as poets, peer through a window at the world or do we step out to meet it?" (19) She goes on to deconstruct the backyard as a symbol of confrontation, but the parlor, by implication the white man's domain, is the domain of silence, where the only witnesses to lives lived and acts undertaken are the eyes of the saints in portraits, looking out over the velvet. Dove says that this passing through "is the moment of ultimate possibility, and of ultimate irresponsibility" (24); however, the moment the poet achieves emotional distancing, being neither inside nor outside, free of defined spaces, she contradicts established definitions of Otherness and consequently of established spaces. Minh-ha says:

> The moment the insider steps out from the inside, she is no longer a mere insider. She necessarily looks in from the outside while also looking out from the inside. Not quite the same, not quite the other, she stands in that undetermined threshold place where she constantly drifts in and out. Undercutting the inside/outside opposition, her intervention is necessarily that of both not quite an insider and not quite an outsider. She is, in other words, this inappropriate "other" or "same" who moves about with always at least two gestures: that of affirming "I am like you" while persisting in her difference and that of reminding "I am different" while unsettling every definition of otherness arrived at. (418)

In undercutting the binary of inside/outside, the poet also undercuts the binaries of self/other, artist/creation. In such a situation, history and her story intertwine to become a self-reflexive process of exploration for the artist. Minh-ha says: "The subjectivity at work in the context of this inappropriate other can hardly be subjected to the old subjectivity/objectivity paradigm" (418). The shift in paradigm results in a blurring of the binaries of the personal and the political, wherein history as narrative merges with the narrative as history. This marks a transition from earlier African American writing, which treated spaces as either places of belonging, or the hostile Other. The Post-Black aesthetic rejects this confinement of space, and traces a genealogy of worlds that extend their contours to include the outside. The recurring motif of the traveler marks space as temporary dwelling, at best passing through, thus challenging "ontological expansiveness" (Shannon 10) as white privilege, and making available to the black man the same privilege of being able to pass between worlds that the white man has.

The second poem in the sequence is titled "The First Book." Words, according to Dove, comprise a world in themselves, and the progression of the intellectual into this lived space is a natural step in historical progression. For her, words are moments caught in time where there is a perfect intersection of facts and interstices. The poet moves from fact to metaphor, from the ground floor to the obscure corridors, a traveler and a philosopher rethinking white privilege and the ownership of lived spaces in a contemplative revisiting of history. In "The First Book," reading is compared to entering unknown spaces, and the fear of a book is the fear of the unknown, yet, once started, it pulls you into its insatiable depths:

> You see, it keeps on opening.
> You may fall in.
>
> Sure, it's hard to get started;
> remember learning to use
>
> knife and fork? Dig in:
> You'll never reach bottom.
>
> It's not like it's the end of the world—
> just the world as you think
>
> you know it.

The poem posits that the book is the traveler's final exploration. Language is presented as lived space, and reading a way to expand contours.

The journey from the word to the book might have been a long one, but the journey from the book to the library is relatively short. In the next poem, titled "Maple Valley Branch Library, 1967," the irresistible lure of the library as the key to a world that opens up to "bliss" is presented in language that resonates with imagery:

> So I read Gone with the Wind because
> it was big, and haiku because they were small.
> I studied history for its rhapsody of dates,
> lingered over Cubist art for the way
> it showed all sides of a guitar at once.
> All the time in the world was there, and sometimes
> all the world on a single page.
> As much as I could hold
> on my plastic card's imprint I took,
>
> greedily;

Reading opens up spaces. So does art, according to the poet. The reference to Cubist art is significant in that it is in Cubism that Dove has found the technique to explore the minor details that form the main part of the historical metanarrative. In Dove's poems, both the word and the image are signifiers. Here, the word becomes the metaphorical sand on which the shift in paradigm will locate itself. The recurring motif of the traveler in quest of worlds to call his own includes the reader. Steffen says that "books are the colorful and colorblind passports to the lyrical self's worlds beyond the local" (146). The shift from the physical to the intellectual is the individual's gateway to freedom. Informing the self through words, these poems lead up to the most important poem in the section, "Freedom: Bird's-Eye View."

The changing contours of lived space and intellectual exploration have prepared the African American for the idea of freedom. Dove's reappropriation of lived space builds on Fanon's idea of the colonization of geographical space being a metaphor for the colonization of psychological space (*White Skin, Black Masks*). In the poems that lead up to this important one, Dove explores the fixity of lived space for African Americans, using the word to destabilize structures that then enable the black person to move in and out of spaces freely, a privilege earlier allowed only to white people. Written in the 1990s while Dove was Poet Laureate of the United States, the poem is her delineation of the view from above. Neither inside nor outside, looking down from a distance that is both literal and metaphorical, the poet uses her vantage position to explore what freedom really means for the African American today:

> To watch
> the tops of 10,000
> heads floating by on sticks
> and not care if one of them
> sees me (though it
> would be a kick!)
> —now, that's
> what I'd call
> freedom,
> and justice,
> and ice cream for all.

The idea of freedom presents a different reality as compared to the ones in the earlier collections. The implication of the historical context of signifiers informs the image. Dove has finally achieved the "delicious sliding moment when one is *neither in nor out but floating*, suspended above the interior and exterior ground" (*The Poet's World* 24). This defines the postethnic—it is at this point that the individual can forsake identity to form voluntary associations across the color-line based on individual choice. The vantage position offers Dove not just a panoramic view of humanity, but also an anonymity that is rare for the black person. Inconspicuous and out of reach of structures of power, the poet is able to reformulate reality from above. This is Dove's definition of real freedom for the black man. Each moment in this process involves a Hegelian dialectics of progression towards knowledge and freedom.

Having established ontological expansiveness as real freedom, Dove celebrates Blackness in the poems that follow, cautioning, however, against the dangers of returning to constricted (ethnocentric) spaces and restricted worlds. It is a Post-Black reconstitution of identity which allows for an individual journey, countering the power-knowledge nexus that presents Blackness as a homogeneous entity. Touré says that in a Post-Black era, "we need to move from exhaustive Blackness to expansive Blackness" (xix). "Rooted in but not restricted by blackness" (Touré 12), the Post-Black poet celebrates Black identity without the cultural constrictions of either racialized ethnocentrism or the racial self-abjection born of double consciousness. The section, "Black on a Saturday Night," centers around the poem of the same name, a celebration of Blackness with all its flaws:

> the wages of living are sin
> and the wages of sin are love
> and the wages of love are pain
> and the wages of pain are philosophy
> and that leads definitely to an attitude
> and an attitude will get you
> nowhere fast so you might as well
> keep dancing dancing till
> tomorrow gives up with a shout,
> 'cause there is only
> Saturday night, and we are in it—
> black as black can,
> black as black does,
> not a concept
> nor a percentage
> but a natural law.

Having transcended double consciousness to accept Blackness as a part of being, the poem is replete with black cultural energy that celebrates the moment. The process, however, stresses on the reversal of the gaze that results in a building up of "attitude" to embrace life boldly—"black as black can,/ black as black does." In realizing potential, Dove repudiates exaggerated pride in an ethnocentric identity, instead accepting the celebration of a rootedness that is not restrictive but as natural as nature.

In celebrating the freedom of the individual to evolve his own definitions of what it means to be Black, the section presents an aerial view of American society that is panoramic in its scope. Race as a socio-cultural way of life is shown to be contingent to individual perceptions and ideas, and the freedom to interpret Blackness rests with the individual. In this reformulation of structures, racial identities do not constrict individual ontological expansiveness, and the political is shown to be subservient to the personal. Righelato observes: "Cultural ideologies are under scrutiny in this section of the volume: the bird's eye view is, in part, an inspection of American values as they impact the young" (182). Steffen confirms the philosophical quest for knowledge and progress that must precede an emotionally detached analysis of reality as the purpose of the poems in the section:

> Poetry demands both diving into the demands of (book) wisdom and breakfasts as well as soaring above and beyond human knowledge in details, even if they refer to the March on Washington in 1968 [...] "Freedom: Bird's-Eye View," the title poem, is the ultimate declaration of independence: "Life, liberty, and the pursuit of happiness." (147)

The poems in this section are Dove's observation of history as a process, the idea carried over into the next poem, "The Musician Talks about 'Process'," where the poet's grandfather's amateur playing of the spoons spreads in Orphic resonance through the forest after his death, when even the birds and animals sing for two days. This, the poet seems to say, is how a movement sustains itself, spreading to become a way of life:

> When my grandfather died,
> every creature sang.
> And when the men went out
> to get him, they kept singing.
> They sung for two days,
> all the birds, all the animals.

The journey is individual, the progression irreversible. In the Hegelian dialectics of progress towards freedom, this process needs to eschew retrospective trauma, instead acknowledging its presence yet moving forward. The next poem, "Sunday," traces freedom as a goal worth any amount of pain:

> They were eating his misery
> like bad medicine meant to help them
> grow. They would have done anything
> not to see his hand jerk like that,
> his belt hissing through the loops and around
> that fist working inside the coils
> like an animal gnawing, an animal
> who knows freedom's worth anything
> you need to leave behind to get to it—
> even your own flesh and blood.

Freedom here is purely individual, precluding pity and favoring action. Dove concludes in the section, "Revenant," that self-pity hinders movement forward, saying, "It gets you nowhere but deeper into/your own shit—pure misery a luxury/ one never learns to enjoy" ("Against Self-Pity"). Freedom becomes part of the individual's existence to such an extent that it becomes almost unnoticeable.

"Revenant," the word referring to a ghost come back from the dead to haunt a particular place, treats the perspective of the poet as the ghost who traverses worlds and centuries to record what she perceives. The first poem in the section, "Best Western Motor Lodge, AAA Approved," sets the tone for such a revisitation, saying: "I tell you, if you feel strange,/strange things will happen to you". Inferring that the memories revisited in such a frame can hardly be anything but moments of horror, the union of man and Nature in a frenzy of the misery in possible (repressed) images of the violence inflicted on slaves is acutely depicted in "The Peach Orchard":

> And branches,
>
> bank upon bank of them brimming
> like a righteous mob, like
> a ventriloquist humming,
> his hand up
> my spine...O these
>
> trees, shedding all
> over themselves.
> Only a fool
> would think such frenzy
> beautiful.

The reference to Nature as the only true witness to the horrors of history recurs here, and the poet allows herself a moment of horror before stating that fear, or grief, or misery, is relative. In the poem, "Against Self-Pity," the idea of trauma as relative, even as politically expedient, is presented: "There's always some // meatier malaise, a misalliance ripe/to burst." Horrors are, thus, contingent upon extenuating circumstances that work to lessen their intensity, the imagination being one. Righelato says:

> The *Revenant* section of *On the Bus with Rosa Parks* comprises a series of disturbing meditations on the soul's intensities and sicknesses, both individual and cultural. To return to the past or to visit again the spectacle of human degradation are occasions from which, like the angel in the poem "Revenant," the human desire is for escape. (199)

This section implies the necessity to uncover the wound, to remove the "gauze bandages over the wounds of State" ("Revenant") to return the world to its natural state.

It is into this surrealistic frame that Dove introduces the persona of freedom. The black man, having come through the arduous process of achieving the ontological expansiveness that is real freedom, must now appreciate and protect it. "Lady Freedom Among Us" is presented as a ghost walking among us in the present. Having crossed time to travel to the present, she manifests her presence in the form of the statue that has "assumed the thick skin of this town/its gritted exhaust its sunscorch and blear." In her, Dove stresses the need to remember trauma yet not be overwhelmed by it:

> don't think you can ever forget her
> don't even try
> she's not going to budge
>
> no choice but to grant her space
> crown her with sky
> for she is one of the many
> and she is each of us

The use of enjambment is significant, stressing continuity. Dove first read this poem at the second centenary commemoration of the U. S. Capitol and the restoration of the Statue of Freedom. When she saw the statue taken down for cleaning, it was caked in dirt, and she says that that was where the metaphor was born. For Dove, the statue became the representative of a Post-Black freedom that was present in every individual's life, yet let each one accept and interpret her presence. Here, the idea of freedom is that "she is each of us," implying that psychological freedom is as important as political freedom. The dialectics of history is a progression towards this psychological freedom. The reminder, too, is of the consciousness of freedom.

In this Hegelian reconstitution of freedom to include the psychological, Dove implies that once the black man is free to exercise the ontological expansiveness that was traditionally white privilege, healing from historical trauma will follow. It is only after being freed of the exhaustive nature of racialized constrictions that the collection revisits Rosa Parks. The last section in the collection, titled "On the Bus with Rosa Parks," begins with the epigraph: "*All history is a negotiation between familiarity and strangeness.*" The poem titled "Rosa" wryly comments on the contradictions that made a great historical moment possible: "Doing nothing was the doing," she says, stressing, too, that this inaction became action only because of the consciousness of the freedom to exercise choice. Thus, the previous moments have all been a preparation for this moment, implying that, for even "doing nothing" to become effective action, the moment and the act must concur: "the time right inside a place/so wrong it was ready." Just as the poem had to traverse the conflict of the earlier moments to reach this moment of revelation, the Post-Black artist too has to contend with a journey that must enter the recesses of historical memory before it can reach the moment of transformation.

Having revisited the Civil Rights movement through the figure of Rosa Parks, the section and the collection end with the statement that the intensity of past trauma cannot be measured in the present, and all that the revisiting can do is make the present confront the past. "QE2. Transatlantic Crossing. Third Day." is a poignant adjunction of past and present frames, and the disconnect between the two—"This is not the exalted fluorescence of the midnight route,/exhaustion sweetening the stops..../Here I float on the lap of existence."

The idea of home recurs here, and the idea of looking for roots in revisiting history is introduced. Although Dove's earlier poems reflect what Pereira terms the "anxious cultural mulatto figure" (94), On the Bus with Rosa Parks sees the blossoming of the Post-Black artist ready to embrace the postmodern fluidity of an ontologically expansive identity. The "free" black woman no longer fears intra-racial censure and can align cultural amalgamation with racial rootedness. The penultimate stanza of the poem demonstrates Dove's final statement on the progression of history—as a descendant of slaves who has never experienced the trauma of slavery firsthand, her literary aesthetics cannot be structured by the original moment of trauma in history. She resigns herself to her moment in time and space—a relatively wealthy black woman living in a time of personal peace and prosperity—"And that, friends, is the difference—/I can't erase an ache I never had." The last line of the poem reveals Dove's final acceptance of her identity as a traveler. She seems not to have a place of her own: "Well. I'd go home if I knew where to get off." And that is the identity of the Post-Black artist in a post-historical world. Post-Blackness is a journey, and an individual one. Finally accepting the impossibility of recapturing a past identity on this journey, the poet celebrates the present, the *real* Rosa Parks emerging from the pages of history in "In the Lobby of the Warner Theatre, Washington, D.C.," saying that "she was *living* history," come to remind the present that the trauma was over:

> She nodded,
> lifted a hand as if to console us
> before letting it drop, slowly, to her lap.
> Resting there. The idea of consolation
> soothing us: her gesture
> already become her touch,
> like the history she made for us sitting there,
> waiting for the moment to take her.

Having returned to a celebration of the present, Dove states the impossibility of recapturing history. This is not just because of the gaps, but because it demands an impossible reconstruction of the affective as well as the factual. Saying, in the last poem of the collection, titled "The Pond, Porch-View: Six P.M., Early Spring," "I've missed the chance/to put things in reverse," she admits that the present might seem unfamiliar, but it is the only reality available to us: "Where I'm at now/is more like riding on a bus/through unfamiliar neighborhoods." This poem seems to capture much of what Dove's work as a whole moves toward. It is about a feeling of displacement, of struggling towards an identity, but of finally resigning oneself to the present moment in history, not ideals, finding oneself in oneself where one is, not where one wishes to be, nor in a group identity. Identity, finally, is shaped by history, and given a final form by the present moment. The present is Dove's final concern, a Post-Black acceptance of the moment.

Thus, Dove's perspective of history is an act of reconstruction that is both political and personal. In her work, the personal cannot be separated from the political—the racial and the individual are not quite separate moments in time. Race remains a recurrent trope in both the collections, but Dove eschews an ethnocentric celebration of Blackness and black history, choosing instead a wide canvas that exemplifies Hollinger's precepts on the need to replace identity with voluntary affiliations across the color-line. Dove is preoccupied with history and, more particularly, with what standard history omits as gaps. Hers is a synthesis of a historical consciousness with a poignant analysis of everyday life, where the lives of ordinary individuals bear the mark of the political situation prevalent at the time. More importantly, history is proven to be a process rather than a collection of singular moments connected by linear temporality.

Dove's attempt to trace how events in history were a powerful force in the lives of ordinary individuals takes her on a journey of exploration that is an ingression into world history and black culture. In her poems, she articulates the everydayness of life while also keeping track of the consequential milestones of human existence. The events in the lives of the characters are set against the backdrop of important historical events; these events, in turn, influence and shape the actions of her characters. Her poems combine history, culture and poetic skill to delve into the semiotics of trauma resolution and a movement towards a postethnic reformulation of identities. However, they are unmistakably black in their essence, drawing from black memory and experience.

Thus, both collections initiate a process which favors a new mode of identity construction that foregrounds the individual over officially recorded public memory. Extending the notion of history as an individual journey, Dove weaves facts and interstices in a Hegelian reconstitution of the dialectics of history whose progression is built through a juxtaposition of frames of imagery where conflict is a necessary part of the movement towards the next stage. This definition of history differs from the traditional framework built on facts and linear temporality, and sets the stage for a redefining of black aesthetics, whose features are clearly visible in the collections of poems that follow.

Works Cited

Anderson, Benedict. *Imagined Communities*. Verso, 1991.
Angelou, Maya. *I Know Why the Caged Bird Sings*. 1969. Virago, 1984.
Block, Melissa. "Touré Discusses What It Means to Be Post-Black." *Touré Discusses What It Means To Be Post-Black*, National Public Radio, September 27, 2011, www.npr.org/2011/09/27/140854965/toure-discusses-what-it-means-to-be-post-black. Accessed October 21, 2017.

Dove, Rita. "An Interview with Rita Dove." By Stephanie Izarek Smith. *Poets and Writers Magazine* 22.2 (March–April 1994): 28.
———. *On the Bus with Rosa Parks*. W.W. Norton, 1999.
———. *Selected Poems*. Vintage, 1993.
———. *The Poet's World*. Library of Congress, 1995.
———. *Thomas and Beulah*. Carnegie Mellon UP, 1986.
———. *The Yellow House on the Corner*. Carnegie Mellon UP, 1989.
Fanon, Frantz. *Black Skin, White Masks*. 1952. Translated by Charles Lam. Pluto, 1986.
Foucault, Michel. *Power/Knowledge: Selected Interviews and Other Writings 1972–1977*. Ed. Colin Gordon. Translated by Gordon, Colin et al. Pantheon, 1980.
Gilroy, Paul. *Against Race: Imagining Political Culture Beyond the Color Line*. The Belknap P of Harvard UP, 2000.
Hall, Joan Wylie, ed. *Conversations with Audre Lorde*. UP of Mississippi, 2004.
Hollinger, David A. *Postethnic America: Beyond Multiculturalism*. Basic, 1995.
Hook, Derek. "The 'Real' of Racializing Embodiment." *Journal of Community and Applied Social Psychology* 18 (2008): 140–51. doi: 10.1002/casp.963.
Ingersoll, Earl G., ed. *Conversations with Rita Dove*. UP of Mississippi, 2003.
Minh-ha, Trinh T. "Not You/Like You: Postcolonial Women and the Interlocking Questions of Identity and Difference." *Dangerous Liaisons: Gender, Nation, and Postcolonial Perspectives*. Ed. McClintock, Anne, et al. U of Minnesota P, 1997.
Morrison, Toni. *Playing in the Dark: Whiteness and the Literary Imagination*. Vintage, 1993.
Moyers, Bill. *The Language of Life. A Festival of Poets*. Ed. James Haba. Doubleday, 1995.
Poster, Mark. "Foucault and History." *Social Research* 49.1 (Modern Masters, spring 1982): 116–42. JSTOR, www.jstor.org/stable/40970855.
Righelato, Pat. *Understanding Rita Dove*. U of South Carolina P, 2006.
Roy, Lekha. "The Personal Is Political: Slavery, Trauma, and the White Man's Legacy." *The English Paradigm in India*. Ed. Shweta Rao Garg and Deepti Gupta. Palgrave Macmillan, 2017. doi: 10.1007/978-981-10-5332-0.
Shannon, Susan. *Revealing Whiteness: The Unconscious Habits of Racial Privilege*. Indiana UP, 2006.
Smith, Roberta. "Kara Walker Traces Slavery's Bitter Legacy with New Ways of Drawing." Review of Kara Walker. *The New York Times*, September 7, 2017, www.nytimes.co/2017/09/07/arts/kara-walker-sikkema-jenkins.html. Accessed October 1, 2018.
Steffen, Therese. *Crossing Color: Transcultural Space and Place in Rita Dove's Poetry, Fiction, and Drama*. Oxford UP, 2001.
Touré. *Who's Afraid of Post-Blackness? What It Means to Be Black Now*. Free P, 2011.
Vendler, Helen. *The Given and the Made: Strategies of Poetic Redefinition*. Harvard UP, 1995.
White, Hayden. "Introduction: Historical Fiction, Fictional History, and Historical Reality." *Rethinking History* 9.2/3 (June–September 2005): 147–57.
———. *Metahistory: The Historical Imagination in Nineteenth-Century Europe*. The John Hopkins UP, 1973.

· 4 ·

DECONSTRUCTING MYTHS IN *GRACE NOTES* AND *MOTHER LOVE*

This chapter studies Dove's deconstruction of myths by presenting them as narrative bridges across concepts of race, space, and time. This is part of the Post-Black effort to free signifiers of their historical associations by proving them to be linguistic constructs that have gained the force of reality through use. Positing that myths function as language, the study contends that myths are one of the most potent bases of signifiers that lend credence to racialized structures by supporting their epistemology with narratives that belong in the past but are perpetuated through recurrence in cultural discourse, becoming associated with a particular culture, and being the source of widely held beliefs about that culture. In most cases, they support modernist binaries by a synchronic immobility across racial and cultural boundaries. In her fourth and fifth collections of poems, *Grace Notes* (1989) and *Mother Love* (1995), Dove deconstructs both the origin and the specific nature of myths by placing them in the transcultural space created in her first collection, wherein the myths exist in a cultural space at the point where the synchronic and the diachronic intersect. The aim is to subvert the politics of consciousness of the self, built through racialized imagery, bringing to the fore myths as a delusionary device intended to preclude the individual's acceptance of reality, and make him strive towards an impossible norm. This outlines Dove's theory, following

Hall's, of race as a "discursive practice" that constructs the norms that govern identity construction, given meaning through the metaphors, anecdotes, and stories that culture spins for us (Hall 2). Race, according to Hall, acquires meaning in the cultural system as a "floating signifier" or "badge" (6-7) through discursive practice. Myths, as a form of story that endures over time, are part of the culture. Dove's poems reveal how myths have been racialized, and race mythologized. By taking a myth out of the relational system of signifiers, Dove alters its racially informed nature to delink it from its cultural associations in the memory. This deconstruction of myths initiates a Post-Black reformulation of the components that inform discourse, the poems crossing over into the psycho-spatial domain of the Other to bridge myth and reality, ancient and contemporary, black and white.

In her earlier collections, Dove deconstructed history as a metanarrative supported by linguistic structures. In *Grace Notes* and *Mother Love*, she deconstructs myths as the specific language through which narratives are propounded. In 1955, Lévi-Strauss proposed the idea that a given mythological pattern possessed a certain signification. His contention was that myths were signifiers that functioned according to Saussurean principles. However, they do not do just that—if myths are akin to language, then the Saussurean principle of the arbitrary nature of every signifier would preclude an individual myth attaining meaning on its own. Further, the nature of the myth would be different in different languages. Lévi-Strauss says: "Myth is the part of language where the formula *traduttore, tradittore* reaches its lowest truth-value" (430). In other words, even in translations where language gets the most distorted, an example of which Lévi-Strauss considers poetry, myths sustain their originality. He concludes, then, that "language in myth unveils specific properties," stating that "those properties are only to be found *above* the ordinary linguistic level; that is, they exhibit more complex features beside those which are to be found in any kind of linguistic expression" (431). Myths thus get meaning, he says, not from constituent units but from *bundles* of constituent units arranged synchronically, that is, different versions of the myth in different cultures, or diachronically, that is, over time (431). This structuralist notion of how myths sustain themselves across different languages and time frames points to their gaining meaning through use, wherein the different structural units combine across time and space to sustain the myth.

In *Mythologies*, Barthes used Lévi-Strauss's principles to explicate myths as a form of speech—"a mode of signification"—saying that "everything can be a myth provided it is conveyed by a discourse" (107). Tracing the epistemological origins of myths, he concludes that every object passes from its objective state to a metaphorical social allusion, an image to which it becomes attached, through discourse. This image and its connoted associations then live as representations in the memory, to be revived through discourse. Stating that there can be no *eternal* myths, Barthes concludes that it is through usage alone that objects attain mythical status. Every myth is, thus, a linguistic construct whose meaning is perpetuated through historical discourse:

> Every object in the world can pass from a closed, silent existence into an oral state, open to appropriation by society, for there is no law, whether natural or not, which forbids talking about things....one can conceive of very ancient myths, but no eternal ones; for it is human history which converts reality into speech, and it alone rules the life and the death of mythical language. Ancient or not, mythology can only have an historical foundation, for myth is a type of speech chosen by history: it cannot possibly evolve from the "nature" of things. (Barthes, *Mythologies* 107–108)

As myths are propagated through usage, it is impossible for them to be sustained without inclusion in social discourse. In the Saussurean world of the constructed nature of language, it is impossible for there to be any natural origin of the mythological; further, if language is a construct consisting of the signifier and the signified, it follows that every myth is a signifier with a historically determined signified. This applies not just to language, but to images as well. Thus, the idea of skin color as a racial identifier is associated not just with "black" and "white" as colors, but the images of slavery that they are associated with in the memory as well.

Myths thus originate in culture and are sustained through discourse, in turn acting as signifiers carrying cultural beliefs. The locality of myths is thus mythical—the idea that Greek myths apply only to a certain people living in a certain place at a certain period in time has been disproved by Dove's transposing them on to black life across the Atlantic. Similarly, Morrison has also used classical myths in her novels, albeit more sparingly than Dove, and usually in relation to the apotropaic. The localization of myths occurs when they are included in discourse by or about a particular people living in a particular area. For example, it can be concluded that myths about Blackness are propagated and become localized through usage in everyday discourse about Black life. This also happens because the narrative takes precedence over facts.

Unlike in the case of ancient myths, more recent ones usually propagate the belief while the actual story that gave rise to the myth is relegated to the background. For example, in research conducted on the nature of the Black

American family in 1974, Peters concluded that the idea of the black family as a dysfunctional unit marked by deviancy and uncontrolled sexuality was a myth propagated by the lack of research and literature about Black families, and the general unawareness of this lack among sociologists. In this case, the myth originates as a belief tied to a specific signifier about a people, and gives rise to narratives that would sustain it. In using classical myths in their work, authors like Morrison and Dove move beyond linguistic defense structures that would render a direct association between cultures improbable. They then use these associations to ponder ontological questions in a racialized world, blurring binaries in the process. In transposing ancient Greek myths on to black life, Dove dismantles myths about Blackness simply by assigning to black people the same cultural signifiers that connote white cultural heritage. In an interview with Bellin, Dove states that myths:

> ...touch the yearning inside us; they explain our impulses on a level deeper than logic but do not require blind faith, because they are allegorical. They explain some of the mysteries of our existence and our relationships with each other. ...For me, to work with myths is a way of getting at the ineffable. (Ingersoll 127–128)

In creating myths of resistance wherein the images associated with the myth are reformulated to allow for a racial reconfiguration of cultural codes, Dove's poems strike at the roots of cultural transmission.

It is interesting that Dove chooses poetry to explicate the nuanced variations in the process that both racializes myths and mythologizes race. According to Lévi-Strauss, poetry is the form most open to distortion in translation because of its use of particular combinations of words in a language to portray an image. However, poetry can also be the most potent form to allow for a reconfiguration of images because of its unusual combinations of words, making it the most suitable for Dove's theory of the expanding of contours. Steffen says of Dove:

> Two aspects govern her worldmaking: Often the protagonists will find a way to expand the space that has been assigned to them by either assimilating or ignoring it, or by using it to their advantage. Often they succeed without the colonizer's noticing it. In terms of writing, of the technique itself—poetry is the tightest writing—Dove calls verse a "colonized space," a narrow rigid cage that represents confinement as well as a chance to challenge the walls and find an incredible freedom both in the mastery and expansion of a given frame. (164)

Dove identifies in poetry a capacity to carry metaphor and allusions in a tangential manner, making it the only form she believes capable of deconstructing "gaps" or "silences" as an active component of the linguistic structure. Poetry bespeaks silences, allowing suggestive allusions that enter ontological discourse as mere probability, thus distancing the form from any accusations of historical inaccuracy. In an interview with McDowell, Dove says: "In poetry, there's so much you can't say because part of the task is to let the silence reverberate, to let each word mean everything that it can mean" (Ingersoll 174). The silence that she identifies as gaps or interstices in the narrative structure informs the narrative content and imagery to a large extent. Barthes contends that apart from the "linguistic message," the image provides a series of "discontinuous signs" that draws on "cultural knowledge" ("The Rhetoric" 34–35). According to him, a reformulation of meaning occurs when there is a contradiction between the "perceptual message" and the "cultural message" conveyed by the image (36). As old links in the memory are broken, the new associations recognize suppressed images in the memory and reformulate the narrative to include these images. The cultural context of the myth is thus altered, and in situations where hegemonic structures are countered, they give rise to new, biracial myths of resistance.

Dove's use of the Greek myths of Eden, Medusa, and Demeter and Persephone in her collections is symbolic of the transatlantic crossing that critics have variously termed "a sense of displacement" (Georgoudaki 419), "a literal and metaphorical nomadism" (Kamionowski 12), a "lack of racial consciousness" (Keller 136), and an "inclusive sensibility" (Rampersad 53), but which in reality is a transition from Black Nationalist protocols to a postethnic affiliation across borders, resulting in the ontological expansiveness to claim inclusivity in white space that symbolizes the Post-Black. Pereira says: "The constant coupling of personal and mythical becomes a dominant strategy in her cosmopolitan, post-*Museum* revisionist, universalism" (117). Classifying Dove both as a cosmopolitan and a "cultural mulatto" (Ellis 198), tracing in her works a strain of anxiety about not conforming to the protocols of racial writing, while delineating ways to transcend the constrictions imposed by Blackness, she identifies her as a "world citizen" (Posnock 12) who uses freely cultural materials in her belief that these belong to all who choose to use them. However, Pereira, Posnock, and even Du Bois, in their definitions of what constitutes Blackness in literary writing, adhere to the binaries of essentialism/cosmopolitanism, black/white, us/them. This is the reason most critical studies have not identified the diverse strains as visible in the works of Dove as part of a composite whole. For Dove neither borrows, uses, nor appropriates cultural materials, but states that binaries suppress the interstices that form part of the tale. Hers is a "cultural amalgamation" (Pereira 197) that does not let go of Blackness, but rather redefines its contours. Her use of Greek myths, in contrast to Morrison's, does not connote deviation from the norm; rather, she propounds these myths as universal across time, space, and race, and in so doing, makes them as much the heritage of the Black American as the Greek. In an interview, she says:

> I was fascinated by the way the concept of fate in Greek myth was analogous to the African American experience. If there's any group of people that knows what it's like to try to find a certain amount of freedom within a cage, it's the African Americans. (Steffen 171)

Dove's inclusion of European myths and her meshing of black subjectivity and cultural inclusiveness resists modernist binaries, bridging European and African American, past and present, black and white, abstract and concrete, to delineate the Post-Black.

Following the deconstruction of European and Japanese myths in her first collection, *The Yellow House on the Corner*, Dove gives a detailed description of the individual lives of Thomas and Beulah foregrounded against moments of great historical importance in *Thomas and Beulah*. In both *Grace Notes* and *Mother Love*, the delineation of the mythical-personal occurs in the transcultural space created in the first collection at the intersection of the synchronic and the diachronic. In *Grace Notes*, Dove creates a bridge through which the life of Beulah initiates a journey into black womanhood, the narrative interspersed with allusions to the mythic. Written in 1989, the collection brings to the fore Dove's concerns as a black woman in America. In an interview with Rubin and Kitchen, she says, "I was in Europe, and I had a way of looking back on America and distancing myself from my experience I could look at history, at the world, in a different way because I had another mind set" (Ingersoll 4). Being part of a different cultural context makes her aware of the cultural connotations of signifiers as localized, and initiates a rethinking of the structures that make race a potent identifier. The collection is a bridge between *Thomas and Beulah* and *Mother Love*, combining the deeply personal note of the previous collection with the mythical journey of the next.

In both *Grace Notes* and *Mother Love*, Dove uses Greek myths to defamiliarize and bring into the sphere of visibility an aspect of slave life whose details have hitherto been suppressed in public memory. Myths of Blackness are revealed as constructed as the suffering on both sides of the color-line equates black and white, and the connotations of white as "just human" (Dyer 2) are transposed on to Blackness. In presenting the black man as being faced with the same ontological questions as the whitest of whites—the Greek—Dove destroys binaries. In *Grace Notes*, she includes details of growing up black, comparing aspects of this process to the mythical search for the Edenic. In adding "grace notes," she stresses the internal coherence of the narrative formed by transposing mythical allusions across the Atlantic. In *Mother Love*, she uses the myth of Demeter and Persephone to foreground the universal nature of a mother's suffering at being violently separated from her child, a common aspect of slave life. Both collections posit acceptance of trauma and of the changed nature of the world, reflecting on the impossibility of ever returning to a pre-traumatic state. In juxtaposing classical and contemporary, black and white worlds, Dove defamiliarizes the familiar to open up language to resistance. Pereira says that "in *Grace Notes*, Dove moves from the personal into archetype, and in *Mother Love* she moves from myth into the personal" (117). The poems in these two collections are more personal, more reflective of the poet's consciousness of Black womanhood, than in the other collections.

Myths can also be the bridge between the factual and the affective. In an interview with Bellin, Dove says: "By following the trajectory of a myth, by re-imagining its principal characters or exploring a tangent, one can stumble upon the crucial stuff—what one really thinks or feels" (Ingersoll 128). This has the effect of bringing historical trauma into the sphere of the affective, allowing for a deeper connection between the personal and the political. It also makes the literary journey a deeply personal one. Dyer infers that "how one thinks and feels is at once lived as intensely personal, yet made up of matters that in themselves are not unique to one" (7). In an interview with Pereira, Dove talks of how the personal connects with the historical:

> I think they both have something to do, a lot to do, with being female and being Black. From as early as I can remember, I always felt that there was a world with lots of "historical" events going on, and that my viewpoint was not a direct one, but I was looking at it from the side. (Ingersoll 151)

Much like Dove's perspective, the allusions to the mythic in *Grace Notes* are tangential, more an obtuse comparison than a bold transposing as in the next collection. Like similes, they serve to open up the contours of the image to a wider range of references. In both the collections, the journey is a personal, feminist encounter with Blackness. The poems trace a path back to personal roots, where trauma resides, to become creative catharsis in the process. In the interview with Pereira, Dove reflects on "filling in the past, trying to get into the past as a person and to humanize it so that eventually I could get in my own past without being self-indulgent" (Ingersoll 150). This concurs with her opinion of myths as a way to explore the self and its relationships. In bridging Greek and African American, Dove is also exploring the racial configurations of her own world, both as an author and as a Black woman.

Grace Notes is the quest for an Eden in a material world. It is divided into five sections, with an introductory poem that acts as the bridge connecting it to the previous collection. This first poem, titled "Summit Blue, 1921," refers to a segregated beach, Summit Lake, in Akron, Ohio, where Dove's grandparents first met, and acts as a "historical marker…and a point of reference from which to move on" (Righelato 110). The inclusion of this poem is a measure of historical progression through individual lives. The poem begins on a nostalgic note, the "oil drum tattoo and a mandolin" bringing to mind Thomas's treasured companion, the mandolin, when he arrived in Akron in the 1920s. In its reference to the early part of the twentieth century, when segregation was firmly in place, the poem acts as a point of reference to gauge achievements in terms of racial and gender equality towards the end of the century. The adolescent Beulah of this poem must adhere to social conventions, and the "shawl moored/by a single fake cameo" and the cast on her knee are symbolic of social constrictions that must resist the temptations posed by "sweaters flying off the finest brown shoulders/this side of the world." Righelato notes that "the cultural terms of segregation frame the volume as well as the poem: the 'invisible wings' of the spirit, the 'skittering' music of sensory delight are the grace notes picked out in a 'mean' context" (112). The single poem that acts as a prologue to the poems that follow, thus, sets the tune to which the grace notes will be added—the notes define dreams while growing up black in a segregated nation at a time when the constrictions of being a woman meant that you were doubly marginalized.

The first section of the collection consists of poems that are autobiographical—snippets in a family album, a series of disconnected images in the memory, music a recurring presence in the images. They are images of growing up as a black child in a bleak landscape bereft of poetry. As an example of the imagination giving image its meaning, the first poem "Silos" talks of representations, detailing what the tall white structures meant to everyone. All that is certain is their prosaic nature: "They were never fingers, never xylophones, although once/a stranger said they put him in mind of Pan's pipes/and all the lost songs of Greece." While the townspeople likened them to cigarettes, to the children they brought to mind a fresh packet of chalk. The poem concludes that everything in the world is gendered, and everything is metaphorical, too: "They were masculine toys. They were tall wishes. They/ were the ribs of the modern world." These buildings, in fact, are a metaphor for perspective, varied as the people in the town.

The next few poems are a journey through childhood experiences. "Fifth Grade Autobiography" talks of the gaps in representations. A childhood picture becomes an entire narrative when the gaps are filled in by memory, combining the factual and the affective: "I am staring jealously at my brother;/The day before he rode his first horse, alone." The role of the affective in informing images is visible in "The Buckeye," where children learn that the state tree actually has a useless, ugly fruit, good only "to kick/along gutters // on the way home." Hiding their vulnerability beneath a tough exterior, the seeds of this tree are represented with racial undertones: "there was the bald/seed with its wheat- // colored eye." "Flash Cards" traces the daily life of a child who is good at math, working at numbers while his father relaxes with a copy of *The Life of Lincoln*. The nondescript domestic scenario is followed by "Crab-Boil," a poem that revisits the scene at the beach, only it is no longer the 1920s, and attitudes have changed.

"Crab-Boil" marks an important punctuation in the series of poems; it is here that the reader must pause and take stock of the distance covered from the time when Beulah waited on the beach. Segregation is no longer legal, but the fear of violence remains. The experience of violence has also de-sensitized the Southerner, especially the older generation who had experienced segregation and its attendant horrors firsthand. Racial hierarchy is also seen from the point of view of the (assumedly) superior being. While the first-generation Northerner dreads being attacked by "them," she readily accepts the older Southerner's assumption that crabs feel no pain while being boiled alive, their exoticism elevated by the method of cooking:

> I don't believe *they* won't come
> and chase us back to the colored-only shore
> crisp with litter and broken glass.
>
> "When do we kill them?"
> "Kill 'em? Hell, the water does *that*.
> They don't feel a thing...no nervous system."

> I decide to believe this: I'm hungry.
> Dismantled, they're merely exotic,
> A blushing meat.

Ironically, eating the crabs after boiling them gives a sense of power—"If/ we're kicked out now, I'm ready." However, what lives on in the memory is the affective: "the scratch,/shell on tin, of their distress," implying that the present generation is not immune to suffering, while those from the South, with its history of the cruelty meted out to slaves, view violence and cruelty less as an aberration. It also points to how easily violence can be perpetrated on the less powerful, and moral doubts overcome by ease of living. Righelato claims:

> The crabs are also a focus for feelings of revenge, and of exorcism of those feelings…. the image retains the desire to reverse the stereotyping, the brutality of "meat," now white meat rather than nigger meat, but the "boil" of feeling is redirected, although hardly contained. (113–114)

Delving into the psychology of the victim-turned-perpetrator, the poem traces the cycle of violence, dismissing as a myth the assumption that there are no gray areas where violence is concerned.

"Hully Gully" is another poem which deludes in its surface calm, lulling into a daydream the image of idyllic summers spent lounging at home, humming *Hully Gully*, a popular song and dance tune, as "porch geraniums/rocked the grandmothers to sleep/as night slugged in." In the same vein, "Fantasy and Science Fiction" is about imagining another world, a parallel life, about entering uncharted territory, and about crossing prescribed borders—imagined, as only a child can: "Sometimes, shutting a book and rising,/you can walk off the back porch/and into the sea." Mythical tales can sometimes blur the boundaries between real and imagined worlds. Steffen says of Dove: "To her, the greatest dangers and temptations lie not in what we can create with the human mind, but in what we choose not to see through the veil of human denial" (128). Myths, in this context, can pierce this veil, revealing the real through the metaphorical.

Denial and acceptance form the theme of the last poem in the section, titled "Poem in Which I Refuse Contemplation." The postcard which a harried Dove receives from her mother after a long drive from Paris to Germany contains details which give rise to associations. In a poem filled with the tiny details that recreate home, language becomes a metaphor for belonging. Once again, the image of the garden recreates the quest for belonging. Thus, in a country where her daughter feels at home with the language, her mother's letter pulls Dove back to her roots, making her find fault with all that is foreign to her, especially the language whose perfection connotes the foreign, and her mother's irritatingly misspelled words connote the familiar:

Mom skips to the garden which is

producing—onions, swiss chard,
lettuce, lettuce, lettuce, turnip greens and more lettuce
so far! The roses are flurishing.

Haven't I always hated gardening? And German,
with its patient, grunting building blocks,
and for that matter, English, too,

Americanese's chewy twang?

The poem ends a section that is deeply personal, tracing a path from childhood to adulthood, intertwining nature and culture in memories wherein associations rise as a vapor to create a narrative from what are otherwise gaps in the memory. The hint at the Edenic as mythical perfection that makes man unable to accept imperfection marks the end of the section.

The second section initiates the journey towards the mythic, with the epigraph to the section forming a bridge between the personal and the mythical. Containing two quotes, one by David McFadden saying, "*The legendary forbidden fruit is the self,*" and the second by Hélène Cixous which says, "*To inhabit was the most natural joy when I was still living inside; all was garden and I had not lost the way in,*" the section begins a journey into the depths of the self. The reference to Eden in the first quote is unmistakable, and, having proved in the first section that one association leads to another, the garden that one searches for within oneself is proven to be the Edenic one. Thus, distinguishing between the inner and outer worlds, Dove locates the quest for the essence of the self within. The reference is also to the artist retreating into the world of Imagination to seek the Muse. The struggle to retreat from the Symbolic is visible in the poems in this section. Fraught with paradoxes, the poems reflect an intense exploration for the self in nature, memory, and the cosmic.

The first poem in the second section, titled "Mississippi," presents an intensely erotic image, bringing to mind the Fall. In this poem, nature and man, light and dark complement each other to initiate a new world and new beginnings in a carnal image that emphasizes the sensual:

> We were falling down
> river, carnal
> slippage and shadow melt.
> We were standing on the deck
> of the New World, before maps:
> tepid seizure of a breeze
> and the spirit hissing away...

The poet seems to imply that to arrive at the New World, the Fall was necessary, a paradoxical ending and beginning of time. Righelato says, "Sexuality here is the engine of being and the metaphor of American discovery" (116). But more than that, it is a bringing together of race memory and Biblical imagery in a search for the self that is significant. The journey down the Mississippi river is significant in that it invokes Hughes's "The Negro speaks of Rivers," in which he says, "My soul has grown deep like the rivers." The "slippage" associated with rivers, thus, associates Biblical genesis with the "shadow"—the darkness—of the Negro's soul, tracing his ancestry back to the beginning of the world.

The next few poems allow for a grappling with the complexities of the new world. "After Storm" juxtaposes the image of rain and virtue struggling for hours, followed by destruction and calm. The image once again resonates with the Biblical myth of Creation, the raging water that covered the earth finally calmed by the Creator and given form. "Dog Days, Jerusalem" follows the poet as she waits for rain, waiting for the Muse to appear, setting out "black tea and oranges—/carefully, though no one will see me." As a mythic parallel to Creation, the quest for the self must grapple with external forces, and both rain and the desert, traveling and waiting, reflect the complexities of adapting to the new world.

The poem "Ozone" wonders whether the world seeks itself in us as we seek ourselves in it. The image in the poem is of a modern waste land, civilization so technologically advanced that all that can be seen when we look up are the wires, the hole in the sky visible where the aerosol cans cut through the ozone layer. The beauty of the sky strangled in the mesh of wires and the earth cramped with houses is very different from the Edenic garden the poet is searching for, and the Rilkean sublime that she quotes in the epigraph to the poem becomes an ironic reflection of the (lost) imagined world of the child. It is a dystopia of contradictions, ugly in its perfection. The world described is more Eliot's than Rilke's, the images dystopian:

> The sky is wired so it won't fall down.
> Each house notches into its neighbor
> and then the next, the whole row scaldingly white,
> unmistakable as a set of bared teeth.
> ....
> If only we could lose ourselves
> in the wreckage of the moment! Forget
> where we stand, dead center, and
> look up, look up,
> track a falling star...

The nostalgia for a lost world is evident in the last line, reflecting the despair evident in Davies's description of "this life...where we have no time to stand and stare" ("Leisure") and Eliot's "unreal city/...each man fixed his eyes before his feet" ("The Waste Land"). The cramped nature of existence points to an inescapable reversal of the Rilkean world where love is at the center of the universe. Dove's poem is a resistance to this world where the mythical can only be imagined as a metaphor. Talking of the imagery in the poem, Righelato says that the present "civilization is not so much the self-mastery that Rilke admired in the Greek sculptors as the inability to escape from the wreckage we have created, whether personal or collective" (118). Thus, the quest for the self needs a Hegelian withdrawal from this dystopian world, into the inner sanctum. Righelato mentions the "sense of lost Rilkean sublimities... the same questioning of existence and of connection between the intimate and the supra-human scale" (118–119), but such intense thoughts are difficult to sustain in the midst of dystopian surroundings. Thus, it transpires that the individual must seek the Garden of Eden within himself.

The next couple of poems detail life in this waste land. "Turning Thirty, I Contemplate Students Bicycling Home" is a juxtaposition of contrasts. Spring, the "weather of change/and clear light" is also "the tired, wise/spring." In this waste land, impurity or the admixture of contradictory ideas seems to be the norm. "Particulars" is a poem about pessimism and misery as the natural emotion to arise out of these dystopian surroundings. The symptoms detailed in the poem are of clinical depression, ceaseless tears that "weren't/tears of relief, and after a few weeks/not even of a particular sorrow." Everything in this waste land, even sadness, had become a mechanical exercise. The emotion came on the poet so systematically that she began to keep a record:

>   She caught herself
> crying every morning, ten sharp, as if
> the weather front had swerved,
> a titanic low pressure system
> moving in as night steamed off
> and left a day with nothing else
> to fill it but moisture. She wept
> steadily, and once
> she recognized the pattern,
> took care to be in one spot waiting
> a few moments before.

The concluding lines of the poem give direction to sorrow, but in a contradictory fashion, it is really not direction at all. The poet considers the uselessness of knowledge that comes only when it is of no use, thus leading to a situation where satisfaction is eternally deferred, or, in other words, a situation of eternal dissatisfaction: "that was what she was weeping over:/the lack of conclusion,/the eternal *dénouement*." The lines reflect Vladimir and Estragon's endless waiting in Beckett's *Waiting for Godot*. This is an existential dilemma, the twentieth century a mythical waste land.

In the waste land that the world has turned into, even events like death do not evoke sadness, but rather evasion. The last two poems in the section deal with death. "Your Death" marks the greatest contradiction presented by the juxtaposition of death and life, the day the poet's father-in-law died being the same day her pregnancy was confirmed. Death overshadows life, and the sorrow makes her feel "robbed": "the tuna fish sandwich/I had bought at the corner/became yours." It is symptomatic of the waste land that mourning takes precedence over celebrations, and absence supersedes presence. The section ends with "The Wake," where absence fills the house even when it is full of mourners, and the image is one of "trying to cover/the silence with weeping." The search for the Edenic in the external world proving futile, the poet finally withdraws into her pregnant self, trying to tap into the garden of life within. Here, she seems to point at the future as the root for healing and regeneration. The second section thus traverses the mythic to return to a deeply personal note, pointing out the contradictions present in every sphere of existence, and ending with the expectation of a new birth and new life. Here again, the end evokes Eliot's *The Waste Land* as providing an alternate set of paradigms to replace the old; this is the symbolic birth in Dove's poem as well.

In the third section, the poems detail the experiences of motherhood, beginning with the desire, expressed in the epigraph to the section, to protect the new life: "*Where's a word, a talisman, to hold against the world?*" The new world needs to be protected against the old, and the journey in this section will be towards this talisman. The quest for this talisman in this new frame of mind will also see the poet finally reach the Edenic. The first poem in the section, titled "The Other Side of the House," begins the journey with a significant stepping out of the kitchen door into the world outside. The stepping out is metaphorical, as Dove says in *The Poet's World:* "Any effective assignment forces you to go where you might have been too lazy, or frightened, to go before" (17). In the poem, the poet steps out determinedly into the world, exiting through the kitchen door, which was the door black people were traditionally supposed to use while entering or exiting a house. The image suggests a return to roots while starting the quest. Talking of the metaphorical significance of space, Dove says, "All the required elements of a psychic landscape—comfort and loss, suffocation and risk—come together in the struggle of enclosure versus exposure" (*The Poet's World* 21). As the poet renounces the security of enclosed space, "the green surreptitious/dusty like a trenchcoat" welcomes her into its sandy folds, and the quest for the self transmutes into the natural world: "Where am I in the stingy/desert broom, where/in the blank soul of the olive?" In the space outside, there is no security, no calm, yet it is here that the poet would seek herself as home metamorphoses into the juxtaposition of nature and thought: "I learned to walk out of a thought/and not snap back the way/railroad cars telescope into a train."

Motherhood reconnects the poet to nature, and the images of the child resonate with awe. At this stage, the child sets the mother free to experience raw, unschooled emotion:

> I liked afterwards best, lying
> outside on a quilt, her new skin
> spread out like meringue. I felt then
> what a young man must feel
> with his first love asleep on his breast:
> desire, and the freedom to imagine it. ("Pastoral")

Here, the freedom to go back to the world of the Imaginary expresses itself in the symbolism of the innocent lover.

In the poem titled "Horse and Tree," desire and the freedom to imagine come up against the constrictions imposed by the Symbolic. The struggle between the two contradictory impulses expresses itself in a whirlwind of images in the poem. Having stepped into the outer world, the poet notes the contradictions invested in it by the opposing forces of nature and culture. The title of the poem is itself an antithesis, connecting two opposite spectra in the social order. While the horse symbolizes cultural order, the tree symbolizes the freedom of nature: "This is why we braid their harsh manes/as if they were children." Implying that the Symbolic carries with it a fear of the Imaginary, which is the natural world, Dove compares the freedom of unbraided horses with their manes flying in the air to children feeling themselves flying freely on life's carousel, in turn akin to the sap rising in the tree to its zenith. The tree symbolizes nature's freedom, where the external (body) must remain grounded while "the luminous sap ascends" within. A metaphor for life, the carousel brings life full circle, a metaphorical joyride which children soon adapt to and enjoy, forgetting their initial hesitation. Unlike Rilke, Dove admits of the carousel's brief existence as a moment of joy rather than of loss: "there is music and then it stops;/the beautiful is always rising and falling." Righelato says that for Dove:

> ...the rise and fall motion is also expressive of the natural and familial cycle in which as sensory beings we are a vital part, and, in caring for our children, in sharing aesthetic delight and loss—"the beautiful is always rising and falling"—we have something that is life giving, a natural joy. (121)

Thus, the natural and the cultural must co-exist, and Dove's focus is on the beauty that, though transient, lights up moments in the circle of life.

The transition from an appreciation of the beauty of life to the pains of acculturation is delineated in the poem, "The Breathing, The Endless News," which traces the process of owning culture from nothingness in the child's eyes at birth to being full of "the myth of ourselves." Here, the poet talks of the ideological schooling that gives even gods their identity through culture, a paradoxical image in which "each god is empty/without us, penitent,/raking our yards into windblown piles." Identity is revealed to be a cultural construct, each child filled with the mythic image of the self, learned through social conditioning. With this mythic knowledge, the children proceed towards violence:

> So we
> give our children dolls, and
> they know just what to do—
>
> line them up and shoot them.
> With every execution

doll and god grow stronger.

The reference in the last line hints at how violence is culturally conditioned and condoned, and how it affects both the victim and the perpetrator. With every incident, both grow stronger, and the violence becomes more acceptable. Power, violence and the internalizing of social hierarchy are seen to be intrinsic to acculturation.

The third section ends with an exploration of the myth of Blackness. The image is that of social learning which equates Blackness with embodiment and objectification, and hence induces racial self-abjection. The exotic nature of the black body as constructed through images is brought out in the poem, ironically titled "Genetic Expedition," where the expedition to genetic roots is limited to the color of the skin. Dove traces the moment when the black child learns that she is an aberration, forbidden from looking at the naked black female body in magazines like the *National Geographic*. Thus conditioned, black skin reinforces "the colour-coded constructedness of beauty as truth" (Roy and Ringo 67). Dove attributes this to the images that were propagated by the media. Growing up, she observed her body becoming more and more like that of the women in the magazine, an image she had been taught to avert her eyes from. As an adult with a mixed-race daughter, she can finally analyze the racially constructed nature of beauty as she observes how people stare at her child, her genetic and cultural mix unfamiliar: *"You can't be cute*, she says. *You're big."* The poem is a refashioning of Elizabeth Bishop's poem "In the Waiting Room," set in Massachusetts in 1918. In Bishop's poem, a young six-year-old girl accompanies her aunt to the dentist and while waiting for her, reads the *National Geographic*. In Dove's poem, the mother notes her body becoming more like the black bodies "from natives in the *National Geographic*/my father forbade us to read." The dread of growing up is the dread of *becoming* the black body, with its connotations of Otherness, exoticism, and difference. Dove, towards the end of the century, has more freedom to "renegotiate cultural stereotypes" (Righelato 123) and to explode the myth of the female black body as exotic, than Bishop did when she was writing. The journey towards finding a talisman to hold against the world as mentioned in the epigraph needs to separate the self from its images, and find the real self *sans* filters.

The last poem in the section, titled "Backyard, 6 A. M.," is a metaphorical acceptance of "space stapled down with every step." In *The Poet's World*, Dove talks of the significance of the backyard, saying, "My backyard emerges as a place for confrontation" (21). Yet the section ends with being "back/home," thankful for the transience that has metamorphosed into the moment, for the poet is aware of how brief moments on the carousel are. She says: "Is there such a thing/as a warning?" and her relief at still being there is palpable. Back from her exploration of outside space—"the possibilities of the Open" (*The Poet's World* 21), she is eager to carry the possibilities into her poems. As she senses the Muse—"I hear wings"—the transition from the personal into the world of art bridges this section and the next.

The fourth section delineates the difference that marks artists and their creations, and outlines the nature of art for the African American poet. The poems in this section are few and well-defined, each marking the nature of African American art and poetry. This is a section that talks of knowledge of the self and of acceptance. The epigraph to the section is from a poem by Claude McKay that admits of difference: "*I know the dark delight of being strange,*" and the banal acceptance itself decenters the exoticism that the image might evoke. The first poem in the section is titled "Dedication," speaking of the poet's dedication to her art: "I am a magic/that can deafen you like a rainstorm or a well." It is also an acceptance of her exoticism, trapping her in her skin. Stating that true knowledge comes from nature, not books, she says: "What are music or books if not ways/to trap us in rumors? The freedom of fine cages!" The myth of freedom and the trappings of language reveal the nature of art.

The next poem, titled "Ars Poetica," is one of the most important poems in Dove's œuvre, and describes the creative genius at work. Taking its title from Horace's "Ars Poetica," written in the form of an epistle to advise poets on the art of writing poetry, the poem is an injunction to the (male) poets of the century to remind themselves that great poetry "involves rising above the masculine ego and acknowledging the resistance of American landscape to the individual mind" (Righelato 124). Following Eliot's theory of impersonality, Dove contends that for great poetry, the poet's persona and emotions must distance themselves from the persona and emotions in the poem. In addition, Dove's theory of language is for every word to convey a world of images, the narrative completed by the gaps:

> What I want is this poem to be small,
> a ghost town
> on the larger map of wills.
> Then you can pencil me in as a hawk:
> a traveling x-marks-the-spot.

Contending that real poetic power comes from brevity and artistic precision, Dove counters the dominant presence of male poets in their poetry. Steffen calls the "x" an "identification with the nameless and forgotten" (5), referring to the characters in Dove's poems being from "the underside of history" (Georgoudaki 421). The poet herself looks down at a distance from above, the metaphorical hawk, a traveler.

The condescending attitude of great poets is the subject of Dove's next poem, "Arrow." Outlining the unbearably masculinist nature of the interaction with a prominent scholar who read through "prize-winning translations of/the Italian Nobel Laureate"—male-centric poems which portrayed women as objects through which men achieved agency—Dove questions the deceptively eclectic nature of poems written by men:

> He explained the poet
> to us: immense difficulty
> with human relationships; sensitive;
> women were a scrim through which he could see
> heaven.
> We sat through it. Quite lovely, these poems.
> We could learn from them although they were saying
> *you women are nothing, nothing at all.*

Having established the constructed nature of male superiority, Dove explores the constructed nature of skin color as a racial identifier in the poem, "Stitches." Contending that black and white are mere colors, she describes how an accident showed her that black was just a surface color:

> When skin opens
> where a scar
> should be, I think nothing but
> "So I *am* white underneath!"

Her example interrogates black skin as signifying identity, the signifier itself just skin deep.

Returning to Greek mythology in "Medusa," Dove chooses this female gorgon to describe the powers of the poet. If Medusa could freeze with a stare, Dove has already established in "Dedication" that the poet can deafen like a rainstorm or a well. Ascribing to the poet the role of the philosopher, Dove asserts that poets need to reach to the depths of places unseen, contending that creative power arises from these depths. In the myth, Medusa's ghost went to the Underworld and frightened the dead there. The metaphorical allusion to the artist being powerful among the spiritually dead gives credence to poetic power immortalizing the artist, as well as to the poet being the harbinger of change. In the myth, Medusa was beheaded by Persius, who used her head as a weapon to freeze his opponents to stone. Dove alludes to the power of the poet to influence, like Medusa, long after she is dead:

> Someday long
> off someone will
> see me
> fling me up
> until I hook
> into sky
>
> drop his memory
>
> My hair
> dry water.

The image of the frozen hair indicates the powerful nature of the poet's countenance even years after she is gone. Steffen says that Dove "lifts Medusa from object to subject position. No longer victim but agent, she writes her own story" (82). Talking of the deliciously sensual nature of the image, Righelato says:

> It has the shiver and chill of a Billie Holiday song: she found, from within, the grace notes of a damaged life, thrown up as she was by the public into stardom. Understatement and compression give the poem a cryptic resonance, a mesmerizing aura distilled in "dry water," the oxymoronic conclusion. (129)

The section ends with "In a Neutral City," which enters calmer waters with the image of old age, nondescript and forgettable, feeding on memories, but remembering only nature, thus reiterating that nature is the only witness to a complete life: "over lunch we will search for a topic/only to remember a hill, a path hushed/in the waxen shade of magnolias." This returns the poet to nature, the only neutral witness. The section ends with the notion of a Derridean acceptance of impurity and contradictions, asserting that the black self needs to celebrate the contradictions that have gone into the framing of a historically complex identity. This garden of contradictions *is* the metaphorical Eden, the traditional myth deluding the black man into a quest for an impossible and unreal state of existence.

The collection ends with the quest for the mythical Edenic translating into a hard questioning of the reality of contemporary American life and its myths. The epigraph to the fifth section destroys the myth of individuality and freedom that forms the basis of the American social structure. It is a quote by Constantine Petrou Cavafy: "...*Don't hope for things elsewhere./Now that you've wasted your life here, in this small corner,/you've destroyed it everywhere in the world.*" The poems in the section explore freedom as a myth, comparing contemporary life with the "freedom of fine cages" ("Dedication").

The first poem in the section, titled "Saints," is a description of Catholic rituals and the importance of religion for the otherwise nondescript black woman who is "fat now, she stinks in warm weather." The description of the children that she bears as "medallions/swinging in the dazed air" are imagined by Righelato as "votive offerings, the ritualized mode of representation transmuting into the political reality" (131), yet the image is eerily close to the scene of lynchings, each justified by religion as the recourse of a divinely ordained superior race to civilize the inferior one. The poem, "The Gorge," details the scene of black family life in a poor town with a railroad. In this poem, little Joe runs away from his father who had shouted at him for forgetting his glass of iced water. Sitting down on the rails to cry so that his father wouldn't see him, he doesn't hear the train approaching and has his toe cut off. The poem ends with the image of poverty, sin, and false swagger. In an interview with Bellin, Dove says, "Myth begins in anecdote" (Ingersoll 129). Describing the mythic nature of black life in the town, she says: "This gorge leaves a trail/Of anecdotes, // The poor man's history." Here, Dove traces both the origin of the mythic nature of the black town as poverty-stricken, squalid and violent, and deconstructs oral history—"anecdotes"—as the poor man's only recourse to a place in history. The implication of official history as a narrative dominated by the rich and powerful is contrasted by the notion of anecdotes as the poor man's history. In this anecdote of the poor man in a poor town, freedom is an illusory label for constricted spaces.

The poem, "Canary," brings to mind music, and bespeaks a talented career in the twilight of its greatness. Billie Holiday, an American jazz singer of the first half of the twentieth century whose real name was Eleanora Fagan, is caged in memory as besieged in life, successful in the public eye yet like Angelou's caged bird (*I Know Why the Caged Bird Sings*), her voice has traveled the road of suffering:

> Billie Holiday's burned voice
> had as many shadows as lights,
> a mournful candelabra against a sleek piano,
> the gardenia her signature under that ruined face.
> ....
> Fact is, the invention of women under siege
> has been to sharpen love in the service of myth.

Contemplating on the mythical quality of celebrities' lives, Dove concludes that it imprisons the celebrity into her public image, saying, "If you can't be free, be a mystery."

The poem, "The Island Women of Paris," returns to the subject of racial objectification, a satirical description of the way black women in Paris stand out in the crowd because of their dark skin. Highlighting the difference in skin color as exotic, their haughty and regal countenance is actually a defense against being stared at for being black. This defensive stance of complete withdrawal into themselves makes them appear more exotic:

> The island women move through Paris
> as if they had just finished inventing
> their destinations. It's better
> not to get in their way. And better
> not look an island woman in the eye—
> unless you like feeling unnecessary.

Differences, Dove seems to say, are born of the unfamiliar. Black women who "skim" and "glide" through Paris, immune to racism, rather drawing attention to themselves by their "ornamental bearing," refusing to let racist objectification break their spirits, are a formidable minority. Referred to as the "island women," these women appear almost surreal, having perfected the art of ignoring the stares that Dove noticed herself on her travels to the Continent. Ironically, Paris is portrayed as the modern Hell in *Mother Love*, and Dove ends *Grace Notes* with an introduction to its racist ambience.

The last three poems in the section close Dove's argument on the reality of life, too short to harbor illusions. Set in Israel, they trace the economic exploitation of slave labor as the basis of all achievements. The last poem, "Old Folk's Home, Jerusalem," reflects on the uselessness of all achievements in dotage, on the road to death:

> So you wrote a few poems. The horned
> thumbnail hooked into an ear doesn't care.

The gray underwear wadded over a belt says So what.

The night air is minimalist,
a needlepoint with raw moon as signature.
In this desert the question's not
Can you see? but How far off?

The collection ends with individual life fading into death. Old age is an endless waiting, the myth of grandeur in life contrasted with the obscurity of old age. The poem completes the anecdotal view of history as a collage of individual snippets, and of myths as born of these snippets. Righelato says that Dove aims to not only convey individual destinies in the "gleamed scraps but also recognize the universal narrative impulse, the impulse of individuals to latch onto an ideology that confers mythic destiny" (140), and in so doing, touches the grace notes of all lives. Like music, the mythic flows through the rise and fall, the demonic and the sublime, in human destiny. Although race is not the central subject of these poems, the narrative is unmistakably black, interspersed with the classical. This collection deconstructs the myth of American identity, and the poet traces the origin of myths in individual lives that have attained mythic status.

Having deconstructed the mythical nature of Eden as a deceptive mirage that precludes acceptance of reality, and concluding that myths often *become* history, saying that "the sad thing about white America is that it often believes its own myths, believes the official versions of history" (Ingersoll 152), Dove carries her exploration of myths into her fifth collection of poems, *Mother Love*. In this collection, she makes the Greek myth of Demeter and Persephone a metaphorical revisitation of the black mother-daughter relationship in the twentieth century. The collection builds itself around the myth of Demeter, the Greek goddess of the earth, and her daughter Persephone, the Greek goddess of fertility, to weave a tale about the grief of a mother separated from her daughter, a common feature of slave life, and the myth of black natal isolation. According to the Greek myth, Persephone is plucking flowers in her garden, and had just stooped to pick a golden narcissus when the earth suddenly opens and Hades, the God of the Underworld, drags her down into his kingdom. Demeter's grief at her daughter's abduction makes her neglect the earth, and all crops begin to wither. Her refusal to accept her fate forces Zeus to ask his brother, Hades, to return Persephone to her mother, and all seems well except for Persephone's act of eating pomegranate seeds, unaware that anyone who consumes these seeds can never return to the world of the living.

The resultant compromise forces her to exist between the two worlds, and this results in the seasons of the year. As Persephone returns to earth each spring and summer, the crops ripen and flowers blossom, but as she returns to the Underworld in the autumn and winter, Demeter grieves and the crops wither.

Exploring the cycle of life from the woman's perspective, tracing in the myth a metaphorical oneness with Nature and a counter to the Orphic nature of poetic creation, the poet navigates the world of classical mythology and the modern world as the mother-daughter tale weaves through time and space in a narrative that is black in essence. Stating in the Foreword that her use of the sonnet challenges the ordered structure of the (Shakespearean or Petrarchan) form as indicative of chaos "lurking just outside the gate" in "a tale of a violated world" (xi), Dove makes it a symbol of the fallacy of mythic tales that insist on the unchanging nature of the world outside as the moment unfolds within. Stating that sonnets seemed the most appropriate form "in homage to and as counterpoint to Rilke's *Sonnets to Orpheus*" (xii), Dove, however, reasons that this is not the main reason for her choice of this form. Talking about the need to push against prescribed borders, she echoes Hollinger and her own earlier poems when she talks about the need to both challenge and defy the limits set by these. In a Lacanian articulation of art as a challenge to the Symbolic, she says in the Foreword:

> I will simply say that I like how the sonnet comforts even while its prim borders (but what a pretty fence!) are stultifying; one is constantly bumping up against Order. The Demeter/Persephone cycle of betrayal and regeneration is ideally suited for this form since all three—mother-goddess, daughter-consort and poet—are struggling to sing in their chains. (xii)

Dove's inclusion of the poet in the trio of women attempting to break through the chains imposed by social order is indicative of the language of poetry trying to break through the order imposed by the sonnet. The choice of the sonnet makes this struggle more visible, and in transposing Greek mythology on to black life, Dove challenges borders in more ways than one. Steffen says that the racial contexts have been interchanged to emphasize parallels:

> Whereas the mythical abduction is played out on a vertical axis of "upper-and-under-world," this worldly modern version develops horizontally between the stereotypes of an innocent America and a Paris of erotic experience. While the Greek model features a white girl in a dark world, *Mother Love* highlights a dark girl in a white world. (131)

The world of the violated does not limit itself to the victims alone—everything on earth must feel the change, even as the victims themselves must accept the in-between as the new fluidity that challenges closed borders as unrealistic in this changed world.

The collection is divided into seven sections, each unnamed. The first section has just one poem in it, titled "Heroes." This poem is not a sonnet, but a narrative that uses abrupt, prosaic language in three-line stanzas and a single line at the end to introduce a violated world which seems the exact opposite of Milton's Paradise. In fact, the title seems to be an ironic overturning of the heroic tradition to project heroic qualities after Paradise has been lost. In such a world, violence seems almost pre-destined, and individual identities don't really seem to matter:

> A flower in a weedy field:
> make it a poppy. You pick it.
> Because it begins to wilt
>
> you run to the nearest house
> to ask for a jar of water.

The act has been committed, and Dove seems to insist on the futility of negation. The mythic connotations surface in the poppy, symbolic of the smoke-filled world of Demeter. As the perpetrator runs to the nearest house to ask for water in an attempt to revive the flower, he finds that this was the last flower in the garden of the lady of the house, who begins to scream at the sight and has to be silenced. One violent act thus leads to another, even more gruesome murder, any evidence of which must be carried away by the perpetrator, merged into the surroundings even as it changes him, a politics of silence surrounding the memory of the act henceforth. The poet indicates that this is where the story must begin—in violence and its repression in the memory: "Already the story's starting to unravel,/the villagers stirring as your heart/pounds into your throat." The last line of the poem—"it was going to die"—standing by itself apart from the earlier three-line stanzas, indicates the objectification that precedes a violent act, the object of violence recovering her subjectivity only to the extent that the act affects the perpetrator. The last line puts the act in stasis, as it were, and the section ends with the outlining of definitions of heroism in a world where ethical norms have been overturned. Righelato states that the progression from "the minor ecological transgression of the opening to the enraged human encounter in which the mundane implodes unexpectedly out of control" initiates a cycle of violence that resonates through the collection. She says:

> These resonances are not only moral and causal, the damaging encounters of humanity and nature, but also literary and mythic. This spare account only allows itself to come at the mythic obliquely, but its frame of reference is ambitious; the apparent simplicity of the poem is artful. (146)

Like *Paradise Lost*, therefore, *Mother Love* begins on a deceptively simple note of a nondescript encounter whose consequences swirl through destinies. Just as Lucifer's fall from grace begins a cycle that overturns the natural order in Milton's epic, the protagonist's simple act in the first poem of Dove's collection causes its ripples to be felt through all of the next creations. This is the crossroads at which the character, like Persephone while eating the pomegranate seeds, chooses her destiny, albeit unknowingly. Dove's rhetorical question in the Foreword to the collection is a reply to those who might question her decision to challenge the contours of the conventional in this collection: "But ah," she says, "can we ever really go back home, as if nothing had happened?" (xii) It signals, too, the crossroads at which the African American poet finds herself in the contemporary world—in a changed world, the traveler must move on, overcoming nostalgia for an imaginary homeland.

Once the credentials of the heroic in a changed world have been established, the second section begins with "Primer," a description of a childhood filled with being bullied, poor and black, not necessarily in that causal order. The second section consists of twelve poems, interspersing voices to weave a tale where past and present, black and white, myth and reality are interchangeable concepts. The irony of being bullied by skinny classmates for being skinny is surpassed only by the irony of rejecting the savior mother because of her cheap car. "Primer" ends on a note of determination to stand up for oneself: "I'd show them all: I would grow up." Clearly, childhood is not an idyllic paradise in this overturned world, and courage is deferred to adulthood.

However, the next poem, "Party Dress for a First Born," warns against the dangers of impending womanhood. It is a world where "men stride like elegant scissors across the lawn," the farcical nature of the interaction revealed in the next lines: "I will smile, all the while wishing them dead." This interaction, with its sexualized overtones, foreshadows the impending disaster. This appears suddenly as the mythic in the next poem, "Persephone, Falling," a sonnet whose sestet is an ironic epilogue about the kind of warnings Persephone (in the modern world) chose to ignore: "Remember: go straight to school./

This is important, stop fooling around!/Don't answer to strangers." Ironically, Persephone followed all but one of the instructions—"She had strayed from the herd." Righelato comments on this by asserting that "the modern Persephone of these poems is wary and alert, enterprising and independent—not victim material. But disaster, like Hades, comes out of nowhere" (149). As she bends to pick a narcissus, pulling hard at it, the unnamed perpetrator "sprung out of the earth/on his glittering terrible/carriage, he claimed his due." The poem concludes by emphasizing the ease with which disaster strikes, the girl a mere object at the hands of destiny.

The poems that follow Persephone's fall are about the disorder that follows a catastrophic destruction of the natural order. In a reversal of the Wordsworthian idyll, Persephone's fall is a warning in itself. "Is there such/a thing as a warning?" asks the mother in the poem, "Protection," as the earth withers, grieving with her. In this oneness, grief transmutes itself into nature's cycle, yet it is not knowing for certain the fate of her daughter that is the most painful for the mother. Righelato says: "Acknowledgment of the process of merging into nature's cycle is a diffusion of the weight of grief. Yet there are still exasperated questionings" (151). As Demeter wanders the earth ignoring her duties, the crops wither. In this world, man and nature are one in loss: "The Hawaiian/mulberry is turning to ash // and the snail has lost its home."

The allusions are mythical, yet memory must choose the path back either to the Greek world or to antebellum America. The loss of the daughter was a common pain inflicted on the slave mother, who had no choice but to see her daughter taken away to be surely violated, yet had no means of knowing for certain what her fate was. The title, "Protection," equates the helplessness of Demeter, the Greek goddess, and Sethe, the slave mother who kills her child rather than give her up to the horrors of slavery in Morrison's *Beloved*. As she lets herself sink into grief, wandering the earth with a dishevelled appearance, her vulnerability is suggestive of the dangers that Demeter has exposed herself to in public. "The Search" enacts the daughter's presumed violation in the form of the mother's. In the myth, Demeter transforms herself into a mare to escape Poseidon's lustful advances, but does not succeed. In Dove's poem, the "tantalized" eyes of men follow her as she frequents the path by the river in her grief-infested wanderings, and the other women's spiteful remark leaves no doubt as to her fate: "*Serves her right, the old mare.*"

Persephone's actual violation is played out in the poem "The Narcissus Flower," fear metamorphosing into hate as she experiences life beyond death:

> And though nothing could chasten
> the plunge, this man
> adamant as a knife easing into
>
> the humblest crevice, I found myself at
> the center of a calm so pure, it was hate.
>
> The mystery is, you can eat fear
> before fear eats you,
>
> you can live beyond dying—

However, hate takes with it the chastity of emotion, leaving behind an indifference that is like living death. Persephone is queen of the Underworld, and the slave who is violated by the white master may be queen of the other slave girls, but the privilege has cost her soul. Persephone is "a queen/whom nothing surprises," a lifeless object of lust whose innocent projection of strength into adulthood has crumbled to dust. "Persephone Abducted" describes her struggle, her cry for her mother that went unheeded, the horror of the event manifest in the transition of the image of the abduction from its Greek allusion in the title to its clear presence in the fields where the slaves are picking cotton, "singing in the field, oblivious/to all but the ache of our own bent backs." In this world where natural laws are broken, time struggles against its limitations just as the sonnet does; the horror of the act struggles against any philosophical arguments to mitigate its effects:

> there are no laws when laws are broken, no names
> to call upon. Some say there's nourishment for pain,
>
> and call it Philosophy.
> That's for the birds, vulture and hawk,
> the large ones who praise
> the miracle of flight because
> they use it so diligently.

The poet leaves it for the reader to conclude whether the omission on the part of those around who did not notice the victim screaming was deliberate or not. In a reversal of the natural order, those who were supposed to hear the screams probably did not, but the sole witness to the incident too is advised by her mother in "Statistic: The Witness" not to speak about it to any but "Jesus." Unable to drive the image of the abduction from her mind, the witness understands that the world will never be the same again—"this faithless earth/which cannot readjust an abyss/into flowering meadow." The ethical order has been overturned, and silence has replaced speech. It is a measure of how language is unable, or unwilling, to communicate trauma, and here we find the gaps in the metanarrative. It is in the witness' silence that the enormity of the crime can be gauged as she wanders, condemned to silence, in an irresolvable quest for "green oblivion," the metaphorical "bottomless lull of her arms" just out of reach as trauma claims her too as its victim. As the personae of victim and witness merge, the inescapable horrors of historical trauma demand resolution in confrontation.

The social order that has been disturbed by the mother's refusal to accept her daughter's fate counters society's opinion of grief as personal and transitory. In the communal meeting described in "Grief: The Council," the council decides that the mother must return to communal life—"Get a hold on yourself, take a lover/help some other unfortunate child." Healing, however, is a prerequisite for moving on, and the enormity of the loss of the last flower in her garden is unrecognized by any but Demeter, who has detached herself from her earthly duties: *"the last frail tendril snapped free/(though the roots still strain toward her)."* This is brought out in the poem, "Mother Love," an ode to mothering that comes as naturally as breathing, and is as impossible to forget:

> Who can forget the attitude of mothering?
> > Toss me a baby and without bothering
> to blink I'll catch her, sling him on a hip.
> > Any woman knows the remedy for grief
> is being needed.

However, the remedy is far from what the violently grieving Demeter needs. And thus, even though she follows society's conventional advice in the first half of the poem, the second half, swinging between the mythic and the modern, describes the violent consequences of trying to engage a mind ravaged by grief in what can only be termed surrogate nurturing, a mocking replica of her child in her arms. The image can bring to mind none but the figure of the strong black Mammy nursing the white mistress' children after her own had been taken away from her to be sold. In the myth, Demeter disguises herself as an old woman and is resting near a well when she is offered hospitality by King Celus's wife and daughters. In return, she offers to care for Queen Metanira's son, Demophon. Projecting her grief and her fear of the loss of a child on to this baby boy, she anoints him with nectar by day and puts him on fire at night to burn out his mortality. Myth and reality converge as Dove describes the chilling details of "a baby sizzling on a spit/as neat as a Virginia ham." The poem ends with his torture and Demeter's almost psychopathic reminder that she has not forgotten—"poor human—/to scream like that, to make me remember." Stating that this scene is a metaphor for cultural assimilation, Righelato traces in the poem a reminder of the suffering that results from it:

> There are uncomfortable historical resonances in the fact that this is a scene of torture in pursuit of a myth of perfectibility and cultural refashioning. History has shown that when humanity has "cured" itself of human feeling, the consequences have been terrible. (154)

This poem also exposes the bitterness that results from trauma left to fester; in a contradictory way, what is supposed to heal makes the loss more acutely felt, the fear resulting from the traumatic experience filtering all other experiences and affecting all future actions. As the person enters the world of the unfeeling, memory takes him back to places wherein the pain resonates. In time, as Demeter tries to return to some mode of normalcy, the unresolved pain spreads through it all:

> I rummage the pantry's
> stock for raisins and cereal as they pull
> honking out of the mist, a sonic hospital graph
> announcing recovery. Arise, it's a brand new morning!
> Though I pour myself the recommended bowlful,
> stones are what I sprinkle among the chaff. ("Breakfast of Champions")

Nothing but a revisiting of the actual wound and closure would suffice for healing to take place. Walker, theorizing historical trauma, says, "The world is not healed in the abstract...Healing begins where the wound was made" (200). In Dove's bridging of the real and the mythical, wounds, especially those covered up and left to fester, *become* worlds, violent and unresolved. Thus, the second part of the collection ends with a social injunction to move on. As in Walker's *The Way Forward is with a Broken Heart*, Dove's *Mother Love* moves into the next sections trying to do just that. As Walker did, Dove interweaves past and present, albeit in a more metaphorical sense than Walker ever meant.

The third section thus begins with an acceptance of reality and an attempt by Persephone and Demeter to move on in their respective worlds.

The section consists of just one poem, "Persephone in Hell," and is divided into seven sections, symbolic of the seven pomegranate seeds Persephone had eaten. It is her own account of her journey into an existence marked by an unbearable "ennui," where Hell is a mother's anxious imagination of modern-day Paris. This is the section where *Mother Love* is "much like T. S. Eliot's *The Waste Land*, a continuous parallel between the modern world and the world of myth" (Pereira 142), a description which prompts Righelato to call it "a Baudelairean miasma" (156), referring to the boredom and apathy that marks existence in the city in Baudelaire's collection of poems, *Les Fleurs du Mal*. Steffen notes the affinity between form and theme in this section:

> Except for the final poem, where two parallel columns of fourteen lines each signal a return to poetic shape, hope, and light, this is no sonnet world but rather the most realistic part of the sequence, a prosaic realm, if not a hell of prose. (135)

Crowded and uninspiring, it is full of temptations in a desolate sequence of events that lead to the meeting with Persephone, as Hades waits to separate one person, "*divertissement*," from the homogeneous crowd:

> Or can I wait for one person
> to separate from the crowd,
> chin lifted for courage, as if to place
> her brave, lost countenance
> under my care…

It is in search of relief from boredom that Hades meets Persephone, their relationship following all the steps of modern courtship, yet the "cold longing" belies the expectations of a passionate union. In Dove's world, language often decides major destinies, and so it is in her version of the myth. Persephone is seduced by Hades's language more than by his physical appearance. Characteristic of union in a spiritual waste land, Persephone and Hades's passion is a metaphorical enervating experience that marks the normal in this reversal of the natural. Righelato says:

> It is characteristic that Dove pulls the myth into the contemporary, with the freight of the modernist metropolis, but with something beyond the modernist ennui and the diffidence and disgust that is a feature of contemporary sexual relationships in *The Waste Land*. The sexual encounter in "Persephone in Hell" is not, however, a grand passion but an erotic game with all manner of cultural interfaces to be negotiated. These contemporary elements are in the ascendancy, yet they metamorphose without gradation into the classical. (158)

As the encounter progresses to the sexual, the cold darkness encompasses everything, the heat of passion crying out for the seed to be subsumed in the earth, for man to be subsumed in nature. In a metaphorical stating of the necessity of both to complete the cycle, the final section of the poem has parallel sections on both sides of the page, the left for Persephone and the right for Hades, an answering voice to each call:

if I whispered to the moon	
	I am waiting
if I whispered to the olive	
	you are on the way
which would hear me?	
	I am listening
the garden gone	
	the seed in darkness
the city around me	
	I am waiting
it was cold I entered	
	You rise into my arms
I entered for warmth	

The positioning of the lines forces the reader to *look*. The lines are as art, a union of light and dark, cold and warm. The poem ends with the union of the two, Persephone unable to forget the warmth and her mother's sorrow as she looks for light in this dark world. The illusory city disappears, and the reality of nothingness overtakes her, merging with the passion of the moment.

The next section begins with an exact parallel in the course of events in the life of the mother and daughter. The first poem in the section, titled "Hades' Pitch," details how Persephone "sighs/just as her mother aboveground stumbles" and both are "bereft in an instant—/while the Great Man drives home his desire." The parallel is unmistakably cultural, the loss in both worlds occurring simultaneously even as one is seduction while the other is a forced surrender. Righelato calls this "a double phallic wounding" (159), and the poems that follow will show the divergent paths in the two worlds after this event.

The next poem in the section, titled "*Wiederkehr*," is an observation of how diverse Persephone and Hades's worlds are. Having been seduced by his language when they met, it is improbable that physical passion alone would be enough to bind her to him. The young girl who had come looking for warmth now quietly "sat to hold the rain untouched/inside," and as Hades looks at her, hoping "in darkness, to smell/rain," Persephone realizes that his dark world was not enough for her:

> He only wanted me for happiness:
> to walk in air
> and not think so much,
> to watch the smile
> begun in his eyes
> end on the lips
> his lips caressed.

This is a modern-day dilemma as well, and the mythic responds to the universal dilemma of male chauvinism and the female spirit fluttering to escape its cage. Lofgren notes that "in a marked departure from the original myth, which focuses on Demeter's grief, Dove allows Persephone to tell her side of the story" (136). Here, Persephone is conferred with subjectivity and allowed to choose. Hades realizes that she is not content to be just his queen, and the poem ends with her choosing to leave him when the opportunity presents itself: "when the choice appeared,/I reached for it." The feeling of being encaged in a world devoid of the light of the eclectic reveals itself in the title, "*Wiederkehr*," which means repetition.

However, escape would not be so easy. "The Bistro Styx," an important poem in Dove's œuvre, traces the changes wrought by experiences and the impossibility of the world ever returning to its former state, as Demeter notes with shock her daughter's changed appearance:

> She was thinner, with a mannered gauntness
> as she paused just inside the double
> glass doors to survey the room, silvery cape
> billowing dramatically behind her. *What's this*,
>
> I thought, lifting a hand until
> she nodded and started across the parquet;
> that's when I saw she was dressed all in gray,
> from a kittenish cashmere skirt and cowl
> down to the graphite signature of her shoes.

The shock soon turns into a cynical, resigned acceptance of the fact that it is not just in outward appearance that her daughter appears to have changed. As Persephone talks of their successful art business which is greatly admired by the tourists who visit Paris, Demeter observes closely how her daughter eats a large meal, venturing to ask if she may come to visit her sometime. Although noting that she looked "ravishing," the description is hardly an admiring mother's:

> She did look ravishing,
> spookily insubstantial, a lipstick ghost on tissue,
> or as if one stood on a fifth-floor terrace
>
> peering through a fringe of rain at Paris'
> dreaming chimney pots, each sooty issue
> wobbling skyward in an ecstatic oracular spiral.

If Persephone looks other-worldly, she does not seem to be opening up psychologically to her mother either, avoiding any answer to her question: "But are you happy?" The anxious mother who, at the beginning, had thought of her as "my blighted child," wanting desperately to cry out: "Are you content to conduct your life/as a cliché and, what's worse, // an anachronism, the brooding artist's demimonde?" realizes towards the end that Persephone was irrecoverable, changed by her experiences: "*I've lost her.*" The poem and the section end on a note of divergence as the two women reach across the umbilical cord to define their places in their respective worlds.

The fifth section of the collection begins in the contemporary world, wherein the poet lives the blues, traversing myth and reality as she contemplates freedom and the suffering that precedes it. As she observes the male chauvinism that seems to cut into a halcyon summer day in "Blue Days," bawdy male jokes breaking through the Arizonan blue, the disjunct between nature and the male world makes the poet wonder what Demeter would have thought of the contemporary world: "Demeter," she says, "here's another one for your basket of mysteries."

This is followed by the image of a restless quest in the next poem, "Nature's Itinerary," which talks of traveling, disrupting the pill-controlled cycles of the body that allow the poet to function, and something as innocuous as "having a beer" is understood to be "a man's invention to numb us so we/can't tell which way the next wind's blowing." Righelato compares Dove's restless wanderings in this poem to Demeter's: "Dove's disorientation and restless transit is a version of Demeter's disconsolate wanderings and Persephone's transient sojourns. In locating the mythic displacements in the modern, such displacements can be embraced" (160).

In tracing displacements, the blues trace their origins to African American musical traditions, and the narrative of Persephone's abduction and Demeter's mourning evokes this expression. In "Demeter Mourning," Demeter declares that she inconsolable, her nostalgic mourning and her acceptance of reality giving rise to contradictory emotions:

> I'll not ask for the impossible;
> one learns to walk by walking.
> In time I'll forget this empty brimming,
> I may laugh again at
> a bird, perhaps, chucking the nest—
> but it will not be happiness,
> for I have known that.

Both Demeter and Persephone are pulled between the past and the present, Demeter unable to reconcile herself to the loss of Persephone, and Persephone unable to completely commit herself to either world. In "Exit," Persephone gets leave to return to the earth, but "provisionally," which means that she must exist forever between the two worlds: "Just when hope withers, a reprieve is granted." The politics of belonging and of being forever between worlds haunts Persephone. Having been granted provisional reprieve, she is to spend half the year on earth with her mother, and the other half as Queen of the Underworld.

Towards the end of the section, the poem "Afield" sees Demeter watching her daughter walking in the fields, trying to find the crack in the earth that would return her to Hades. Her time with Hades has changed her, so that coming back, home no longer feels the same. Persephone is like the immigrant who must find her identity in the shifting sands of the in-between—belonging to both worlds, she is at once part of neither. Demeter notices this as Persephone wanders the fields where she herself had wandered in grief:

> Out where crows dip to their kill
> under the clouds' languid white oars
> she wanders, hands pocketed, hair combed tight
> so she won't feel the breeze quickening—
> as if she were trying to get back to him,
> find the breech in the green
> that would let her slip through,
> then tug meadow over the wound like a sheet.

The octave presents a strange reversal of the familiar, the protection against the breeze bringing to mind Persephone's first experience of Hell in the third section:

> After the wind, this air
> imploded down my throat,
> a hot, rank syrup swirled with smoke
> from a hundred cigarettes.
> Soft chatter roaring. French nothings.
> I don't belong here. ("Persephone in Hell")

Clearly, the familiar has become unfamiliar, and the nature of belonging must find a place devoid of the binaries of inside/outside. The section ends with a strangely nostalgic remembrance of the abduction, the memory of the shrieks interspersed with the memory of the soothing gray. In "Lost Brilliance," Persephone remembers the day, but with a different emotion associated to it this time: "I miss that corridor drenched in shadow,/sweat of centuries steeped into stone." At the end, the poet concurs that it is easier to belong to an alien world than to continuously move between worlds, never to call either your own. Righelato concludes: "Whatever Hades has taken, he has conferred a physical self upon Persephone" (162). This new self can never call the earth her own as the old one did.

Identities need to accept changing realities, just as the reality of trauma needs to be confronted as leaving a permanent mark on the victim, the perpetrator, and the laws of the universe. The sixth section of the volume deals with the changed laws of the universe, confronting the political and the historical in its analysis of the nature of freedom and its contentious conditions which foster art. Dedicated to Breyten Breytenbach, a South African writer and painter who was imprisoned by the South African government in 1975 for his opposition to apartheid, the first poem in the section, "Political," determines the nature of Hell, designating it an abstract form that arises from its basic opposition to freedom: "There's a way to study freedom but few have found/it; you must talk yourself to death and then beyond,/destroy time, then refashion it." In this refashioning of time, the linearity of events is challenged, and the desire to find the original world remains: "Even Demeter keeps digging/towards that darkest miracle,/the hope of finding her child unmolested." The definitions of freedom decide the contours of imprisonment, but it would be wise to say that imprisonment changes the nature of both the person and freedom itself.

However, while Persephone finds herself between worlds, Demeter is unable to let go of the longing for a perfect past. This conflict is played out each autumn and winter when Persephone returns to the Underworld as its Queen, and Demeter wanders the earth, inconsolable in loss. "Demeter, Waiting" shows a mother in eternal waiting, unable to break the ties of the umbilical cord to let her daughter step into adulthood:

> No. Who can bear it. Only someone
> who hates herself, who believes
> to pull a hand back from a daughter's cheek
> is to put love into her pocket.

The poem "Lamentations" resonates with the consequences of not accepting reality. There can be no ladder back into the past, the poem seems to say, and to hold on to an unachievable state of past existence would only lead to self-destruction: *"To refuse to be born is one thing—/but once you are here,/you'd do well to stop crying."* This attitude of looking to the future permeates all the poems in this section. The poem "History," though it deals less with history than Dove's other poems, seems to underline the fact that the same principle that underlies myths underscores history as well. Both are metanarratives formed of flashes of facts and a lot of gaps which allow space for perspectives. Recognizing the interwoven nature of the narrative allows for a reformulation of history, understanding that every narrative is a metaphor, and the choice to look forward resides with the individual:

> Everything's a metaphor, some wise
> guy said, and his woman nodded, wisely.
> Why was this such a discovery
> to him? Why did history
> happen only on the outside?

This poem is the fulcrum on which the collection turns towards an acceptance of the present rather than a mourning for a lost past. History, then, is a metaphor like all other narratives, and, like the others, can be read only by taking into account the silences as well as the raw facts. Further, the resolution of historical trauma demands a revisiting of the site of trauma, but *sans* the chains that tie us to the past. The poet seems to say that the attempt to recreate the past only results in further trauma. In "Rusks," Persephone finally admits the futility of trying to exist in two worlds, saying:

> Spring wore on my nerves—
> ....
> I got tired of tearing myself down.
> ....
> As my mama always said:
> half a happiness is better
> than none at goddam all.

Unlike Demeter, Persephone understands that the choice of one world does not mean that she must sever ties with the other—she accepts her affiliations across borders while keeping her roots secure, but without the illusion of return to an imaginary past. For the truth is, that when she did return, the world had changed, and so had she. This is Dove's statement on how the myth reveals just the bare sketch of a story, conditioning ideals and behavior without revealing the struggles that require an impossible fortitude to sustain these ideals in reality. Further, the past can never be re-created, and the "half a happiness" that reality holds out to us must not be lost in the quest for a mythic past.

However, trauma demands closure, and the last poem in the section, titled "Demeter's Prayer to Hades," is about links to the past. Finally accepting destiny's choice, Demeter reconciles to change. With Persephone pregnant, Demeter reformulates the link between past and future by handing it to Hades. This is where the poems diverge from the mythic. While *Grace Notes* ended with the realization that the (pure) world of myths acted as a structural impediment to an acceptance of a real world filled with contradictions, *Mother Love* decides to renounce the quest for perfection, and accept the half-world of happiness that reality offers. In this real world, Demeter, renouncing her hatred, urges Hades to move forward on the path he would share with Persephone. This is an acceptance of existence in a liminal space, and an acceptance of the contradictions that existence in the space demanded. The journey would be both individual and lead to a future unknown, but Demeter understands that it is the only way forward. Following Walker's theory of healing, she forgives the perpetrator, looking to the future:

> There are no curses—only mirrors
> held up to the souls of gods and mortals.
> And so I give up this fate, too.
> Believe in yourself,
> go ahead—see where it gets you.

If history is about control and forging links, Demeter seems to be saying, she is ready for new knowledge. This is also a transition from the ethnocentric to the postethnic, the acceptance of a cultural affiliation between the victim and the perpetrator for a shared future, a Post-Black rejection of separate spaces and an acceptance of a reformulation of identities that does not insist on binaries. However, the poem is also about the journey being an individual one. Just as Demeter has traveled hers, Hades must forge his path. Righelato notes:

> The "traveling," the restlessness that is a keynote of *Mother Love*, indicative of its preoccupation with changing states, with metamorphosis, infects the characters not only with the desire to move beyond the present state but also with a longing to recover an earlier phase that will somehow bring them a beginning again. (162)

Longing, however, turns into melancholia, and leads to an understanding that healing will not take place in this condition. Forever in a state of impossible mourning, the character cannot forge his identity in the new world. Further, the state of dynamic progression ensures that the past the individual longs for will always be an *imaginary* one, a world that does not exist anymore. In this context, Dove's deconstruction of a disconnected, disjointed frame where past and present, mythic and contemporary, are always separate is a deliberate attempt to sift through the politics of identity formation. Her choice of the epigraph to this section from Muriel Rukeyser's "The Poem as Mask" celebrates fragments, and she quotes him, saying, "the fragments join in me with their own music." In Rukeyser's poem, Orpheus repudiates masks, and this, says Righelato, "paradoxically liberates him into artistic power" (164). This is the liberating power that Dove seeks through her renunciation of a mythical past in favor of a present reality fraught with contradictions.

Having returned to the present, the seventh section returns the sonnet to its traditional form. The spaces have changed their contours to fit acceptance, and the inhabitant is now able to revisit traumatic sites in history as a *black* descendant comfortable in his own skin. The poems in this section exhibit continuity in subject and form, a *liaison* in the way each concluding line of a poem forms the opening line of the next one, reflecting the newfound continuity with the past that comes with acceptance. The poems trace Dove's search for the ruins of Demeter's temple near Agrigento in Sicily. The epigraph to this section, significantly a description of Hell from Milton's *Paradise Lost*, contemplates the desolation of the seat exchanged for Heaven. This section celebrates fragments as the only evidence from the past that the poet finds.

The first poem in this section, titled "Her Island," describes the tourist's quest for the remains of the past in a region as desolate as the one described in the previous sections. It begins with the description of "blazed stones, closed ground," and moves through inhospitable ground to find scattered pieces of the past which the poet can only describe as "litter": "Everywhere temples, or pieces of them,/lay scattered across the countryside....Sicily's most exalted litter." The tone is irreverent but practical, and firmly poised in the present. The penultimate part of the poem talks of rules, this time about driving, yet the collection ends on a note of empathy for the one who did follow the rules yet could not be saved:

> Through sunlight into flowers
> she walked, and was pulled down.
> A simple story, a mother's deepest
> dread—that her child could drown
> in sweetness.

Even though empathetic, the tone accepts that the exact details of the abduction, including the exact place where Persephone went down, will perhaps never be known. The earth keeps its secrets, Dove seems to say, even as it is the only true witness to history:

> Water keeps its horrors
> while Sky proclaims his, hangs them
> in stars. Only Earth—
> ....
>   —knows
> no story's ever finished; it just goes
> on, unnoticed in the dark that's all
> around us: blazed stones, the ground closed.

"No story's ever finished," the collection concludes, and the motif of travel recurs yet again. The section, while revisiting the first poem in the collection, "Heroes," in the state of the world described, also completes the cycle to end on a note of postmodern uncertainty. Yet it is in an altered state of mind that the cycle is completed. Stating that history is a continuous process that will go on, it celebrates the blazing stones and the closed ground, treating them as part of the ride on the carousel, the beauty that can be found not just in a mythic past, but in the imperfect reality of the present.

Both *Grace Notes* and *Mother Love* deconstruct the mythic as the perfect world that is surreal, in the past, and unachievable, functioning as a signifier that pulls the individual into an ever-descending spiral of anticipation, an ever-deferred dream of satisfaction, and a state of perennial anticipation. Myths as signifiers form part of the racialized structure that presents Whiteness as the norm, and white myths as symbolic of a perfect resolution. Juxtaposing the Greek frame of myths and black contemporary reality, Dove deconstructs the racialized nature of myths to posit them as denoting universal attributes and emotions. Following Lévi-Strauss and Barthes, she deconstructs them as signifiers that both inform and are informed by cultural contexts. Transposing them on to black life, she proves the universal nature of these myths. Yet, she also proves that as signifiers of idyllic perfection, these myths also inform racial identities by setting unrealistic ideals of existence and behavior. The two collections finally resolve the need for Blackness to trace its own path, after a point diverging from the mythic to an acceptance of its history and its difference from the white. However, unlike the artists of the Black Arts Movement, Dove insists that this acceptance of Black reality should be *sans* any claim to a parallel idealistic frame. Celebrating the postmodern fissures of contemporary existence, Dove decides not to hanker after an impossible past, accepting that trauma *did* happen, and the half happiness that Blacks can have today is better than running after a mythical past.

The two collections form an important part of Dove's œuvre, outlining her theory for healing from trauma. Dove follows Walker in her theory of the revisiting of sites of historical trauma, blurring binaries as she searches for resolution. Her quest takes her on a mythical journey where black and white, past and present, are intertwined in a narrative where each reflects the other. In her assertion that everything is a metaphor, she correlates the personal and the political in a linguistic structure that posits the liminal as the designated space for change in a world constantly in flux. Her position on the threshold and floating above allow her the vantage point of both insider and outsider, which not only allows for emotional distancing but also allows her to make comparisons, juxtapose images, and deconstruct perspectives. This position also allows her to alter the cultural context to examine how myths and narratives inform cultural knowledge. However, it is also this position that finally makes her realize the impossibility of regaining the past. She understands that there must come a point in the narrative where black and white paths must merge to accept contemporary reality. However, it is only when Blackness takes root as a distinct entity can it embrace the Other without the bitterness that a refusal to acknowledge a shared past would engender. In investing Blackness with a new Post-Black place in the relational system of signifiers, Dove frees it from its reactionary mode of existence with reference to Whiteness. Freed of its place as the Other in the system of binaries, Blackness can now exist without being a *relational* signifier, thus providing closure to a conflicted identity. Only when the two frames merge does identity enter a post-mythic, post-historical phase.

Works Cited

Angelou, Maya. *I Know Why the Caged Bird Sings*. 1969. Virago, 1984.
Barthes, Roland. *Mythologies*. 1957. Translated by Annette Lavers. The Noonday Press, 1991.
———. "Rhetoric of the Image." *Image—Music—Text*. Translated by Stephen Heath. Hill and Wang, 1977. 32–51.
Beckett, Samuel. *Waiting for Godot: A Tragicomedy in Two Acts*. 1952. Faber & Faber, 1978.
Bishop, Elizabeth. "In the Waiting Room." *The Complete Poems 1927–1979*. Farrar, Straus & Giroux, 1983.
Davies, William Henry. "Leisure." *Songs of Joy and Others*. 1911. BiblioLife, 2009. 15.
Dove, Rita. *Grace Notes*. W. W. Norton, 1989.
———. *Mother Love*. 1995. W. W. Norton, 1996.
———. *The Poet's World*. Library of Congress, 1995.
———. *The Yellow House on the Corner*. Carnegie Mellon UP, 1989.
Dyer, Richard. *White: Essays on Race and Culture*. Routledge, 1997.
Eliot, T. S. *The Waste Land*. Horace Liveright, 1922.
Ellis, Trey. "The New Black Aesthetic." *Callaloo* 12.1 (1989): 233–51.
Georgoudaki, Ekaterini. "Rita Dove: Crossing Boundaries." *Callaloo* 14.2 (Spring 1991): 419–33.
Hall, Stuart. "Race, the Floating Signifier: Featuring Stuart Hall." *Media Education Foundation*. www.mediaed.org/transcripts/Stuart-Hall-Race-the-Floating-Signifier-Transcript.pdf. Accessed July 5, 2015.
Hollinger, David A. *Postethnic America: Beyond Multiculturalism*. Basic, 1995.
Hughes, Langston. *The Collected Poems of Langston Hughes*. 1921. Knopf, 1994, www.poets.org/poetsorg/poem/negro-speaks-rivers.
Ingersoll, Earl G., ed. *Conversations with Rita Dove*. UP of Mississippi, 2003.
Kamionowski, Jerzy. "Homeward Dove: Nomadism, 'World'-Travelling, and Rita Dove's Homecoming(s)." *Crossroads: A Journal of English Studies* 3 (2013): 12–21.
Keller, Lynn. *Forms of Expansion: Recent Long Poems by Women*. U of Chicago P, 1997.
Lévi-Strauss, Claude. "The Structural Study of Myth." *The Journal of American Folklore* 68.270 (Myth: A Symposium, October–December 1955): 428–44. *JSTOR*, www.jstor.org/stable/536768.
Lofgren, Lotta. "Partial Horror: Fragmentation and Healing in Rita Dove's 'Mother Love'." *Callaloo* 19.1 (Winter 1996): 135–42.

Morrison, Toni. *Beloved*. 1987. Vintage, 2007.
Pereira, Malin. *Rita Dove's Cosmopolitanism*. U of Illinois P, 2003.
Peters, Marie Ferguson. "The Black Family—Perpetuating the Myths: An Analysis of family Sociology Textbook Treatment of Black Families." *The Family Coordinator* 23.4 (October 1974): 349–57. JSTOR, https://www.jstor.org/stable/583109. doi:10.2307/583109.
Posnock, Ross. *Color & Culture: Black Writers and the Making of the Modern Intellectual*. Harvard UP, 1998.
Rampersad, Arnold. "The Poems of Rita Dove." *Callaloo* 9.1 (1986): 52–56.
Righelato, Pat. *Understanding Rita Dove*. U of South Carolina P, 2006.
Rilke, Rainer Maria. *Sonnets to Orpheus*. Insel-Verlag, 1923.
Roy, Lekha and Rano Ringo. "Interrogating Racialized Perceptions in Toni Morrison's *The Bluest Eye* and *God Help the Child*." *Dialog* 29 (Spring 2016): 65–78.
Steffen, Therese. *Crossing Color: Transcultural Space and Place in Rita Dove's Poetry, Fiction, and Drama*. Oxford UP, 2001.
Walker, Alice. *The Way Forward Is with a Broken Heart*. Ballantine, 2000.

· 5 ·

REDEFINING BLACK AESTHETICS IN *AMERICAN SMOOTH* AND *SONATA MULATTICA*

> People have come to believe that concentrating on themes releases them from the necessities of form. In returning to form, I've had to address the question of why pattern exists. Why do meter and rhythm beguile us? Conversely, what are we denying in language by going against formal verse? If we are trying to address emotions, surely we must admit that so much verbiage stands for the ineffable, what you can't really "get at." (Steffen 175)

This chapter outlines how Dove's poems exemplify the metamorphosis of Black aesthetics into the Post-Black, resolving the conflict between form and content in a redefining of poetic aesthetics that rejects the separation between the two. In an interview with Steffen, Dove muses on this disjunct, stating that the traditional notion of free verse allowing a person to think deeply while attention to form detracted from the seriousness of its contents was a fallacy, saying: "In a sense, the space of the poem is a narrow cage whose bars I am always trying to bend" (Steffen 176). This expansion of contours is a conscious effort started by Dove in her first collection, *The Yellow House on the Corner*, and culminates in the two collections, *American Smooth* (2004) and *Sonata Mulattica* (2009), in the final stage towards ontological freedom for the black man—the acceptance of the fallacy of binaries and the reality of miscegenation. Post-Blackness rejects binaries, and Dove's aesthetics follow the Post-Black trajectory to infuse Black life and Black content into structured European forms like the sonnet, the lyric, and, at one place, the villanelle. For the purpose of blurring binaries, she chooses music, experimenting, in *American Smooth* and *Sonata Mulattica*, with the double contradiction of a juxtaposition of rapturous, rhapsodic opposites straining against the walls of a contradictory structured form. This exemplifies the Post-Black movement away from the free verse of traditional black forms to fit black subject matter into traditional European forms. Further, the straining of the former against the fixed structure of the latter serves to emphasize the affective, as well as expand aesthetic contours. The circular movement of the subject in each collection, the last poem ending at the point where the first began, represents a Post-Black rejection of temporal linearity, representing the notion of the non-linear progression of history. The chapter traces how these two collections of poems indicate a final movement towards the Post-Black, incorporating all the features of the aesthetic—universal in nature yet black in subject and tone, contradictions juxtaposed to emphasize the notion of the impure as pure, rich in metaphor and imagery, and stressing the need to decenter race through an acceptance of intersectionality.

Both black art and literature have traditionally adhered to racially prescriptive forces wherein artistic representation struggled to escape from the Du Boisian "double consciousness" (194) that an acceptance of the color-line necessitated. However, in recent years, there has been a realization that the color-line was a code for constructing and representing reality, negating cultural and biological miscegenation as a legacy of slavery. In the visual arts, artists like Glenn Ligon, Kara Walker, and Rashid Johnson reveal this code by stressing gaps and dark spaces, insisting that the act of *looking* would reveal the symbolic nature of the elements that composed the historical metanarrative. Straining against conventional art forms, these artists explore existence in the in-between, incorporating light and shadow, text and image, black and white. In the literary sphere, Langston Hughes, Sterling Brown, Gwendolyn Brooks, Robert Hayden, Maya Angelou, Rita Dove, Yusef Komunyakaa, and Kevin Powell are poets who reflect on the complex nature of Blackness, and the impossibility of attaining individual consciousness without accepting the fallacious nature of binaries. Their poems revisit trauma and celebrate the complex nature of Blackness as literary and cultural catharsis.

Black aesthetics historically originated in the visual arts, and the Black cultural revolution centered around Harlem. The Black Aesthetic Movement, also known as the Black Arts Movement, grew alongside the Civil Rights movement in the 1960s, and was pronounced by Larry Neal in 1968 as the aesthetic and spiritual sister of the Black Power movement. Starting in the visual arts, it called upon poets and artists alike to depict social issues faced by the community, stressing the need to define a specifically African American aesthetic in opposition to the white one. Characterized by music, color, and symbolic imagery, it promoted a closed ethnocentric return to roots. Poets like

Larry Neal, Amiri Baraka, Langston Hughes, Sonia Sanchez, Askia Touré, and Ntozake Shange celebrated the cultural definitiveness of African American literature, music and the arts as opposed to white literary and artistic traditions. Their poems spoke to the black man directly for the first time, inviting him to take pride in a therapeutic return to roots. Hughes, known as one of the main poets of the Harlem Renaissance, invited the black man to dream in a period characterized by everyday racism, asking:

> What happens to a dream deferred?
> > Does it dry up
> > like a raisin in the sun?
> > Or fester like a sore—
> > And then run?
> > Does it stink like rotten meat?
> > Or crust and sugar over—
> > like a syrupy sweet?
> > Maybe it just sags
> > like a heavy load.
> > *Or does it explode?* ("Harlem")

Hughes's poem inspired Martin Luther King's famous 1963 speech, *I Have a Dream*. It also inspired Lorraine Hansberry to write her famous play, *A Raisin in the Sun*, in 1959, exploring the effects of deferred dreams on identity and relationships in a racist society. Realizing that the Thirteenth Amendment had provided them Emancipation from slavery but not social acceptance as equal citizens of the United States, these poets and artists spoke to and of the moment, providing a cultural impetus to the call for change. The poems of this period used African imagery; using specifically black forms and black colloquial language, they conjured up a closed Black identity through their writing.

The Black Aesthetic Movement followed the Harlem Renaissance and lasted for about a decade, from the mid-1960s to the mid-1970s, when Dove was growing up. It was a time when "strategic essentialism" (Spivak 214) was seen as necessary for survival in a racist world, and consequently, the protocols of Black Nationalism aimed to create a specifically Black identity, purpose, and direction in the literary and artistic sphere. It was an attempt to free the literary and artistic self from the cultural strangleholds of the colonizer, and saw a diversity of ethnic voices become part of the mainstream, with black theater groups, poetry, music, and dance giving voice and expression to a distinctly black identity. This, however, meant that both artistic and literary representation had separate historical narratives for the two races.

The Black Arts Movement began to fade in the mid-1970s when Dove started writing. A new generation of artists and writers, who had not experienced slavery firsthand, began to question an identity that only strengthened hegemonic structures, negating the fluidity of experience. Further, young black artists such as Robert Colescott expressed discomfort with the idea of a black art that did not encompass difference. Campbell writes:

> Many of these successful young artists found the label "black art" imprisoning, culturally and esthetically. They expressed the need to participate more expansively in a world that, in their eyes, had grown more connected, geographically mobile, culturally fluid, and porous. (317-318)

These artists and poets repudiated what they felt was an exaggerated nationalism that promoted Black identity as a closed ethnocentric space, reinforcing marginalization and limiting artistic representation. This generation grew up in "a multi-racial mix of cultures" and felt no "need to deny or suppress any part of our complicated and sometimes contradictory cultural baggage to please either white people or black" (Ellis 189). They believed that since *de jure* equality had become a reality, stressing on difference would seal off cultural borders, thus reinforcing hegemonic structures. Terming them "cultural mulattoes" (189), people who tended more toward universalism, navigating both black and white worlds with ease, Ellis called these artists of the seventies and eighties "a minority's minority mushrooming with the current black bourgeoisie boom," stating that they "have inherited an open-ended New Black Aesthetic from a few Seventies pioneers that shamelessly borrows and reassembles across both race and class lines" (187). In effect, the belief was that being a cultural mulatto was being true to the black. This is reflected in Campbell's observation that:

> ...the rebelliousness of a phrase like "post-black art", in part, is resistance to habits of mind that inhibit the ability of viewers to have an opportunity to see and experience the work of black artists unmediated by a predisposition of one kind or another. (321)

Although the term would be coined much later, its seeds were visible when Dove started writing.

The African American poets who rose to prominence during the 1980s employed stylistic traditions that stretched back to Langston Hughes and other Harlem Renaissance writers. Though the themes of survival and freedom remained pronounced in their works, the major difference was that they faced the effects of time and history on the individual, and stressed on the personal as opposed to the political. Using imagery that was universal, they confronted their nightmares. The poems of this period were mostly written in free verse, reflecting the breaking of boundaries and the free flow of subject matter. Audre Lorde, in an interview with Tate, spoke against the Black Arts Movement's stress on representation of the global experience of blacks and the oppressed, stating that poetry was a reflection of the personal: "...our *real power* comes from the personal; our real insights about living come from the deep knowledge within us that arises from our feelings" (91). In his 1989 essay, Ellis tried to give a coherent expression to this way of thinking about authenticity that was emerging among the African American artists of the time, terming it the "New Black Aesthetic" or NBA (187). The NBA built itself up against the Black Aesthetic, and was characterized by a parodying of the Black Nationalist movement that contrasted with the reverent enthusiasm of its predecessor. Ellis says: "NBA artists aren't afraid to flout publicly the official, positivist black party line" (191). Writing about artists freeing themselves of both the white gaze and the black, he says:

> NBA artists are now defining blacks in black contexts—so we are no longer preoccupied with the subjects of interracial dating or integration. And these artists aren't flinching before they lift the hood on our collective psyches now that they have liberated themselves from both white envy and self-hate. (194)

The NBA artists celebrated Blackness, yet did not flinch from exploring intraracial differences and lesions. However, even as they examined the warts, the pride in an essentialist Blackness remained unfazed:

> Nationalist pride continues to be one of the strongest forces in the black community and the New Black Aesthetic stems straight from that tradition. It is not an apolitical, art-for-art's sake fantasy. ...Neither are the new black artists shocked by the persistence of racism as were those of the Harlem Renaissance, nor are we preoccupied with it as were those of the Black Arts Movement. For us, racism is a hard and little-changing constant that neither surprises nor enrages. (Ellis 96–97)

However, there was still one major drawback preventing a complete overcoming of trauma that would negate differences. The acceptance of racism (and the need to counter it), combined with a nationalist pride in Blackness, resulted in the persistence of the binaries of black/white, us/them, inside/outside in the NBA, preventing any but an outsider's view of Whiteness, and also preventing a more complete dismembering of the gaze in formulating black identities. This resulted in the cultural mulatto turning into what Ellis terms "assimilationist nightmares; neutered mutations instead of thriving hybrids... Trying to please both worlds instead of themselves, they end up truly pleasing neither" (201). Thus, even though the NBA artists rejected Black ethnocentric attitudes on the surface, the feeling of being different persevered. Race continued to be the central organizer in their representations.

The realization of the failure of black artists to successfully navigate both black and white worlds while allowing neither to impinge on one's sense of self lead to the emergence of Hollinger's proposition for a "postethnic America" in the 1990s. The realization of the role of binaries in fostering difference made Hollinger term race an "anachronistic" construct and propose a replacing of "identity," which he considered a static concept, with voluntary "affiliations" (7) across the color-line, making it a dynamic proposition which would take into account the postmodern fluidity of existence in the twentieth century. Postethnicity followed Gilroy's contention that cultures could not be "sealed off hermetically" ("The Black Atlantic" 2), and the binaries that divided black and white as separate cultural domains were untenable in a postmodern world.

Dove's poems present a contradictory array of subjects and lyrical modes that signal the postethnic, yet critics have been wary of assigning to her writing an aesthetics that is definitively African American. Dove repudiates the Black Nationalist protocols of writing, yet Ellis stops short of calling her an NBA artist. The consciousness of being in an in-between place is visible in Dove's poems, but there is a determined avowal to reject binaries without being uprooted. The in-between, or transnational, space is, for Dove, the only way to re-negotiate movement between racially circumscribed spaces. This, her poems seem to state, is the only way forward, to frame a distinct African American ethos that is Black, yet not circumscribed by predefined notions of Blackness. Critics have interpreted this in various ways. Vendler says that "Dove has taken on the daunting aesthetic question of how to be faithful to, and yet unconstrained by, the presence—always already given in a black American—of blackness" (88). On the other hand, Georgoudaki interprets it as part of a parallel feminist tradition, tracing in Dove's poetry a distinctly Womanist strain, saying that she "shares certain dilemmas and concerns with previous Afro-American women poets, such as their feelings of displacement, fragmentation, and isolation, and their distaste for conventional stereotypes, hierarchies, divisions, and boundaries" (419). Similarly, while Rampersad places Dove squarely against the traditions of the Black Arts Movement,

Pereira calls her poems a more personal exploration of space and identity, saying, "For Dove, the tension between individual desire and the protocols of race plays out against the backdrop of the Black Arts Movement (approximately 1964–1975) and her middle-class upbringing" (197).

However, Dove's use of individualism and the reformulation of black aesthetics is neither purely personal nor purely political, but a mix of both, resulting from a realization of the constrictive nature of ethnocentric identities as well as the need to give expression to a traumatic past without being prisoner to it. She contends that the personal can never be separated from the political; each informs the other in a reciprocal schema of interrelated signifiers. Growing up in a relatively prosperous middle-class family with the benefits of education and travel, Dove became aware on her travels in Europe of the complexities of the Du Boisian "double consciousness" in life and in literature. For the first time, she found herself objectified as a black woman, and the transatlantic crossing opened up to her the hegemonic underscoring of Blackness as a category. In an interview with Steffen, she says:

> ...the insistence on black arts is just a device, a way of establishing territory. It was necessary at one time to underscore that "otherness" in order to get any kind of respect whatsoever, but the insistence on difference also requires one to erect certain walls, all of which is anathema to the artist. (169)

The realization that change must be initiated in and through art causes Dove to refrain from erecting walls, allowing a cultural porosity that reflects on binaries. At the same time, her poetry diverges from both the Black Aesthetic and the NBA in that it does not enclose identity within the prescriptive limits defined by race. This is what Golden and Ligon would term the "Post-Black" in 2001.

Thus, Dove's refusal to subscribe to racially defined binaries builds on the realization that the ethnocentrism of the earlier movements had precluded the possibility of affiliations across the color-line by refuting the reality of culturally porous borders. The insistence on binaries meant that artists had to choose between an ethnocentric or a cosmopolitan stance. This meant that one could occupy either the inside or the outside, refuting postmodern fluidity to remain ensconced in the fixity of identity formation. This "otherness" is a limitation in a postethnic world, and it is the poet who must lead the change. The change, however, does not lead to a certain re-defining of Blackness, but rather celebrates the uncertainties of being in a liminal position. By positing it a journey that celebrates uncertainties and fissures, Dove makes the

Post-Black journey an individual one. Crawford says: "Black anticipatory aesthetics is the art of not knowing what blackness will be; it is the art situated within the sustained dissonance of the earlier chords being heard, simultaneously, with the sounds that are just beginning to emerge" (36). In other words, the Post-Black does not constitute a clear break from the past. Rather, it incorporates in itself notes that existed as "gaps" in the earlier narrative, meshing it with postethnic reality to anticipate a new music. This is reflected in poems that use the structured forms of the European lyric and the sonnet while infusing these with Black subjectivity. This contradictory admixture serves two purposes—first, blurring binaries both in form and content and presenting the double contradiction as the new antithetical reality that is the Post-Black aesthetic, and second, emphasizing the affective and allowing it to change the contours of lived space in the structured original.

American Smooth and *Sonata Mulattica* exhibit most clearly the Post-Black Aesthetic. In making music the tenor for change, Dove follows Black tradition, but deviates from it in including *all* music, not just black music, as free for the African American to inherit. However, hers is not a cultural borrowing; it is, rather, an extending of cultural borders to admit the Other. It is an acceptance and a celebration of miscegenation in all its forms. Further, in making music not just the vehicle, but the tenor, for change, Dove's poems follow Gilroy's identification of the stages towards self-realization in black cultural representations to indicate a shift in the status of music as an independent cultural variant in the politics of representation. In *The Black Atlantic*, Gilroy states:

> The first stage would be identified by the attempt to liberate the body of the slave from a rather deeper experience of reification than anything that can be mapped through the concept of the fetishism of commodities, and the second phase by the liberation of culture, especially language, as a means of social self-creation. Though music plays a significant role in both of the earlier phases, the third can be defined by the project of liberating music from its status as mere commodity and by the associated desire to use it to demonstrate the reconciliation of art and life, that is, by exploring its pursuit of artistic and even aesthetic experience not just as a form of compensation, paid as the price of an internal exile from modernity, but as the favoured vehicle for communal self-development. (124)

This tenor for change is political in the tradition of African American literary writing; even as *American Smooth* takes the reader through the metaphorical twists and turns of ballroom dancing, *Sonata Mulattica* is a culmination of musical cadence that confronts the core of the problem of identity resolution for African Americans at the end of the twentieth century—miscegenation, both biological and cultural, and the politics of silence surrounding it. However, it is also a personal journey tracing the dynamics of identity for mixed race individuals. Music carries the individual into this rhythmic journey of exploration. *American Smooth* sets the rules for the dance as a partnership where each sets the other free to dance individually, initiating the metaphorical journey that is Post-Black in its stress on individual freedom as the condition for a confrontation with trauma. This confrontation, outlined in *Sonata Mulattica*, will allow for the "ontological expansiveness" (Shannon 10), or the freedom to move in and out of spaces, that Post-Blackness posits as the essential nature of a Black identity freed from the trauma of the past.

Dove's seventh collection of poems, *American Smooth*, is divided into five sections, three of which comprise poems on dance. The sections are an exercise in grace and rhythmic movement, an experiment in balancing community and individual freedom. Dove, a musician, accomplished singer and ballroom dancer herself, says that "musical structure affects how the poems are ordered in a book" (Ingersoll 154). The first section of the collection, "Fox Trot Fridays," the title taken from Nat Cole's song, is all about the ecstasy of ballroom dancing, a form Dove excelled at, in a changed world. The poems, much like the form they represent, liberate the spirit with the individuality of the rhythmic self, carrying the self into a Paradise of Hegelian withdrawal:

> one man and
> one woman,
>
> rib to rib,
> with no heartbreak in sight—
>
> just the sweep of Paradise
> and the space of a song
>
> to count all the wonders in it. ("Fox Trot Fridays")

The lines move as beats in a song, rising and falling with the syncopated rhythm. The poem, the first in the section, introduces dance as the medium through which the Self withdraws from the world to reconstitute reality. This, according to Hegel, is a necessary step in the movement towards self-actualization. This is followed by a quickening of steps as the music steps up. The next poem, "Ta Ta Cha Cha," extends this musical ecstasy to Nature, as "five doves/scatter before a wingtip's/distracted tread." "Brown" carries the racial in the swish of a colored dress, pointing out the ironic absence of the black from polite society, where the (white) dress lady needs to point out to the (black) poet that she looks good in every color. The fact that a black person dancing the waltz to perfection in a room with only two other black people in it is taken to be an exception is an ironic comment on the fallacy of color blindness:

> Why you look good in every color!
> the dress lady gurgled, just before
> I stepped onto the parquet
> for a waltz. I demurred;
> ....
>   Don't
> get me wrong: I've always loved
> my skin, the way it glows against
> citron and fuchsia, the difficult hues,
> but the difference I cause
> whenever I walk into a polite space
> is why I prefer grand entrances—

The insistence on color in everyday rhetoric is an inescapable reality for the African American, the insistence on color as an identity marker even for a skilled dancer a reminder that "in a totally racialized society, it is impossible to escape racially inflected language" (Morrison, *Playing* 13). Yet the celebration of color here reveals a determination to move beyond it without negating its existence. "Heart to Heart" follows this abomination of color as the poet examines red as the color which the heart is not, and language as a poetic construct that does not reflect reality. The fallacy of accepting as truth that which is merely a signifier in a relational structure is brought out here. Proverbs are deconstructed as linguistic constructs that have gained meaning through use. Thus, while "the bottom of it," that is, the heart, does not exist, "there's no key" to unlock it either, because the proverbial lock does not exist except in the speaker's or listener's mind. Deconstructing the epistemology of proverbial constructions, the poem ends with the reminder that the reality is the person, not the constructs built around him:

> It's neither red
> Nor sweet....
> it's all yours, now—
> but you'll have
> to take me,

too.

Music here is a language in itself. With the alternating rising and falling of notes, the music shapes contradictory notions into a whole. The rhythm mimics the beats of the heart, expressing desires that cannot be fulfilled without accepting the complete person. In an interview, Dove says:

> The way that a chord will resolve itself, is something that applies to my poems—the way that, if it works, the last line of the poem, or the last word, will resolve something that has been hanging for a while. (Ingersoll 154)

This is the case in most of her poems, although the resolution is not always certain.

The last poem in the section, "American Smooth," representing a form of dance that allows individual freedom to each partner, stresses the individual nature of the journey that music takes each person on, where one partner is filled with "ecstatic mimicry/...the *sine qua non*/of American Smooth," while the other becomes "still." It is an acceptance of contradictions into the Self. The flight into the Self culminates in a return to reality—"the earth/remembered who we were/and brought us down." In an interview with McDowell, Dove stresses the similarity between poetry and dance, assigning to both the status of the romantic sublime:

> Poetry is a kind of dance already. Technically, there's the play of contemporary speech against the bass-line of the iambic, but there's also the expression of desire that is continually restrained by the limits of the page, the breath, the very structure of the language—just as dance is limited by the capabilities of our physical bodies as well as by gravity. (Interview)

Poetic sublimity here involves a Hegelian reconstitution of the world through poetry or dance, when one merges into the other, the purpose of both a reconstitution of reality through a reconstitution of the Self in relation to reality. Righelato says of Dove: "Music is, indeed, the keynote of her poetry; it is the life of her poems about musicians as well as the poems rhythmically animated by blues, jazz, or classical forms" (4). The first section of *American Smooth* introduces music as an independent cultural entity before commencing on a journey that shows how it has been used as a vehicle in earlier moments in history. Music formulates here a renegotiation of both social and personal space.

The second section of the collection, titled "Not Welcome Here," is a historical revisiting of World War I, to a time when African Americans fought in the American Expeditionary Force in Europe. However, the poems focus not on the fighting soldiers, but on the players in the dance-hall bands, tracing their experiences before and during the war. This was a time when both *de jure* and *de facto* segregation were firmly in place in America, and black soldiers were subjected to the same treatment in Europe. Dove recaptures the spirit of their experiences, making music the vehicle for their resilience of spirit, "energizing and restorative in the face of racism in their own culture and the hardships and dangers of a soldier's existence" (Righelato 210). The bands are witness to history, their journey across the Atlantic and back a significant foray into the group dynamics of racism across cultures. They also reverse the gaze, music lending them subjectivity in a racist situation.

The first poem in the second section, titled "The Castle Walk," achieves narrative probability through an analysis of the attitudes of wealthy New Yorkers by the bandleader, James Reese Europe, who was hired in 1915 to provide music to the dance team of Vernon and Irene Castle, the favorites of the elites in the city. Reese's Negro jazz band would later accompany the African American soldiers of the 369th Infantry to Europe in the First World War. The poem marks his observations on the absence of musical sensibilities among wealthy whites, correlating racial insensitivity to a general lack of aesthetic discerning:

> These white folks stalk
> through privilege
> just like they dance:
>
> one-two, stop, pose,
> over and over.

The poem follows the bandleader's thoughts as he observes a people for whom the music is important only for its associations with privileged membership; the mechanical ballroom dancing is in direct contrast to the "crazy quilt of rage/and honor" across the Atlantic that stands at a distance from this privileged world. This contrast is built up in the following poems that follow the band as it joins the war in Europe, the Negro jazz band having gained immense popularity in France where it played for the soldiers. *The Memoirs of Lieutenant "Jim" Europe* finds place in the exhibition titled *The African American Odyssey: A Quest for Full Citizenship* at the Library of Congress. The exhibit states: "These army bands became immensely popular in France, both among American troops and the French public, introducing many Europeans to jazz and ragtime rhythm and the African American performance styles" ("World War I and Postwar Society"). Dove's poem inverts the gaze that records history, presenting Reese's account of white elitism and privilege measured through the barometer of musical (in)sensitivity.

In a poem towards the end of this section, titled "The Return of Lieutenant James Reese Europe," Lieutenant James Reese Europe returns to America with his music, but to a very different audience. He, too, is a changed man. In this poem, Dove traces the effects of the transatlantic crossing and the experiences of war on the black man's perception of himself and of the racism prevalent back home. Fighting in the war has made Reese aware of his own subjectivity and power. As he plays to celebrate the return of the black soldiers from the ravages of war in a victory parade across New York City in February 1919, the difference in tone reflects the change in perspective:

> You didn't want us when we left but we went.
> You didn't want us coming back but here we are,
> ....
> No jazz for you: We'll play a brisk French march
> and show our ribbons, flash our *Croix de Guerre*.

Reese's memoirs contain much detail about the racial climate in the United States and in France at the time. Dove's poem reflects the change in the attitude of the black man after the war. He is no longer willing to dilute his music to "pay 'em back—pour on // the violins, insinuate/a little cello" ("The Castle Walk"). The transatlantic crossing has been instrumental in making him appreciate the good things like the warm sun, but it has also made him *think* about race. Righelato says: "Returning is returning to racism, and it is only when they see the 'brown faces' of Lenox Avenue, are they really at home" (214). The music has also changed; aware of its own subjectivity, it refuses to let racism at home dilute it to suit its aesthetics.

The intervening poems in the section, between Reese's playing in New York City before the War and after his return, outline the experiences of war of African American soldiers who fought in Europe. The second poem in the section, titled "The Passage," is a longer description of going off to fight in the war. Written in the form of a journal entry, it is based on Dove's conversations with Cpl. Orval E. Peyton, a war veteran who fought in the 372nd infantry, and whom she met in Tucson in 1987. The poem consists of nine parts, each a journal entry written between 30 March and 7 April 1917 by an African American soldier on the transatlantic journey to Europe. The poem moves from idealistic romantic notions of gallantry to a realization of the stark realities of life as a (black) soldier. The conditions on the voyage are an unmistakable reminder of the tortuous journey of their ancestors across the Atlantic as slaves. It is a personal and political moment of contention with the past—reliving it, albeit with a different purpose.

The first part of the poem sets the personal moment against the political. While there is hardly anybody to see off the soldiers, the day marks a momentous event in the lives of the men themselves—"This will be a day never to be forgotten." Their anxious anticipation is made more prominent by the absence of any of the traditional symbols of public recognition: "No cheering nor tears shed, no one/to see us off, to kiss and cry over." The image of the black men marching off alone to a foreign land, reminding themselves, "We were soldiers," is strangely pathetic in its uncertainty, the traditional definitions of heroic patriotism suddenly crushed beneath the sight of a segregated people seeking belonging in a transatlantic crossing to a strange land.

As the journey commences, the second part of the poem, "The Passage," sees the soldiers celebrate Easter Sunday below deck on the ship after services held by a chaplain, in quarters whose suffocating nature brings to mind the original transatlantic journey of the slaves. The next part contrasts the conditions on board with descriptions of food—"Good breakfast—/bacon, eggs, grits, and of course coffee," and again at night—"potatoes, corned beef, apple butter and coffee." The description of food marks the only change that is noted in detail—"The food seems better here than/in camp. Our boys do not complain much." The irony of the reverse crossing as heroic is brought out in the abysmal conditions that mark the facilities allowed to these soldiers. Danger fosters bravado—"Some of the boys have put on life preservers/but most don't seem to be afraid and are as jolly/as if they were on shore." The poems are a tribute to the resilience of the soldiers in the harsh conditions that are physically as well as psychologically trying. The reality of the hardships, however, seems to have stripped the journey of romantic notions of travel to faraway lands as a gallant enterprise: "When I think that I am a thousand miles/from land, in the middle of the Ocean,/I am not a bit impressed as I imagined I would be." The certainty of gallant fame seems to have been replaced by the uncertainty of harsh reality. The soldier's earlier words, "*The future will always be with me*," have changed into an uncertain "I wonder where I'll be this time next year." As the hardships increase, even the meals are cut down to two a day, and people fall sick, nostalgia gripping the mind to be relieved only by memories of racism and segregation back home. These memories act as an ironic aside to make the journey bearable, even enjoyable:

> I am tired of the voyage.
> I suppose there are lonesome days before me,
> But no more so than those that have already passed.
> I can make myself contented.
> We are having very good weather.

The poem is a poignant expression of the need to escape from a racist structure, and Dove's delineation of the wretched conditions on board serves to emphasize the abject conditions back home which are seen as worse than the present sickness and misery. The conditions on board, ameliorated by the provision of ample food and freedom of movement, also bring to mind the contrasting conditions under which captured slaves were transported during the transatlantic slave trade.

The last poem in the section, titled "Ripont," is a very significant moment in the Post-Black journey, bridging past and present, personal and political. The title of the poem refers to the village of Ripont in north-east France which was destroyed during the First World War. As Dove recounts her travels through Europe, the poem creates a personal bridge for her daughter, Aviva, whose grandparents are both American and German. The family revisits the village where the soldiers of the 369th Infantry "fought like tigers," the image one of animated resilience—they were "joking as the shells fell around them/so that the French told the Americans/Send us more like these." Calling them the "Harlem Hellfighters," Dove contends that "we were descendants too." The emotional distancing that the poet has maintained till now breaks down as Blackness traces a path back into a political minefield that is personal. As she and her husband travel with their baby daughter across what is a literal and metaphorical minefield, the past connects with the present, each ruined village a memento and a witness to a search that leaves Dove unable to write anything about the visit "for thirteen years" until the day when her daughter "*leaving home*" connects personal memory with communal memory. The recollection of her baby daughter "waving back" bridges past and present: "where we turned left they turned right/some of them waving/our daughter waving back." The paths that merged and diverged in the memory do so again in the present, and the suffering of parting, though of a different kind, connects the two, acting as "a fortuitous and benign parallel of the wartime fellowship of the French and African American soldiers" (Righelato 215). This connection is accentuated by a lack of punctuation throughout the poem, where the words seem to be extended moments in time, set free for associations in the memory to chart their own paths. Vendler says that Dove has discovered:

> ...that life exhibits a "lack of conclusion," and presents an "eternal *dénouement*".... The newly learned "secret" of life—that it lacks conclusion, is always unknotting what it has knotted—is the most devastating secret a poet like Dove, drawn to conclusiveness, could learn. (83)

This poem is the moment when Dove finds a personal connection with her communal past, transcending what Rampersad found disturbing in her earlier poems—"One might say that she apparently declines to dwell on the links between past history and present history" (55). The poet whose earlier poems insisted on the dialectics of history as ever progressing to newer crossroads towards individual freedom, realizes that these crossroads also challenge the teleology of the historical metanarrative, and that the *trace* of moments past can never be eliminated from the present, leading to the idea of identity as *différance*, an ever-deferred reality. This signals the Post-Black moment as an acceptance of identity being strongly linked to memory, and freeing itself of its constrictions through this acceptance of the interplay of images.

The interplay of images is further stressed in the next section of the book, titled "Twelve Chairs." Written as if on the back of a chair, the thirteen poems in this section represent the perspectives of twelve jurors seated around a table, and an extra one for an alternate juror not called to serve. It is significant that Dove chooses to eschew linearity to stress that these poems, carved on the back of the marble chairs at the Federal Court House in Sacramento, California, can be read in any order, the structure of a round table acting as an indemnity against influence. The section, placed at the center of five sections, serves the purpose of acting as the "'fulcrum' of a collection that 'is all about our particular, American brand of justice'" (Dove qtd. in Righelato 217).

If justice is the enduring theme of the collection, the poems celebrate individual resilience as triumphing over social injustices. The fourth section, titled "Blues In Half-Tones, ¾ Time," introduces the importance of accepting the wounds in the epigraph: "[Our] heart was forged out of barbarism and violence. We learned to control it, but it is still a part of us. To pretend it does not exist is to create an opportunity for it to escape." It is a woman's acceptance of the past. The emphasis is on the sensuous, the world perceived through the senses. The first poem in the section, "Chocolate," identifies pleasure as the seeker, seeking women to tempt:

> Knotted smoke, dark punch
> of earth and night and leaf,
> for a taste of you
>
> any woman would gladly
> crumble to ruin.

This abstract image of the cost of worldly pleasures metamorphoses into a more serious examination of the costs of success in the next poems.

The cost at which pleasure and success are achieved, especially for a black woman in segregated America, form the subject of the next poem, titled "Bolero." Based on the life of Bessie Smith, the American blues singer of the 1920s and 1930s, nicknamed the Empress of the Blues, Bessie's popularity forms the backdrop to a life lived in pain to achieve perfection. As Bessie "holds nothing back/but the hurt // she takes with her as she dips, grinds, then rises sweetly," the poem foregrounds the effort that goes into being a famed dancer: "How everything hurts!"

The story of Hattie McDaniel, the first African American to win an Oscar as best supporting actress for her role as Mammy in the film *Gone with the Wind* is another example of effort and recognition. What was notable about McDaniel's achievement was that she won it at a time when segregation was the norm and African Americans were treated as secondary characters—when the film premiered in Atlanta in 1939, McDaniel was not even invited. Dove's poem, "Hattie McDaniel Arrives at the Coconut Grove," celebrates McDaniel's arrival at the Academy Awards dinner despite the racism that refused to accord her equal status:

> what can she be
> thinking of, striding into the ballroom
> where no black face has ever showed itself
> except above a serving tray?

Dove contends that more commendable than winning the Academy Award was McDaniel's courage in defying segregation to attend the Awards dinner as an equal. Stating that McDaniel's real achievement lies in her journey, she addresses her directly across time:

> Three million dishes,
> a truckload of aprons and headrags later, and here
> you are: poised, between husbands
> and factions, no corset wide enough

to hold you in, your face a dark moon split
by that spontaneous smile—

These tales of female achievement are celebrated towards the end of the section in the poem "Rhumba," which is a perfect example of unity in dance. The poem is structured like a dance, with both dancers following parallel lines on either side of the page. It marks the perfect communion that music and dance can achieve for both the man and the woman, a fitting finalé to years of excruciating practice and a struggle to survive racist structures.

The fifth and final section in the collection, titled "Evening Primrose," is a communion between man and Nature. Unlike the Romantics, however, Dove does not treat the two as separate entities in time. Here, Nature acts as a metaphor for man's actions, serving to identify a Post-Black deferring of actions that marks the African American's quest for identity. The first poem in the section, "Evening Primrose," presents the mediocre looks of the primrose in comparison to the cowslip and the "extravagant fuchsia." Blazing forth at night, the flower chooses to be different—"Sun blathers its baronial/endorsement, but they refuse/to join the ranks." The primrose is one of the earliest spring flowers in Europe. Yet, not adhering to nature's rules, it cannot be seen during the day even in summers when there is a profusion of flowers all over. Righelato says that:

> the flower, blazing at night, is implicitly an image not only of the writer's own secret labor (Dove likes to work at night) but also of deferral, the storing of experience to come into expression out of darkness, at a later time. (219)

Akin to Wordsworth's creative process, the primrose chooses to bring forth creation in the tranquillity of deferral. In *The Poet's World*, Dove uses Rilke's example of the rose in his poem *Die Rosenchale* (translated as "The Bowl of Roses" by Edward Snow) to anticipate "postmodern cynicism" (52) and the consequent need to identify "the interior connection" (54) between the world and the self. This, she says, is what poetry needs to do:

> I don't believe Rilke is arguing here for pure art. If anything, he is saying that self-containment—true self-containment—also contains Walt Whitman's multitudes. The poet's task, if we were to take Rilke's poem as credo, is to show us the handful of inwardness in each and every instance of outward worldly activity—even in "the changing and flying and fleeing of the clouds." (53)

This journey from outward worldly activity to inwardness is what the next few poems trace. Following the metaphorical flower, the poet outlines the process of creative flowering in the poems that follow. "Reverie in Open Air" acknowledges that the poet often finds herself an oddity, "out of sync with wasp and wren." Saying, "I prefer books to moonlight, statuary to trees," she brings herself up against the Romantics in their reverence for Nature, yet finds a strange communion in the touch of green grass against bare feet, the air "a tonic of absence." The objective contemplation of nature in the first stanza has moved to a contemplative internalizing of Nature. "Desk Dreams" trace the creative process in places from Arizona to Paris, North Carolina, Bellagio, and finally, Charlottesville. Each place has its own associations in the memory, like the cicada in Arizona, the midnight traffic in Paris, the green and the single jay calling out in the solitude of North Carolina, the chill Cyclopean blue of Lake Como in Italy, and finally, the charred remains of the poet's desk in Charlottesville, Virginia, after the fire that destroyed her house.

In the last poem in the collection, "Looking Up from the Page, I Am Reminded of This Mortal Coil," the tired poet contemplates dawn—"daybreak/or end, I can't tell." Sounding a note of contradiction, the poem is significant for its refusal to end on a conclusive note. Signifying the ever-deferred *dénouement*, the poem is also significant for its celebration of a Derridean impurity. Dawn, the end to a day of writing, is also the beginning of a new day, a time when "play's over," but the "blaze freshens," and the music renews as "five or six miniature birds/strike up the band." In this communion of man and Nature, Nature's refusal to signal a *dénouement* signifies open-ended definitions.

Dawn also signals continuity in the journey. Likening creativity to life, Dove admits that the journey cannot be easy. Despite the advances made by science, phenomenological questions remain the same. The musings of the creative mind are also a metaphorical quest for identity in the real world, and the deferred nature of the quest is a feature of the postmodern celebration of inconclusiveness: "I suspect we don't/travel easily at all, though we keep making better wheels—/smaller phones and wider webs" ("Looking Up from the Page, I Am Reminded of This Mortal Coil"). Yet, Dove seems to imply, the answers lie in the quest, asking a rhetorical question, "What good is the brain without traveling shoes?" This correlates to her idea of "imaginative truth" which she defines as "an ability to connect to our inarticulate emotions and a willingness to admit that there are feelings that go beyond the catch-phrases of civilized discourse" (*The Poet's World* 55). These are the interstices in the narrative that complete reality, and which any quest for identity must include in its definitions.

American Smooth, then, practices the title dance by becoming a quest that celebrates both individuality and identity. Beginning with the ecstasy of dance, it takes its readers to sites in memory awakened by music. Although it does not make race an overt identifier, the journey is an unmistakably black one to the depths of African American history, uncovering history from the perspective of the individual, connecting man and nature in a journey of which music is the primary motif. The collection also follows Gilroy's delineation of the third stage in self-realization, freeing music from being a mere commodity to being the tenor which carries the narrative, bridging past and present to lead to the most contentious issue in the process of self-actualization in contemporary America—miscegenation and its complicated underscoring of identity. The next collection of poems arrives at this moment.

Dove's next collection, titled *Sonata Mulattica*, written in 2009, is a specifically Post-Black quest for identity in a postethnic world. The collection tells the story of George Augustus Polgreen Bridgetower (1778–1860), the biracial violinist who is best remembered for being the first performer of Beethoven's "Kreutzer" Sonata. Born of a Polish woman and an African prince, Bridgetower was a talented violinist who made his debut in Paris at the age of nine. In 1803, he traveled to Vienna to meet Beethoven, performing with him on stage on 24 May at the Augarten Theatre, Beethoven on the piano and Bridgetower on the violin. Beethoven, impressed by Bridgetower's talent, dedicated his Violin Sonata no. 9 to him, with the dedication "*Sonata per un mulattico lunatico,*" translated as "sonata for a lunatic mulatto." Undoubtedly, the use of the term "mulattica" in the title of Dove's collection is an ironic reference to Beethoven's calling Bridgetower a lunatic and a mulatto. Unfortunately, the two fell out over a woman, and Beethoven rededicated the sonata to the French violinist Rudolphe Kreutzer, who declared that it was impossible to play. The strangely important figure of Blackness in a white artist's world motivated Dove to investigate the connection between the two. In an interview with Schwartz, Dove says that art is "about the artist seeking common ground with his subject as well as a meditation on being 'exotic,' being thought of as 'other'" (personal interview). In another interview with Hanna and Basosi, she says:

> When I began work on *Sonata Mulattica*, I didn't approach the story of George Bridgetower from the outside. I didn't think: What an interesting historical character; let's see if I can give him flesh! No, I wanted to get to know him personally; and

> though I began researching like a historian, I soon began searching for details that would help me imagine what it would be like to walk the streets of London in 1790 as a little dark-skinned boy with a violin tucked under his arm. The end effect may appear to be a personalization of the grand historical narrative, but the very nature of poetry is to confound the notion that you can stand back and look at what's happening; with poetry, you are put deep in the thick of things. (Hanna 259)

The collection recreates Bridgetower's life and art and his dramatic relationship with Beethoven. Although not overt, the implications of racial prejudice are there among the possibilities. Also indicated are the possibilities of Bridgetower being naught but Beethoven's suppressed (black) self. This Freudian suppression of (the racially abject) part of the (miscegenated) self results in the destruction of the artist.

This collection signals the arrival of the Post-Black poet, including in itself all the features of the Post-Black Aesthetic. Without making an overt reference to race, the collection celebrates biracial identity as a given, stressing on art and the idiosyncrasies of the artistic temperament rather than race as an identity marker. The struggles played out in the sonata, composed by Beethoven but part of which was improvised by Bridgetower and which could be played only by him, form a metaphorical tale of both the extending of limits and their closing-in, in a tempestuous relationship whose end is a loss for both. The Kreutzer sonata is at once playful and intense, defying linear progression to always return to the starting point. Opening with four bars in A major, it shifts suddenly to A minor, careering precariously between the two in defiant anguish, both piano and violin alternating between the notes, punctuated by uncontrolled flights of musical ecstasy, before finally closing on an anguished coda. This, in the collection, is the first poem, where life comes full circle. In a tightly controlled mimetic journey that rises and falls with the music, Dove emphasizes possibilities and imagination, even though her story is well-researched. In doing so, she protects herself from the protocols of Black Nationalism in her portrayal of a black artist of the nineteenth century. Steffen says:

> In moving from the historically informed political occasion to the most beautiful imagery, she ties herself to a sense of urgency yet at the same time keeps a safe distance from the limited and limiting essentialism of the black aesthetics. Hence Dove opposes, even fights tyranny both in a broader and more subtle way. (8)

Dove's portrayal is thus an antinomic un-naming of the racial, antinomic in that it portrays the necessity of accepting the black-white for the healthy functioning of the psyche, without overt emphasis on race. In a juxtaposition of black and white frames, the emphasis is on musical genius, racial identity being secondary, although the implication of racial discrimination being the reason for the separation of frames lurks in the background. It is the practice of generating new signs that transgress dominant cultural norms, and recognizing that every new expression, no matter how subjective, is historically hybrid, related genealogically to all those utterances that came before it and are developed around it. It is not a moment in itself, but is a moment built up by all the historical events preceding it. In her interview with Schwartz, Dove says, "I'm not after the actual artifact. I'm after what swirls around that artifact—all of the preconceptions that inform it" (personal interview). The subtitle of the collection, "A Life in Five Movements and a Short Play," juxtaposes motion and stasis, a rhapsody that captures the grandiosity and the melancholy of the artist's existence. Dove uses the five moments associated with the sonata in her exploration of Bridgetower's life—an introduction, exposition, elaboration, recapitulation, and a coda. Foregrounding the black genius, Dove also explores the (supposedly) white genius in the background, and how the two psyches are creatively enmeshed. In a celebration of hybridity, the collection uses all the registers—nursery rhymes, diary entries, drama—recreating voices from the past to make it a metaphorical celebration of all facets that comprise creation, even as it accepts the ephemeral nature of fame. Calling it "a virtuosic treatment of a virtuoso's life," *The New Yorker* (2009) says that the collection is "stuffed with historical and musical arcana" (review). Exhibiting a predilection for paradox and aporia, the collection symbolizes the features of the Post-Black. Vendler says that Dove's purpose is to explore "how the inner life of that time—our time—can be accurately and compellingly represented in brief verbal patterns" (x). In the Preface to the collection, Dove claims historical probability rather than historical accuracy, her main purpose being to explore possibilities, of how one who could have become "one of the most revered musical virtuosos of all time" was reduced to "fifteen minutes of fame" (15), dying in its shadows.

The collection begins with a Prologue that centers around possibilities. Beginning with "If" ("The Bridgetower"), it mulls on what would have happened if Bridgetower had not been black, young, and a genius. Or, if he had remained one, but had not fought ridiculously with Beethoven over a woman, perhaps "we would find/rafts of black kids scratching out scales/on their matchbox violins." The next poem in the Prologue calls on the reader to extend the imagination to further imagine possibilities. Stressing that what followed would be a story—"a lost story/but we will be imagining it, anyway" ("Prologue of the Rambling Sort"), Dove builds on narrative probability, suggesting that history is a narrative built from bare facts, the final story a product of the narrator's perspective. In this imaginative state, there is a suggestion of racial injustice having permeated the plot of Bridgetower's (or Beethoven's?) life, but it is quickly rejected by the consciousness:

> This is a story
> about music and what it does to those
> who make it, whom it enslaves…yes,
> slavery of all kinds enters into the mix,
> although the skin of our protagonist
> does not play so great a role
> in his advancement and subsequent
> fade from grace as might be imagined.
> Or does it? ("Prologue of the Rambling Sort")

This is, definitely, a cautionary prologue—"a tale of light and shadow," the vital links to be found in the gaps. Pointing out that the only thing that separated Bridgetower and Beethoven, both musical prodigies at a young age, with "absent" mothers and "all-too-present," exploitative fathers, was skin color, Dove paints the canvas with images of traveling with, as she is careful to point out, "background music." The concluding line (in parenthesis) belies the assertion of the music's quotidian obscurity, though: "(Ah, but what heavenly music *that* was…)." Dove's travels bridge the gap between the extremes as she "reinstates, for twenty-first century readers, a rival to Beethoven's dominance of European mystical romanticism" (Nanda 84), bringing to life a man who, but for his one brush with fame, was destined to be relegated to obscurity in the annals of musical history. This is also a Freudian tale of the psychological suppression of any traces of color in the psyche, and the eventual destruction of creative genius it leads to. This, however, is just a probability, as the poet cautions in the prologue. It is a story in silhouette, much like Kara Walker's, and the shadows must be lighted up. The poet, in the liminal space, is free to both look in and look out, weaving a tale that builds on the binary of presence/absence and its resultant conflict in the psyche of the miscegenated person. This is the Post-Black artist's contention with history as a selective frame.

Dove's poems do not arrive at a moment suddenly, but rather trace the events that lead up to it. The first section, titled "The Prodigy," begins with a poem titled, significantly, "(Re) Naissance." Crawford calls the word "the *pregnant* state of anticipation," literal and metaphorical. She says, "Anticipation is the force of giving birth to expression that has not been named and fully realized, but it is nonetheless a part of you the entire time it is being formed" (33). The poem describes peasants digging in a frost-covered field, the icy East wind creating a "fuzzed silence" as they worked, "mere blood and burbling humors/ trussed into a package of skin." The fields are white, each step a dangerous crack in the ice, and the silence spreads across it all. It is in this frozen void— "on this day of no accounting,/no different than yesterday or tomorrow" that the "answering cry/...tiny, enraged" brings forth the warmth of life. This is not a life to be welcomed, however; described as:

>   Another soul
> quickened to misery,
> dark as our shadows lurching
> over the snow-riddled furrows.
> Another spirit cursed to walk
> this glacial crust, another body
> some day to bury.

This dark-skinned child, born of a peasant working in the fields, is an unwelcome addition to the already-suffering race. However, there is a possibility that this child, black or biracial, would yet achieve greatness in life.

The next poem, "Capriccio," presents Lieutenant Field Marshall of the Austrian empire giving Haydn the task of assembling nature's eccentricities for his court. Tracing the childhood of Bridgetower, the poem "Friedrich Augustus Bridgetower Discovers the Purposes of Fatherhood" opens with the elder Bridgetower's identification of the child's musical talent: "The boy is smitten with tiny sounds:/purring bees and crickets, sighing leaves,/hammer clack from the courtyard." "Maestro" Haydn concurs: "*There's music in here*," and so begins the child's musical journey. "Recollection, Preempted" recounts Bridgetower's days at the palace of the Prince, as he absorbs all sounds, from the singing of the crickets to the "inconsequential music" that reached his ears as he hid in the puppet theater, listening to the operas at night: "But oh, the witchery of orchestral strings—/the full *body* of sound gathering you in,/ as to a mother's bosom." The child prodigy debuts in Paris at the age of nine, astonishing young and old alike in a performance that *Le Mercure de France* commends for "maturity of playing." Introducing "*Mr. Bridge-Tower, young Negro from the Colonies*," the poem alternates between Bridgetower and Dove as narrators, the child praising himself at the end of the concert: "Praise me. I am small" ("Paris, Panting"). The title is an ironic reference to the exoticizing of Blackness, the child introduced as an oddity, a genius belying the color of his skin.

The next poem, titled "What Doesn't Happen," introduces Bridgetower as he goes to perform at the *Salle des Machines* in Paris in a carriage, his violin case "like an animal trapped under the hunter's eye" as he "ignores his heart's thudding and steps out/onto the flickering stage, deep and treacherous/as a lake still frozen at sunset." Racial ignominy is a danger as the crowd awaits his small frame—"(*let's see the toy bear jump his hoops!*)"—but then he sees one of the two girls beside him, "who fastens her solemn black gaze on the boy as if to say/*you are what I am, what I yearn to be.*" The prodigy might falter, but the idol with the black gaze fastened on him plays, and even with all the applause that is his when he stops, it is the gaze that matters.

"Windsor," the next poem in the section, brings forth the irony of artistic success circumscribed by a racialized structure. Race as a social regulatory occupies central position in this section. The black man, genius though he may be, is still at the bottom of the social hierarchy. Not only is Bridgetower "told to practice/*out of sight*, in the servants' wing," he is also required to perfect "a gentleman's curtsy, deep as a girl's." All the preparations are for a performance at the Queen's Lodge, and Bridgetower is told along the way, "*You're quite the lucky lad to be here;/the feather in your cap, boy, remember.*" The allusion to Blackness is not lost on him, and even as he walks down the passageways and paths at Windsor, he cannot help but think of ships. The image, bringing to mind the slave ship as a chronotope in Gilroy's *The Black Atlantic*, is Dove's ironic assertion of the play of images in historical memory. It is also an image of the racialized nature of lived space in the nineteenth century, reminiscent of slave ships, the black man relegated to a space out of sight. Towards the end of the section, Bridgetower is hailed as a musical prodigy, yet his identity remains circumscribed by the racial identifier, "mulatto." Hailed as the grandson of an "African prince," his exoticism combines with his talent to make him appear almost an aberration: "a phenomenal musical talent: the mulatto George Bridgetower" ("The Seaside Concerts"). The section ends with "Disappearance," emphasizing that underneath all the fame lives just a young boy who is one with his violin, both unremarkable until he starts playing.

The second section, titled "Bread & Butter, Turbans & Chinoiserie," begins with "Hear Ye!" introducing "Little Mulatto Prince George" playing onstage at the Drury Lane Theater, an exotic choice amongst many others in London. This section describes, with variation in details, the concerts where

Bridgetower performs, and his rapid ascension to fame. The poems serve to bring out the fact that the audience Bridgetower performed for was mainly white and, while his talent was admired, at no time was he accepted as an insider. "Concert at Hanover Square" presents him as the perennial outsider looking in on the circles from which he could smell the appraisal, tinged with hatred:

> We knew hatred
> because we could smell it
> all around us, it sang in the cool glasses
> tinkling over our heads,
> the carefully tended laughter,
> the curious glint
> of a widow's appraisal.

Dove is careful to point out that even as Bridgetower walks through the fields of hatred, music both gives him succor and draws succor from him. For Bridgetower's playing is a spiritual ascension that tugs at the soul, effecting a cathartic expulsion of grief at the failings of the world. Haydn describes the enthralling quality of the notes in "Pulling the Organ Stops":

> But the organ
> climbs into your chest, squeezing
> as it shudders—a great lung
> hauling its grief through the void
> until we can hear how profoundly
> the world has failed us.

In a cathartic union, man and instrument become one in a journey towards healing. Paradoxically, music liberates itself through this union.

The section also contains the confessions of Haydn in "Haydn, Overheard," in which he ruminates on slavery, and on the difference between being enslaved to music, and being enslaved to a man, stating his reluctance to risk life beyond the known, fearing hunger. The enslavement of the mind is complete when the slave prefers to stay on out of choice, even though his talent might earn him his bread somewhere else: "if slave I must, better/the oboe's clarion tyranny // than a man's cruel whims." But though Haydn calls his enslavement to music better than being slave to a man, Dove points out that one is really a synonym for the other, in this case.

"Mrs. Papendiek's Diary" is a sequence of poems that recurs in every section of the collection to provide a background for the preparations for Bridgetower's travels on the path towards fame. The poems are a sequence describing the social life of the Bridgetowers, and serve to remind the readers that musical genius cannot make Bridgetower an insider in London society. The third part in this sequence describes the Bridgetowers' reception and dinner at Mr. Papendiek's house one winter evening. The very next poem, however, is the Father's aside on the exoticism that makes him and his son attractive to London society. Titled "The Dressing," it is a poignant exposition of the "fear and longing" that symbolizes the exotic allure of black skin. Evoking Said, Dove makes the objectification and self-abjection complete in the black man's realization that the color of his skin makes him not a "man" but a "thing":

> Outside, I am not a man.
> I am a thing
> which in fine company
> arouses awe:
> that curious fusion of fear and longing
> I have learned to make use of.

Exoticism frames much of the elder Bridgetower's identity for white society—a black man and an African prince, he understands that he is "no more/than a mere phantasm,/a swarthy figment of their guilt." This rejection of autonomy or even identity for the black man except in subservience to white systems proposes an "othering" of Blackness for the purpose of completing the white self. Critics such as Dyer and Morrison have studied the reducing of the black man to his body (effectively the color of his skin), and conclude that black embodiment is necessary to white systems of identification. Dyer states:

> White discourse implacably reduces the non-white subject to being a function of the white subject, not allowing her/him space or autonomy, permitting neither the recognition of similarities nor the acceptance of differences except as a means of knowing the white self (13).

Oddly, the exoticizing of the black body as a site of knowledge for the white man also limits the black man's knowledge of his own self beyond his body. Morrison states that this effectively dehumanizes the black man, colonizing him in the white man's imagination: "Imaginary Africa was a cornucopia of imponderables that resisted explanation. …Even when Africa was ostensibly a subject, its people were oddly dehumanized in ways both pejorative and admiring" (120–121). Bridgetower understands this racialized structure of identification that exoticizes and ultimately reduces the black man to a single identifier—the color of the skin, thus permanently reducing him to the level of the sub-human—a "thing"—in the white normative.

"Mrs. Papendiek's Diary (4)" follows up the social invitation to Bridgetower with shock when he assumes familiarity. The "African impresario" is seen to be forward, assuming an equal acquaintance that shocks the genteel folks unused to such effrontery. However, the wily Prince has a plan—he puts George in their care, planning for George to pour out his woes to them, wherein they pay the Prince to be rid of his presence. This is followed by "The Undressing," where the young Bridgetower, rid of his Father, rejoices on no longer having to dress up in his "Sir Monkey Jacket," but would "become a proper British/gentleman: cuffed and buckled/with breeches and a fine cravat." Glad to shed his exotic apparel, he awaits with eagerness his transformation into a gentleman. However, and here Dove reveals the intricate interweaving of the color of the skin with identity to overshadow all other identifiers, the minute he undresses, the sight of his naked skin against the white sheets reinforces racial self-abjection: "I—I am a smudge,/A quenched wick,/A twig shrouded in snow." The binaries of black/white reinforce themselves as internalized systems of identification that decide self-worth and racial belonging, wherein "the black body becomes the locus of an emotionally vulnerable self at an age when the visible plays a significant role" (Roy and Ringo 72). Dyer calls this "the persistence of the Manichean dualism of black:white that could be mapped on to skin colour difference" (17). Black skin and a gentleman are an antinomy for young Bridgetower, and he cannot reconcile the two despite possessing all the qualities that would credit him a gentleman. For him, the color of the skin is the main identity marker, corroborating the observation that "as the black self-determines its worth in relation to a white centre, and symbols come into play, the colour of the skin becomes the sole determinant in a perspectival framework within which identity construction takes place" (Roy and Ringo 68). The child grows up, firmly entrenched in racial self-abjection, and the color of his skin *becomes* his identity. Having learned this at a very early age, Bridgetower, for all his success, cannot dissociate himself from the racial self-abjection that the sight of his dark skin evokes. On the contrary, he exoticizes this difference by further objectifying his body:

>   promenading
>
> his bright skin and curls
>   his agreeably knobbed nose,
>   eyes black and brown lips
> plush enough to sink
>   a lady's dreams into. ("Pretty Boy")

This hegemonic system of identity formation makes any escape from embodiment impossible for the black man. The section ends with the image of the "glutted Prince" ("New Century Aubade"), walking lightly through it all, drunk with success.

The third section, titled "*Sturm und Drang*," translated as "Storm and Stress," refers to the proto-Romantic movement in Germany in the late eighteenth century that rebelled against the Reason of the Enlightenment and stressed on nature, feeling, and individualism. C minus was Beethoven's key of *Sturm und Drang*. Beethoven was not only a musical genius *sans pareil*, but also a man of intense passions very much under the influence of Haydn. This section of Dove's collection, dedicated to Beethoven, is rife with melancholia, a desperate longing for recognition. Beethoven's increasing deafness at this time instilled in him a fear of losing all that he had achieved, and the first poem in the section, titled "The Petition," is an expression of this fear:

> Because there comes a time.
> Because there was a time.
>
> Because I want to be known as a gentleman
> everywhere.
> Because Haydn came from there; came, and went back.
> Because I am no longer a *Wunderkind*.

The poem expresses fear of loss of power; for the artist is powerful when wedded to fame, but divorced from it, he loses his identity. The section on Beethoven begins as a quest, wherein the composer searches for fulfillment. The poem "To the Continent" is an unravelling of the addictive nature of the fame that fuels ambition: "I played to keep the noise going,/to fill me up." Yet success does not fill the void that exists, and it will not be filled by anything except a "love that resists, notes that will not fit." In other words, the ego demands the acceptance of the impure that will make it whole. The music composer wants music that will leave him exhausted in its intensity:

> I want to be appalled & staggered
> in equal measures, I want blood
> & blood's aftermath—
>
> Weariness & affliction, *sans* mercy.

This awareness of a void and the quest for a passion to fill it makes the journey as much internal as it is literal.

Traveling through cities in this state of mind, Beethoven reaches Vienna, going to a quiet village "where he had been ordered to recover," the poem "Ludwig van Beethoven's Return to Vienna" tracing the impossibility of quelling the rage that reflected the void in him, the music coming so fast that he was unable to record the swell, filling him with a sense of loss and further rage at the deepening clamor that had begun to obstruct composition:

> At first I raged. Then music raged in me,
> rising so swiftly I could not write quickly enough
> to ease the roiling. I would stop
> to light a lamp, and whatever I'd missed—
> larks flying to nest, church bells, the shepherd's
> home-toward-evening song—rushed in, and I
> would rage again.

However, in response to the true spirit of *Sturm und Drang*, Beethoven is unable to reason the rage away. He understands that the void within him is a fear of losing his place in the limelight because of his inability to listen. Filled with conflicting emotions, he inverts every tender passion he has known, the absence evoking an ache that demands an acceptance that he does not understand. For as long as he has known, music is the only thing that has awakened his passions:

> Every tenderness I have ever known
> has been nothing
> but thwarted violence, an ache
> so permanent and deep, the lightest touch
> awakens it....It is impossible
>
> to care enough.

For the void to be filled, the fractured ego needs to heal. And when Bridgetower walks into this void, Beethoven is forced, in the poem titled

"Vienna Spring," to revise his initial racist assessment of the "mulatto musician/magician most monstrous" to "twilight stranger/who has given me myself again." In the black man, he is forced to accept the darkness that will fill the void. He recognizes his savior in the violinist he would dedicate his sonata to—"all that I know and know I am losing,/have been losing,/have lost." The image is reminiscent of Morrison's description of the black man's presence as the necessary Other to the white man's sense of Self, that "one can see that a real or fabricated Africanist presence was crucial to their sense of Americanness" (*Playing* 6). Bridgetower appears to fill the void in Beethoven's life as this metaphorical Other presence. Probability states that he is also the repressed darkness in the racialized psyche of the (miscegenated) self that demands acceptance.

The next poem, "Polgreen, Sight-Reading," sees the two musicians playing together for the first time. Bridgetower is awed, and not a little frightened, at the violent contradictions present in Beethoven's music, saying:

> He frightens me. I've never heard music
> like this man's, this sobbing
> in the midst of triumphal chords,
> such ambrosial anguish
> jigs danced on simmering coals.

Beethoven, in the true spirit of *Sturm und Drang*, surrenders completely to passion. Bridgetower feels the sheer violence of the rendering, saying, "it's as if I'm skating/on his heart, blood tracks/looping everywhere." Beethoven is impressed as Bridgetower manages to accompany him on an impossibly difficult piece. He has drawn the blood he needed to thrive as an artist, and the frame expands to encompass a black-white sequence that reaches a crescendo of creative excellence.

The next poem, "Beethoven Summons His Copyist," follows the two as they prepare for their concert together, two halves of a whole, Beethoven's feverish composing—"propped/in a mound of blotched papers, humming," contrasted with Bridgetower's nervous demeanor—"perched in the corner like an enormous crow,/fiddling the air and grinning with fear." Beethoven has composed the sonata to open with the violin, and "Augarten, 7 AM" records the audience's bewilderment as the two commence a dialogue that is as plaintive as lovers reaching out to each other:

Spectator Two
>
> Curious beginning—solo violin,
> reminiscent of Bach but wilder, a supplication—
> and the piano's reply is almost a lover's,
> a bird on a cliff returning its true mate's call.
> ....
> That's it—a father to his prodigal son,
> Come home at last.

The music, classical notes with the soul of the black man seeping into it, renders it a strange mixture that will later be unintelligible to Kreutzer. It is the miscegenated whole that can be made intelligible only by the true halves of the same ego. This is the Post-Black, neither white nor black, defying duplication. Curiously, it is the violin that seems to lead the piece and Bridgetower, drawing all the attention, partly because of his black skin and partly because of his perfect playing, is Beethoven's equal in talent and performance. The poem, however, in the form of comments from various sections of the audience, brings out Bridgetower's appearance and Beethoven's temperament as the main focus. Bridgetower, although Beethoven's equal in musical genius, is unable to transcend his black body, the admixture of exoticism and genius too overpowering to be ignored:

> For a savage he plays quite nicely.
> As for his figure—tall, slim,
> dare I say elegant? I'd heard
> he was a charmer, but never thought
> chimney soot applied to countenance
> could be considered handsome.

Race is a subtle but central force in the spectacle, and Bridgetower's exoticism is always at the forefront of his persona as a musician. Dove introduces racial learning as beginning in childhood, when, in the midst of comments from the spectators, even a child can be heard wondering, "How can he see out/ from all that darkness?" As the reader is taken down the path back in memory to a century when slavery was still a legal institution backed by the force of social institutions such as the Church and the intellectual and philosophical force of the Enlightenment thinkers, the image of Bridgetower sharing stage, nay, even paralleling Beethoven in the exercise of musical talent leaves the audience gasping in disbelief. Dove forces her readers to confront race as a necessary part of everyday discourse in the nineteenth century, an accepted system of classification defining social hierarchy, in the process forcing a confrontation of the "metaphysical necessity" (Morrison, *Playing* 64) of racially inflected visual and linguistic codes that continue in the present. For Dove, as for Morrison, "imagining is not merely looking or looking at; nor is it taking oneself intact into the other. It is, for the purposes of the work, *becoming*" (Morrison, *Playing* 4). What the audience discerns and tries to understand is the working of a genius with a healed psyche, and the heights of possibility it reaches underlines the earlier ruptures. This is shown in the next section, where a return to the fractured state spells destruction for both parts.

The next section begins after a brief interlude in the form of a short play, titled "Volkstheater," wherein Beethoven is shown to be enraged over Bridgetower's treatment of a woman, and the two fall out over the transgression, with Beethoven tearing up his dedication of the sonata to Bridgetower and storming off in a fit of rage. This section is the fulcrum around which Destiny turns its back on Bridgetower, and the frames separate. What follows proves the incompleteness that marks both black and white frames as they follow disparate paths. Neither will attain separately the zenith of musical excellence that they did together.

The section, titled "All is Ashes," begins with an image of ruin. The first poem in the section, titled "Tail Tucked," follows Bridgetower as he exits the city in disgrace:

> Not much left to do
> but pay your respects
> —bow, genuflect?—
> to the ochre façades of a city
> you'd wanted to conquer…

Bridgetower's bewilderment is palpable as he returns to his hometown to find everything changed. Silence reigns where once the sound of operas and concerts filled the rooms. In the poem, "Home Again," he tries to explain to his mother why he would no longer be playing, skimming over his quarrel with Beethoven, trying to understand himself what had gone wrong, not realizing that despite being admitted into white space, he had never been an equal:

> The concert was a sensation. I was feted.
> We went out on the town.
> (Weren't we comrades? True brothers,
> who can drink and curse the night through
> yet swear loyalty all the more fiercely
> come morning?)

White space as a privileged and closed sphere (mediated by the white man) precludes equality, and this is evident in Bridgetower's fall from grace.

Deprived of music, Bridgetower sounds lost. The homecoming is not a celebratory event, marked as it is with loss and alienation. Steffen deconstructs the poetic layers even as Bridgetower tries to understand the cultural, saying: "The saving grace of art is that it offers a home for all who are dispossessed" (175). Bridgetower, the repressed part of the miscegenated psyche, must make sense of the obscurity that fills his world now. Music for him was lived space, making him belong in a racist world, allowing him the freedom to move in and out of spaces freely, a freedom that countered black embodiment and racial self-abjection. For a while, music had made him identify with the white man and become part of the closed world of privilege. It had allowed him to cross the color-line and identify as black-white. The loss is thus more than just a loss of patronage—it is a failure to transcend black embodiment through art.

Forced to play for the pleasure of nobility with nary an ear for music, Bridgetower finds it a soulless enterprise. In "Panopticon," an ironic title for a man rendered invisible by destiny, Bridgetower says:

> Music played for the soul is sheer pleasure;
> to play merely for pleasure is nothing
> but work. Is anyone listening? I am
> the First Violinist of the Prince Regent's
>
> Prized Private Orchestra, playing
> for your satisfaction—except
> His Mad Majesty's son is a gluttonous fool,
> And I'm as invisible as a statue of a moor.

Having lost the support of his patrons, Bridgetower can never hope to touch greatness again. The society that had prized him as an exotic catch throws him off as the darkness that had dared to transcend its own shadow. He, and the music he plays, are reduced once again to the level of service rendered for the elite. He is reduced to the lifeless panopticon, surveying all around him, yet deprived of subjectivity himself. The racial self-abjection that has always filled him at the sight of his black skin ensures that he would always reject Blackness, while social norms ensure that he is rejected by Whiteness. By the end of the section, we see bitterness engulf him at his loss, as he is rendered invisible, his music a useless remnant of glory past. He has lost the only identity marker that allowed him to occupy white space, and his abject rejection of black space completes the unmooring.

The last section in the collection, "Nomadia," traces Bridgetower's last days in obscurity and poverty, a nomad "in search of pasture, a place to lie down in" ("Nomadia"), with neither success nor family to relieve the pain of passing through the world, unloved and uncared for in his final hours. The figure of the cultural mulatto as a nomad is a warning against universalism without being anchored to the roots. Bridgetower is Ellis's "assimilationist nightmare" (201), failing to negotiate identity and space, leaving him belonging to neither the black world nor the white. At the end, he leaves the world with not a soul to care that he had lived. With him, his music dies too:

> Yeah, that's him, Bridgetower.
> Didn't know his given name.
> ....
> So he was a fiddler,
> something of a stunner in his day.
> "Day's done, gone the sun"—
> ain't that a German song? Heard it
> Somewhere. Kinda mournful.
>
> Wonder could he play that. ("The Witness")

The poem charts Dove's fear for the artist and the mulatto who fails to renegotiate identities. The man who could have been a legend is remembered as a "fiddler," his artistry and the sonata buried with him.

In this volume, music can be read as the vehicle that takes Bridgetower to fame in a racist society where he might have been working in the fields but for his talent. However, the end does not portray him as a victor, and the journey, even at the peak of success, does not allow him to forget that he is an immensely privileged *black* man. Music, rather, is the narrator in this collection, as in *American Smooth*, of a tale in which Bridgetower is but a circumspect observer, a tenor viol. This collection marks the point where art observes the artist, the violin playing Bridgetower, each indistinguishable from the other, the downfall of both the tragic coda of the sonata. Like the sonata, the end takes us back to the point where it all started: "This is a story/about music and what it does to those/who make it, whom it enslaves" ("Prologue of the Rambling Sort"), and the last few lines of the final poem, titled "The End, with MapQuest," come back to the same uncertain position, the poet no surer about what really had happened than she was at the beginning, the entire sequence a play of possibilities:

> I don't know if your playing was truly gorgeous
> or if it was just you, the sheer miracle of all
> that darkness swaying close enough to *touch*,
> palm tree and Sambo and glistening tiger
> running circles into golden oil. Ah,
> Master B, great little man, tell me:
> How does a shadow shine?

In restoring to him the glory that should have been his, Dove signs off not by describing the poverty and obscurity that marked Bridgetower's last days, but by handing to him the agency of success. Reminding history of the "sheer miracle" of Bridgetower's success, she ends on a note of wonder at the possibility of the dark shadow managing to become the light, albeit for a brief moment.

Sonata Mulattica is Dove's *meisterstück*, a masterpiece that rises to match the tenor of Beethoven and Bridgetower's compositions. It is also the Post-Black artist's moment of contention with history. The juxtaposition of black and white frames lights the image up just long enough to prove the irreducibility of historical frames to racially disjunct pieces. The bridge that the poet builds between the past and the present must necessarily light up uncomfortable areas, and at some point, lead to a definition of Blackness (buried as a gap in the historical archive) independent of the Other. In an interview with Rowell, Dove says:

> I wanted to convey the sensation of how history had buried him. The only way to do that was to not make the story simple and straightforward, but to show the many different factors that influenced his life, and how much of not only his life but of the lives which touched his we'll never know at all—And so it dawns on us that history itself is a fiction. We think of history as a narrative, but all we have are little flashes, like Morse code; we connect the dots into the narrative line we call History. So there I was, trying to keep this whole book up in the air as I wrote it. I found it counterproductive to even think about it in the kind of terms one would use to answer the question: "What's it about?" I could have said, "If I tell you his story, that's not what it's about at all." (696)

In this recounting of the narrative, Dove negotiates the delicate line separating nationalist, essentialist notions of Blackness from a cosmopolitan universalism, using the liminal space created in the first collection as she fills in the gaps, claiming poetic license to do so in the Preface. Historical facts and the literary imagination are interwoven in this tale to stress the racialized nature of historical memory. Stressing that race is an inescapable presence that need not restrict but need not be denied either, Dove's poems are a response to Morrison's concern that "in matters of race, silence and evasion have historically ruled literary discourse. Evasion has fostered another, substitute language in which the issues are encoded, foreclosing open debate" (*Playing* 9). Accepting the role of race in shaping identities frees up the category from the constrictive forces of both the white gaze and the black, achieving ontological expansiveness to allow an individual reformulation of definitions of Blackness. The revelation of history as a metanarrative also frees the black man from absolute definitions of truth, revealing perspectival constructs that operate as absolute entities rather than relational signifiers.

In both *American Smooth* and *Sonata Mulattica*, Dove aims to free Blackness from its pejorative associations with slavery, instead lighting up areas of real achievement, resilience, and artistic excellence. The poet is conscious of the interpretive force of language and images, and succeeds in forcing race into public memory without being termed ethnocentric only because she has carefully prepared a transcultural space in her first collection, which subsequently functions as heterotopic space for a reformulation of collective memory. Like Morrison, her project "is an effort to avert the critical gaze from the racial object to the racial subject; from the described and imagined to the describers and imaginers; from the serving to the served" (*Playing* 90). In a return to the Black Aesthetics Movement of the 1960s and 1970s, Dove reintroduces layers to black identity, while countering its dominance in all discourse related to black people. In making music the tenor to integrate the two halves of the miscegenated self, the poet not just points out the limitations of a racialized identity for the artist, but also liberates music from its role in preserving ethnocentric identities. Rejecting teleological progression by going back to where the poems began their journey, she traces a path towards a Post-Black acceptance of biological, cultural and historical miscegenation.

The Post-Black Aesthetic, thus, does not radically break off from its predecessors, instead including an acceptance of postethnic affiliations and a realization of the destructive nature of closed, exclusive spaces that are racially defined. There is also an attempt to decenter race through an opening up of space rather than a countering of the signifier. Dove, more than any other contemporary poet, has carefully charted the course toward the Post-Black through a conscious expansion of artistic space and an acceptance of postethnic fluidity. Vendler, while eschewing labels, identifies Dove as the proponent of the Post-Black Aesthetic when she says: "More than any other contemporary black poet, Dove has taken on the daunting aesthetic question of how to be faithful to, and yet unconstrained by, the presence—always already given in a black American—of blackness" (87). Looking neither to Africa nor Europe for roots, this form of writing proposes to bridge both in a transatlantic crossing that emphasizes the ever-dual nature of African American identity. Stressing that an acceptance of cultural and biological miscegenation is necessary for creativity and for the healthy functioning of the ego, Dove's poems present the black-white as the *only* way forward. For the purpose, she chooses music to circumvent linguistic structures in the memory, moving towards un-naming rather than countering existing labels. Music, as the two collections verify, initiates this Post-Black un-naming, in the process freeing itself as well.

Works Cited

Campbell, Mary Schmidt. "African American Art in a Post-Black Era." *Women & Performance: A Journal of Feminist Theory* 17.3 (2007): 317–30, doi: 10.1080/07407700701621541.

Crawford, Margo Natalie. *Black Post-Blackness*. U of Illinois P, 2017.

———. "What Was Is." *The Trouble with Post-Blackness*. Ed. Houston A. Baker and K. Merinda Simmons. Columbia UP, 2015. 21–43.

Dove, Rita. *American Smooth*. W. W. Norton, 2004.

———. "An Interview with Rita Dove." By Claire Schwartz. *VQR: A National Journal of Literature and Discussion* 94. 2 (Winter 2016), www.vqronline.org/interviews-articles/2016/01/interview-rita-dove. Accessed August 22, 2018.

———. *The Poet's World*. Library of Congress, 1995.

———. *Sonata Mulattica: A Life in Five Movements and a Short Play*. W. W. Norton, 2010.

Du Bois, W. E. B. "Strivings of the Negro People." *The Atlantic Monthly* 80.478 (1897): 194–98.

Dyer, Richard. *White*. Routledge, 1997.

Ellis, Trey. *Platitudes & The New Black Aesthetic*. 1988. Northeastern UP, 2003.

Georgoudaki, Ekaterini. "Rita Dove: Crossing Boundaries". *Callaloo* 14.2 (1991): 419–33.

Gilroy, Paul. *Against Race: Imagining Political Culture Beyond the Color Line*. The Belknap P of Harvard UP, 2000.

———. *The Black Atlantic: Modernity and Double Consciousness*. Harvard UP, 1993.

Golden, Thelma. Freestyle, exhibition catalogue, April 28–June 24, 2001, Studio Museum, Harlem, New York.

Hall, Joan Wylie, ed.. *Conversations with Audre Lorde*. UP of Mississippi, 2004.

Hanna, Sally Michael. "An Interview with Rita Dove." *Scientific Journal of October 6 University* 2.2 (2014): 255–64.

Hughes, Langston. "Harlem." *Poetry Foundation*, www.poetryfoundation.org/poems/46548/harlem. Accessed December 2, 2013.

Ingersoll, Earl G., ed. *Conversations with Rita Dove*. UP of Mississippi, 2003.

McDowell, Robert. *Poet at the Dance: Rita Dove in Conversation*. Personal interview, October 28, 2003, www.poets.org/poetsorg/text/poet-dance-rita-dove-conversation. Accessed August 13, 2016.

Morrison, Toni. *Playing in the Dark: Whiteness and the Literary Imagination*. Vintage, 1993.

———. *What Moves at the Margin*. UP of Mississippi, 2008.

Nanda, Aparajita. "Legacy/Trauma/Healing." *Ethnic Literatures and Transnationalism: Critical Imaginaries for a Global Age*. Routledge, 2015.

Pereira, Malin. *Rita Dove's Cosmopolitanism: POEMS*. U of Illinois P, 2003.

———. "When the Pear Blossoms/Cast their Pale Faces on/the Darker Face of the Earth: Miscegenation, the Primal Scene and the Incest Motif in Rita Dove's Work." *African American Review* 36.2 (Summer 2002): 195–211.

Rampersad, Arnold. "The Poems of Rita Dove." *Callaloo* 26 (Winter 1986): 52–60. JSTOR, www.jstor.org/stable/pdf/2931043.pdf?refreqid=excelsior%3A38bf085251e   1e539a 7f4f2327af36095.

Righelato, Pat. *Understanding Rita Dove*. U of South Carolina P, 2006.

Rowell, Charles Henry. "Interview with Rita Dove: Part 1." *Callaloo* 31.3 (2008): 695–706.

Roy and Ringo. "Interrogating Racialized Perceptions in Toni Morrison's *The Bluest Eye* and *God Help the Child*." *Dialog* 29 (Spring 2016): 65–78.

Said, Edward W. *Orientalism*. Penguin, 1995.

Shannon, Susan. *Revealing Whiteness: The Unconscious Habits of Racial Privilege*. Indiana UP, 2006.

"Sonata Mulattica." Review of *Sonata Mulattica*. *The New Yorker*, April 27, 2009. Newspaper Source, www.newyorker.com/magazine/2009/04/27/sonata-mulattica. Accessed June 16, 2018.

Spivak, Gayatri Chakravorty. "Subaltern Studies: Deconstructing Historiography." *In Other Worlds*, 1987. Routledge, 1988. 197–221.

Steffen, Therese. *Crossing Color: Transcultural Space and Place in Rita Dove's Poetry, Fiction, and Drama*. Oxford, 2001.

Vendler, Helen. *The Given and the Made: Strategies of Poetic Redefinition*. Harvard UP, 1995.

"World War I and Postwar Society." *The African American Odyssey: A Quest for Full Citizenship*, memory.loc.gov/ammem/aaohtml/exhibit/aopart7.html. Accessed February 8, 2018.

· 6 ·

JOUISSANCE: THE PHILOSOPHER'S *PLAYLIST FOR THE APOCALYPSE*

This chapter traces the journey of the free black man in Dove's latest collection of poems, *Playlist for the Apocalypse*. Having traversed a path towards self-realization in the previous collections, the ontological expansiveness that the black man has finally achieved frees him from the constraints of prescriptive Blackness. In this post-racial, post-historical world, the contemporary African American is free to visit history as a sightseer, freed of the constraints of his own static identity. With a wide array of allusions, this collection merges the persona of the artist with the subjects of her poems. Reverberating with Post-Black symbols, the poems affirm Steffen's assertion of Dove's celebration of Blackness as "black *jouissance* beyond sociocultural concepts, affirmative action, and the like," saying that "it simply and uniquely *is* a celebration of black nature in its beauty, humanity, and joy of life" (149).

The title of Dove's latest collection is a postmodern celebration of the fluidity of life and signifiers. In choosing to call her collection *Playlist for the Apocalypse*, Dove continues the stress on individual interpretation. The collection, divided into six sections, is a philosopher's musings on the nature of the free world. Assuming multiple personae and perspectives, the poet explores ontological questions, moving freely between spaces to bridge past-present, personal-political, man-nature. The images allow for individual associations as the reader accompanies the poet on her travels. The introductory "Prose in a Small Space" justifies straining against the confines of poetic form, stating that though prose accommodates a flood of words, it is in poetry's spaces, its allusions, and its ability to expand contours that imagination triumphs over verbosity.

The first section in the collection, titled "Time's Arrow," is a quest for identity as the free black man savors freedom from a bird's-eye view. The first poem in the section sees Henry Martin, a former slave at Monticello born on the same day that Thomas Jefferson died, talk of looking for belonging as a free man in a world where his mixed-race features arouse discomfort:

> I know my appearance
> frightens some of the boys—the high cheeks
>
> and freckles and not-quite-Negro eyes
> flaring gray as storm-washed skies
> back home; it shames them to be reminded. ("Bellringer")

Miscegenation places the individual in a trans-space where the quest for belonging is fraught with the notion of a complex group dynamics. Henry rather chooses to rise above the dynamics of group binaries, and finds his own place in the "stone rookery perched above/the citadels of knowledge." The irony of people mourning Jefferson's passing while silence surrounds his legacy, the mixed-race children of his estate, is made the opening poem, and the reader is left in no doubt that the playlist for the apocalypse intends to light up the shadows on its journey into what Blackness means for the free black man.

Miscegenation occupies central place in "Family Reunion," which is a personal observation on the impossibility of having one "Black" appearance, accent, experience, or even taste in food. Varied as the features that signify "the beautiful geometry of Mendel's peas/and their grim logic—," the African American experience is a joyous amalgamation of shades and inflections. This poem is a celebration of community, symbolized by shared food, a cultural mix that defies definitions or boundaries. As both onlooker and participant, Dove synthesizes intimate and exterior space. Bachelard, whose theory of lived space informs Dove's images, says: "The two kinds of space, intimate space and exterior space, keep encouraging each other, as it were, in their growth" (201). Standing on the threshold, the poet's tone is full of wonder, even as she introspects: "Who are all these children?/Who had them, and with whom?" It is an unabashed avowal of the heterogeneity that refuses definition: "The sheer plasticity of Blackness, the way it conforms to such a bewildering array of identities and struggles, and defeats the attempt to bind its meanings to any one camp or creature, makes a lot of Black folk nervous and defensive" (Touré xiv). The free Black man, Dove seems to say, no longer shies away from accepting the diversity that is the necessary legacy of miscegenation.

"Eurydice, Turning" is another personal poem that builds on memories of the poet's calling up home and her mother unable to recognize her through her mental fog. Comparing her reaction to her mother's voice to Orpheus's reaction to Eurydice's, Dove projects the idea of home as a person:

> No wonder Orpheus, when he heard
> the voice he'd played his lyre for
> in the only season of his life that mattered,
> could not believe she was anything
> but who she'd always been to him, for him....

Dove's synthesis of intimate and exterior space dares to expose the vulnerabilities of the black person in public space. In using the Greek myth of Orpheus and Eurydice to bring out the vulnerability of personal loss, Dove once again posits trauma as universal, bridging racial boundaries as in *Mother Love*. The symbolic recognition of the past is also a firm assertion of rootedness.

The stepping-out of the black woman into public space is manifest in the poem titled "Girls on the Town, 1946." This poem is unabashedly feminist, celebrating black womanhood as an equal counterpart to "Nigger Song: An Odyssey" in her first collection, *The Yellow House on the Corner*. The joyous celebration of life in the midst of poverty in the earlier poem has translated into a celebration of the strong black woman, whose red lips and minimal jewellery complement the power of the "patent-leather/Mary Janes" (15–16). With idols like Rosie, black woman power in the 1940s is shown to be a far cry from the portrayal in Lee's "Blackwoman":

> This is the only power you hold onto,
> ripped from the dreams none of you believe
> are worth the telling. Instead of mumbling,
> why not decorate?

This poem brings to mind Mari Evans's "I Am a Black Woman"; Dove's black woman has Evans's as an ancestor, and is ready to celebrate the freedom won through years of struggle and of being doubly marginalized. Race and gender have taken years to be decentered, and the free Post-Black woman carries within her generations of struggle. Images recur from Dove's earlier collections, only to stress the changed circumstances. Thomas's scarf, gifted to Beulah, travels generations to settle "across a bare neck" in a sensual appreciation of silk that only prosperity and the freedom to enjoy its fruits can heighten.

Another image that recurs from Dove's first collection is that of the woman on the threshold, herself in the shadows while she observes both the figure within and the one without, herself unseen ("Small Town"). However, the poem "From the Sidelines" is a more overt gaze turned on the man. Once again, the image is one of stepping out of the shadows. No longer using the shadows to shield her, she advocates movement: "Why fret? All/you're doing is walking." The image of the mirror brings out the fallacy of the black body as "harbor" and "avalanche," depending on perspective. The reference to Dove's earlier poem "Genetic Expedition" in *Grace Notes* is visible in the portrayal of the body on both sides of the mirror. However, while the earlier poem referenced the *dread* of becoming the black body, the later poem is an *exploration* of the blackness of the black body. By exploring both sides, the body as signifier is proven to be but just that—its surface. In both these poems, the image is both the signifier and the signified, freed of associations with historical trauma.

Continuing the celebration of Blackness in its varied forms, the next poem talks of all the forms of hair and its styles through the centuries. Hair as a symbol of race is a potent one, with the Black Arts Movement celebrating natural hair as beautiful. Dove's poem, "Found Sonnet: The Wig," shuns the binaries of good hair/bad hair, and accepts it all as natural:

> 100% human hair, natural; Yaki synthetic, Brazilian blend,
> Malaysian, Kanekalon, Peruvian Virgin, Pure Indian;
> iron-friendly, heat-resistant; bounce, volume, featherweight,
> Short 'n' Sassy, Swirls & Twirls, Smooth & Sleek and Sleek & Straight,
>
> Wet and Wavy, Futura fibre, weave-a-wig or Shake-n-Go;
> classic, trendy, micro-kink, frosted pixie, tight cornrow;
> full, three-quarter, half, stretch cap, drawstring, ear tabs, combs;
> chignon, headband, clip-n-bangs; easy extensions and ponytail
>   domes—

This freedom from prescriptive ideas of beauty frees the idea of beauty as well from the binaries of beautiful/ugly. A celebration of all looks is a definite movement from homogeneity to heterogeneity. Crawford says:

> To destroy the "good hair/bad hair" residue of the colonized mind that happened during slavery and was passed on throughout generations, the BAM mobilized the "natural" as a value system that made many young black women in the 1960s realize, for the first time, that they could *show* their unprocessed hair and defy the gaze that made their very bodies a source of shame. (204)

However, the celebration of natural hair also served to accentuate difference and reinforce binaries. In a study of images informing the constructed notion of beauty, Roy and Ringo observe:

> The white normative informs racial hierarchy and the social order, and identity is conditioned by racialized symbols in early childhood. The presence/absence of these coded norms is shown to mark the presence/absence of the "beautiful," an adjectival construct that entraps black identity in a vicious cycle of embodiment. (67)

This vicious cycle kept the black man trapped in his body, his identity defined by the gaze. The Post-Black celebration of *all* kinds of hair decenters race and dismantles binaries by removing the black body from the gaze. Hair becomes just hair, rather than a signifier of prescriptive Blackness. All forms are Black, and neither detract from a person's Blackness nor add value to it. The image of hair as a signifier dissociated from its historical associations in the memory also dissociates it from racial identification and makes it a matter of individual choice. This is a choice that only the free black person can exercise.

Freedom from embodiment not just frees the black man from the binaries of color, but also from prescriptive gender identities. The Black Arts Movement was seen by many as marginalizing gender-fluid voices, and being largely male-dominated, and images were presented mainly as seen through the male gaze. In the poem titled "Trans-," Dove presents the moon as gender-fluid, existing in a trans-space, referred to as both male and female: "He's belligerent. She's in a funk./When he fades, the world teeters./When she burgeons, crime blossoms." The comfort with fluidity is a hallmark of the post-modern and Post-Black experience:

> We might say that to be post-black is to experience the contingency and fluidity of black identity, to have to wrestle with the question of how to orient one's self to the various options for black self-consciousness, and to do all of this while relating one's self to the similarly fluid meanings and practices of the wider society. (Taylor, 627)

The acceptance of the fluidity of identity having been established, the poet turns the gaze on the art of creation in the next poem. Titled "Climacteric," the poem is replete with images of creativity. The act of writing is likened to cooking, the syllables stirred in the thickening gruel far from the madding crowd. Dove says:

>   …as long as the pages
> keep thickening I stir, lick a finger to test the edges
>
> (illicit snacking, calorie-free)—but I'll confess this
> once: If loving every minute spent jostling syllables
> while out in the world others slog through their messes
> implies such shuttered industry is selfish or irresponsible,
>
> then I'm the one who's fled.

As a form of interior monologue, the poem explores the poet's musings as she creates, stirring in syllables, thickening the mix, testing the edges, the images a woman's rendering of the act of creation. Creativity needs space, and the next poem, "Island," talks of "a room in one's head" needed for "thinking/outside of the box." The images are feminist, the image of the mind as lived space recurring. Woolf's need for a room of one's own has translated into the need for mental space free of all constrictions. The image is of the metaphorical lived space, free to inhabit and to move in.

Having established identity as fluid and freedom as given, the collection then revisits reality for the contemporary black man. In "Trayvon, Redux," Dove revisits the shooting of Trayvon Martin in his own neighborhood, in an incident that exposes the racism inherent in the present:

> *Move along, you don't belong here.*
> This is what you're thinking. Thinking
> drives you nuts these days, all that
> talk about rights and law abidance when
> you can't even walk your own neighbourhood
> in peace and quiet, *get your black ass gone.*

The thinking black man, Dove's intellectual, cannot help but think about the futility of activism when a person can still be shot for the color of his skin. This poem is a stark reminder that freedom is a process, and race an insidious element that continually changes form.

The thinking black man in this collection, having accepted his reality, *thinks* about racism. In "Philadelphia," he realizes, unflinching, that confrontation is not the solution, but decentering race is:

> They say we bring it on ourselves
> and trauma is what *they* feel
> when they rage up flashing
> in their spit-shined cars
> shouting *who do you think you are?*
> Until everybody's hoarse.

A confrontation of racist attitudes admits of the temptation to reinstate the binaries of us/them, victim/perpetrator, before reason steps in:

> Next time I promise I'll watch my step.
> I'll disappear before they can't
> unsee me: better gone
> than one more drop in a sea of red.

Thus, the black intellectual has moved on from a demand for freedom to an understanding of the responsibility to protect it. Ontological freedom has made him understand and accept diversity in Whiteness as in Blackness, and he realizes that he too has the power to break the cycle of violence. What sustains him "in the midst of horror," says Dove, was the "beauty" of "the house that music built" ("Transit").

Having thus celebrated the self in a Hegelian withdrawal in a racist world, the next section portrays Nature, in the form of the spring cricket, dwelling on philosophical questions. Stating that "this is Hell," the daily struggle is portrayed as an existential vacuum, where thoughts need to be suspended: "All wisdom/is afterthought, a sort of helpless relief" ("The Spring Cricket Repudiates His Parable of Negritude"). The cricket's observation of the state of the world, though, is a wise one. He knows that his existence matters to none more than to him: "You prefer me invisible, no more than/a crisp salute far away from/your silks and firewood and woolens," but then admits, too, that his existence is his own lifetime: "I've got ten weeks left to croon though./What you hear is a lifetime of song" ("Postlude"). Nature and the Self entwine as one in this Hegelian withdrawal, and the realization of mortality is the poet's own.

The next section, titled "A Standing Witness," is an expedition to witness history. History, as earlier stated in *Museum*, is "inside us, pacing/our lungs" ("The Hill has Something to Say"). The wheel, a powerful image in *Thomas and Beulah*, recurs, but this time with an acceptance of its powerlessness: "Who comforts you now that the wheel has broken?" Illusions shattered, dreams broken, reality is the only constant: "Now that the wheel has broken, // grief is the constant. Hope: the last word spoken" ("Your Tired, Your Poor…"). Freedom from embodiment does not translate into the right of the woman over her own body, and this is questioned in "Woman, Aflame," a debate on the right to abortion. The contemporary world, with its technological emptiness and the images of 9/11, dominates in this section as Obama's election revives the "magic" ("Send These to Me"). With Trump's election, the sun sets on a varied era, and the image of Lady Freedom ends the section with a call to again "listen": "I stand ready to tell you what I have seen. // Who among you is ready to listen?" ("The Sunset Gates"). This section is followed by the "Eight Angry Odes," a section where poetry is filled with nostalgia in a world where beauty no longer exists to give purpose to the odes. The form from a lost world must seek mundane subjects like the knee to express itself.

The transition to the personal happens suddenly as a fall. The next section, titled "Little Book of Woe," begins with "Soup," an extended treatise on the art of making soup that couches the desire to escape from the dreaded news of illness and mortality. Suddenly, the diagnosis of illness makes Time seem like a pearl, hidden and unnoticed as moments:

> We made these environments we cling to—
> unlike the lion who accepts the zebra as meat,
> or the zebra who understands he's meat
> just as much or as little as he understands
> the grasses he hides in or the sky's sickening lurch
> when death comes. Does he fear it? You betcha.
> Maybe he thinks about death all the time, too,
> but I doubt it. We're the species wired for that,
> and our only comfort's the world we've built
> to fuss over, the props and affections
> we mourn all the time we have them, practicing. ("Pearl on Wednesdays")

Reminiscent of the image of the "baseless fabric" in Shakespeare's *The Tempest*, from which Dove significantly quotes the epigraph to the previous section, the lines are a philosopher's musings on the "props and affections" that we worry about in a lifetime, a baseless vision, a temporary refuge that we forget to enjoy in a limited lifetime. Much as Prospero's, Dove's thoughts too muse the end of life. The philosopher-magician's greatest feat has been in demarcating the journey into a Post-Black world, and the poem "Last Words" follows Prospero's desire to finally give up his power:

> I don't want to die in a poem
> the words burning in eulogy
> ....
> let the end come
> as the best parts of living have come
> unsought & undeserved

Yet reflecting that the magic can never disappear, the poet returns in "This Is the Poem I Did Not Write" to lived space, "mounting the elliptical: stairs up, stairs down." Stressing yet again on walls and their function of making sure there was "no hillside," the poem "Rive d'Urale" warns against ignoring the gaps:

> ...do not believe
> what you see before you: The very eyeball can deceive.
> Somewhere in the picture
> there is a bird, but not where
> you'd have it.

The image of the bird just outside the window brings to mind the caged bird in an earlier poem, yet now the bird is outside the poet's window, free, outside the expanded space. Implying that the journey is not yet done, the poem ends with the injunction to movement forward: "each step/a bead."

Yet even as Post-Blackness must move forward, the poet's individual journey must end. Out in the open, Dove's prayer to Nature is Prospero's plea to the Heavens. The poem "Mercy" is a prayer to look up at the sky without magical powers, and see just its beauty:

> Such soft ululations,
> such a drumroll of feathers!
> Yet it was no other weather
> than Wind. I looked up; the sky
> lay blue as always, Biblical
> and terrifying, just where
> it was supposed to be.

The philosopher retires into the lap of Nature, ending the collection on a deeply personal note. The poem, "Wayfarer's Night Song," signals a waiting that is the culmination of an individual journey:

Among the treetops
you can feel
barely a breath—
birds in the forest, stripped of song.
Just wait: before long
you, too, shall rest.

Though the stillness is Goethe's, the birds are Prospero's, set free of their powers. All is quiet, and Nature waits, with the poet. In this oneness of man and Nature, this collection posits the final steps in the Post-Black movement's journey towards a Hegelian freedom: the blurring of the final binary between inside and outside, that of man and Nature, one in quietness, still in movement. The poet has reached the summit: "Above the mountaintops/all is still." This is the view from above, neither inside nor outside, and not in a trans-space either. The poet has finally achieved freedom, the moment of *jouissance*. Here, like Prospero, the philosopher ascends.

Works Cited

Bachelard, Gaston. *The Poetics of Space*. Translated by Maria Jolas, Beacon P, 1994.
Campbell, Mary Schmidt. "African American Art in a Post-Black Era." *Women & Performance: A Journal of Feminist Theory* 17.3 (2007): 317–30.
Crawford, Margo Natalie. *Black Post-Blackness*. U of Illinois P, 2017.
Dove, Rita. *Grace Notes*. W. W. Norton, 1989.
———. *Mother Love*. 1995. W. W. Norton, 1996.
———. *Museum*. Carnegie Mellon UP, 1983.
———. *Playlist for the Apocalypse: Poems*. W. W. Norton, 2021.
———. *Thomas and Beulah*. Carnegie Mellon UP, 1986.
———. *The Yellow House on the Corner*. Carnegie Mellon UP, 1980.
Evans, Mari. "I am a Black Woman." *The Black Arts Movement*, https://blackartsmovementumf.wordpress.com/mari-evans-i-am-a-black-woman. Accessed January 2, 2022.
Roy and Ringo. "Interrogating Racialized Perceptions in Toni Morrison's *The Bluest Eye* and *God Help the Child*." *Dialog* 29 (Spring 2016): 65–78.
Shakespeare, William. *The Tempest*. 1623. Harvard UP, 1958.
Steffen, Therese. *Crossing Color: Transcultural Space and Place in Rita Dove's Poetry, Fiction, and Drama*. Oxford UP, 2001.
Taylor, Paul C. "Post-Black, Old Black." *African American Review* 41.4 (Winter 2007): 625–40.
Touré. *Who's Afraid of Post-Blackness? What It Means to Be Black Now*. Free P, 2011.
Woolf, Virginia. *A Room of One's Own*. Penguin, 2004.

· 7 ·

CONCLUSION

Even as Post-Blackness moved from the world of art to become a general philosophy governing the politics surrounding identity construction and its representation in cultural productions for African Americans in the latter part of the twentieth century and the beginning of the twenty-first, it has faced challenges from critics who found the term too vague. Questions have also been raised about its relevance outside institutionalized art spheres. This book has attempted to answer these questions to some extent. Outlining the features of Post-Blackness as it moved from the sphere of the visual arts to become a literary and philosophical movement, it has delineated the journey towards Post-Blackness as evidenced in the poetry of Rita Dove, positing that each collection of her poems is a step forward in the reformulation of Black aesthetics. Stating that poetry was the most suitable form to carry the shift over from the world of art into the literary, it argues that poetry's ability to carry metaphor and imagery in itself made it a bridge for the movement to enter the literary world in a way that prose might not have facilitated. Further, Dove's poems not only define the features of the Post-Black, but actually clear the path—the symbolic cobwebs in the memory—to mark out every step of the journey towards freeing identity from being centered around race. Although much of the criticism surrounding the Post-Black appeared at the beginning of the present century, the term itself defined by Golden and Ligon in 2001, the study has argued that Dove's reformulation of Black aesthetics foreshadowed the definitions that followed most of her work. Even before Hollinger defined the need to transcend prescriptive ethno-racial boundaries as "postethnic" (7), and Golden and Ligon defined this resistance to prescriptive labels as "post-black," Dove's poems were talking about the fallacy of having separate historical and cultural frames of reference for both races.

The dissatisfaction with an ethnocentric, homogeneous racial identity can also be seen in the works of some earlier artists. The argument that the term "Post-Black" was a vague one that did not specify its exact features or the need for departure from the earlier aesthetics finds an answer in the works of artists like William T. Williams, Robert Colescott, and David Hammons, that experimented with divergent aspects of Blackness. Saunders, as early as in 1967, in a pamphlet titled *Black is a color*, stated:

> i am an artist; examples of my work can be seen in American museums; I have been the recipient of national awards; I have just enjoyed the 'priviledge' of my fourth one-man show at an uptown gallery (reviewed p. 60 of arts magazine, may, 1967); and i also happen to be black. i fail to see any profound significance in the mere conjunction of these circumstances. (pamphlet)

Saunders's distaste of labels is later echoed by Dove in her interview with Thomas in 1995, and reflects what Golden notes was the defining feature of Post-Black art, "characterized by artists who were adamant about not being labeled as 'black' artists, though their work was steeped, in fact, deeply interested, in redefining complex notions of blackness" (14). Campbell examines the reasons for this discomfort with labels, and concludes that:

> ...the rebelliousness of a phrase like 'post-black art', in part, is resistance to habits of mind that inhibit the ability of viewers to have an opportunity to see and experience the work of black artists unmediated by a predisposition of one kind or another. (321)

Post-Blackness, however, is much more than a simplistic rejection of labels or a new pluralism replacing collective identity. It is a philosophy of being, a process, a quest for self-knowledge, symbolized by what Campbell had termed "resistance to habits of mind" (321). Using the arguments of Arthur Danto, Taylor examines this quest that does not remain limited to the world of art but must necessarily progress beyond it. Art, according to Danto, had entered a "post-historical phase" (qtd. in Taylor 636) and no longer played a role in pushing history forward in the Hegelian sense. Thus, concludes Taylor, art is no longer under the compulsion to promote Black self-consciousness, and can finally be freed of the burden of carrying history forward. Taylor says:

> This innovation collapsed the distance between art and the philosophy of art, and turned the enterprise into a quest for self-knowledge. Art began to evolve by working out different ideas about what it was, and eventually found an answer that closed the cognitive-historical circle: just as world history is the history of Geist's journey to self-awareness, and of Geist positing increasingly adequate worldly embodiments along the way, art history is the history of art's continual reflection on its own nature—of artists producing objects that correspond to their various stages of progress toward true self-consciousness. And when artists figure this out, art history is really over. (637)

Post-Blackness, then, is more the journey of art than the artist. In this sense, the philosophy cannot be restricted just to the world of art but must apply to life in general. Further, it not just becomes a philosophy of life but guides the philosophy of race as well. Moving forward in quest of their identity in a postethnic world, African Americans must contend with the role of history in the process and their role in the process of history. As the black man moves towards an awareness of his journey towards self-knowledge, and transcends the color-line to form postethnic affiliations, the role of race enters a post-historical phase. Much like art, race, too, has been freed of the burden of carrying history forward, and must now reflect on itself and its own constitution. This results in a decentering of race in history, and is the realization of the Post-Black moment. "A practice ceases to be historically progressive when it no longer plays a role in moving history toward some goal that is external to the practice," says Taylor, or "when its participants come to see that the history of the practice is the product and embodiment of their own reflection on the practice" (638). In this Hegelian progression, Post-Blackness also signals the end of the history of race. This does not mean that race has come to an end. Rather, with the advent of the Post-Black, race has been decentered, a fact that is reflected in Post-Black art. Reflections on Blackness now do not need to carry forward the history of the black man. Post-Blackness can thus be seen through the Hegelian lens as a philosophy of race, and it is in this sense that Post-Blackness can be said to be post-racial.

A number of critics have questioned the possibility of Post-Blackness becoming a literary aesthetic. However, even though the Post-Black movement is still in its nascent stage in the literary sphere, Dove's poems show that much of Post-Black literature functions like the visual arts, through imagery. Post-Black literature exists at the intersection of art and language, encouraging the reader to *look*, instead of just read. Li contends that "black literature can never be post-black because the signifyin(g) language of black narrative affirms history," and "the tradition of African American literary expression refuses the unmooring of racial identity" (45). Dove's poems recognize precisely this problem and the need to first create a transcultural space where the dissociation of signifiers from their historical and cultural contexts can take place. As these signifiers are dissociated from their traditional contexts in the Saussurean chain, their path back to associated sites in the memory is also obliterated. Signifiers that traditionally emphasized Blackness can now be examined and reformulated, freed from historical associations in the memory. This is the reason Dove chose poetry as the form best suited to explore linguistic gaps that allowed metanarratives to be formulated. Using these gaps in much the same way that Post-Black art uses shadows and dark areas, Dove allows tangential referents to surface in the image, tracing its origin back to sites in the memory. Further, her concept of race as both language and lived space makes it possible for her to expand contours to "imagine the unimaginable" (Crawford 218), using metaphors and images to reconfigure signifiers in much the same way that art does. Beginning with the realization that much of the poetry and art of the earlier part of the twentieth century had adhered to aesthetic traditions that built on difference, the new aesthetic concludes that the Black Arts Movement, which was meant to celebrate Blackness as an aesthetically enriching sphere of artistic, musical and literary tradition, had actually reaffirmed binaries instead of repudiating them. This allowed Whiteness to posit Blackness as a different category, with all its attendant connotations of color, historical trauma, and the hierarchical descension that the Enlightenment thinkers had ascribed to the race. Unable to escape race or transcend it, African Americans soon found their identity circumscribed by the color of the skin as the sole identifier. The myth of Blackness was further perpetuated by cultural productions in the first half of the twentieth century.

The repudiation of race through a decentering of it took place in the visual arts towards the end of the twentieth century, when artists like Kara Walker deconstructed romantic descriptions of slave life in the novels of the nineteenth century. Using paper cut-outs, Walker reconstructed the scene in the novels, but this time with the gaps clearly visible against a stark background. The use of light and shadow, black and white by Post-Black artists was a way to repudiate color, a potent signifier of race, and in the process, decenter race itself as being part of the narrative used to perpetuate myths about black and white life. Intertextuality as a way of informing context was a technique used by Post-Black artists to deconstruct the narrative as suppressing gaps in adherence to literary traditions in place at the time, and Dove also used this technique in the poems in her collection, *Mother Love*, which were mostly written "in homage and as counterpoint to Rilke's *Sonnets to Orpheus*" (Righelato 1).

Dove began writing in the eighties, when Black Nationalist protocols were still firmly in place. However, this was also a time when a new generation of artists were beginning to find these protocols claustrophobic and artistically limiting. The politics of silence surrounding miscegenation and the existence of difference made ethnocentric definitions of identity unrealistic in the new era. Growing up in an integrated neighborhood, Dove was not exposed to objectification as a Black woman till she went to Germany on a Fulbright scholarship and found herself having become the representative of all the slaves who had suffered historical trauma. The reducing of identity to a mere label made her feel the walls closing in, something she described as "anathema to the artist" (Steffen 169). Realizing the need to expand contours rather than simply counter existing binaries, hers is a careful charting of the course that the Post-Black artist must take to be able to decenter race and repudiate the structure of modernist binaries that marginalized the black man and made it impossible to escape racially inflected language and imagery. Realizing that these were rooted in historical associations in the memory, Dove carefully isolates racially inflected signifiers, so that they no longer invoke Blackness as given. In expanding the metaphorical contours of lived space, Dove also admits of the gaps or dark areas in the memory which the imagination is free to fill. In an interview, she said, "That's the distinction I'm trying to make. …One appropriates certain gestures from the factual life to reinforce a larger sense of truth that is not, strictly speaking, reality" (Ingersoll 66).

Dove's concept of race as "occupied space" that functioned like language was built on Bachelard's theory of the affinity between language and space. Bachelard's comparison of the metaphorical flights that make for poetry to the garret of the house, and poetic contemplation to the cellars, gave Dove the idea of language as including suppressed areas that are buried and rarely visited, but which act as a storehouse of memories (*The Poet's World* 18). Stating that the official historical archive is a metanarrative made up of linguistic structures informed by the dominant language, Dove steps out of confined spaces into the open to deconstruct history through a communion with Nature that allows her to see the gaps or interstices suppressed in the metanarrative, and which were essential to understand the complete story. Her analysis of myths shows how myths are constructed, and how, functioning as signifiers, they form part of the structure through which culture gets its meaning. The racializing of signifiers, she infers, happens through association with an established cultural context. Once dissociated from this context, the signifier empties itself of historical associations, and it is in this state that new meanings and associations can be formulated. This was evidenced most explicitly in her deconstruction of music as a racialized category, where the traditional intertwining of the music with the persona of the musician often resulted in the music becoming a victim of racism. This is what happened to the Kreutzer sonata, which remained an inexplicable mystery once it was separated from its original dedicatee. Moreover, music reached the greatest heights in a mixed frame where both races functioned as the vehicle of its conjoined tenor.

Thus, in the Hegelian progression towards self-awareness in Dove's poems, it is not just the black man who is freed of racial identification and the burden of being a representative of the race. Music, art, and race are also freed of their role in history. As these, the greatest signifiers of Blackness, enter a post-historical phase, we can argue that the Post-Black artists can finally be free to reflect on themes that would not be construed as racially inflected. This would, of course, mean an individual journey towards self-knowledge, and an individual representation of such a journey. This is what Touré means when he says, "Who I am is indelibly shaped by Blackness, so I have to examine Blackness to know who I am. But I am much more than a repository for Blackness" (17). It is, thus, an examination of Blackness (a term that itself centers race, based on the color of the skin) and the journey of its unmooring from its roots in the memory. In its post-racial, or post-historical form, Post-Blackness, a term that indicates a moving on that is still a process, is a Hegelian progression towards self-knowledge. Touré reiterates this when he says:

> ...we are in a post-Black era, which means simply that the definitions and boundaries of Blackness are expanding in forty million directions—or really, into infinity. It does not mean we are leaving Blackness behind, it means we're leaving behind the vision of Blackness as something narrowly definable and we're embracing every conception of Blackness as legitimate. (12)

This journey of exploring what Blackness means is a metaphysical one, an individual journey towards self-awareness. In this Hegelian journey towards self-knowledge, the possibilities are not restricted by the contours of space, language, or memory.

CONCLUSION

Dove's journey, or rather, the journey of race towards complete freedom, characterized by ontological expansiveness, is brought out through nine collections of poems, each a step forward on the path towards self-knowledge. However, like the theory, the collections too eschew fixed boundaries. Thus, though each collection focuses on the path towards the decentering of race through the reformulation of specific signifiers that make up historical memory, they also make use of learned knowledge till they finally face up to the destruction that a negation of Derridean (im)purity would result in, thus freeing race, and in the process, their own identity.

Thus, the study traces how Dove charts a path towards a Post-Black reconfiguration of Black aesthetics in her poems, decentering race and revealing the nature of the earlier racialized world, where the fissures in the metanarrative of history suppressed individual lives as gaps, so that a tale was woven with race as the center, further hegemonizing the margins in its representations. Dove's method of reconstructing the past is shown to be the ancient African method of weaving. In reformulating the past, she is shown to foreshadow the Post-Black aesthetic. Even though her earlier poems show traces of the New Black Aesthetic through use of satire, it is satire with a purpose, a thread towards the final fabric. This justifies the use of "post"—the Post-Black symbolizes a continuity of the Black Aesthetic, but without the center/margin dichotomy.

Admitting that although Post-Blackness is a philosophical movement that finds expression in visual and literary representations, Dove posits it as an individual journey in the spirit of Hegel. Prose writers like Morrison and theorists like Hollinger, Dyer, and Hall have stressed the need to decenter race in cultural representations and everyday discourse, and Dove's poems painstakingly delineate the path for this journey. This places her squarely in the tradition of African American poets and makes her the harbinger of a new Post-Black Aesthetic in African American literature. Responding to the realities of a postethnic world, her works provide the method to Morrison's precepts. If Morrison identified the problem, Dove provided the solution. In placing her squarely against the Black Arts Movement and stating that "her poems are exactly the opposite of those that have come to be considered quintessentially black verse in recent years" (53), Rampersad recognizes Dove's reformulation of the Black aesthetic tradition. Steffen too studies "her aesthetic and thematic departure" from the Black Arts Movement (7), and identifies her celebration of Blackness as "black *jouissance* beyond sociocultural concepts, affirmative action, and the like," saying that "it simply and uniquely *is* a celebration of black nature in its beauty, humanity, and joy of life"

(149). Dove's bridging of form and content, personal and political, European and African American, is part of her larger strategy of blurring binaries and admitting the Other in the reformulated, expansive space of the newly formulated Post-Black.

However, the study agrees with Vendler that repudiating race could not have been easy, especially for a black poet. Vendler says: "Any black writer in America must confront, as an adult, the enraging truth that the inescapable social accusation of blackness becomes, too early for the child to resist it, a strong element of inner self-definition" (61). Dove's poems are proven to be as much an attempt to understand her own identity as a Black woman in America as it is to incorporate the realities of postethnicity and cultural miscegenation in her works.

In conclusion, there must be no doubt that Dove's positing of the Post-Black as post-racial should not be confused with color blindness. Admitting that the need to decenter race in cultural discourse would need an understanding of the way Whiteness hegemonized identities, she delineates the process through which a reformulation of spatial contours and linguistic associations was necessary to admit of new meanings in a Hegelian journey that is individual. Although the study limits itself to Dove's poetry, it does so on the premise that the language of prose would admit of a different strategy for the reformulation of identity markers. It also posits that the hyphenated domain of the Post-Black has not broken off completely from the Black Aesthetic Movement, but proposes to fill in the gaps left by the Movement. The study ends on a note of hope for race relations and trauma resolution, but does not propose that the present movement suggests a utopian solution to issues concerning race in the United States. Rather, in positing the journey as an individual one, it makes the quest the destination.

Works Cited

Bachelard, Gaston. *The Poetics of Space*. Translated by Maria Jolas. Beacon P, 1994.
Campbell, Mary Schmidt. "African American Art in a Post-Black Era." *Women & Performance: A Journal of Feminist Theory* 17.3 (2007): 317–30.
Crawford, Margo Natalie. *Black Post-Blackness*. U of Illinois P, 2017.
Dove, Rita. *Mother Love*. 1995. W. W. Norton, 1996.
———. *The Poet's World*. Library of Congress, 1995.
Dyer, Richard. *White: Essays on Race and Culture*. Routledge, 1997.

Golden, Thelma. *Freestyle*, exhibition catalogue, April 28–June 24, 2001, Studio Museum, Harlem, New York.

Hall, Stuart. "Race, the Floating Signifier: Featuring Stuart Hall." *Media Education Foundation*, 1996, www.mediaed.org/transcripts/Stuart-Hall-Race-the-Floating-Signifier-Transcript.pdf. Accessed August 18, 2016.

Hollinger, David A. *Postethnic America: Beyond Multiculturalism*. Basic, 1995.

Ingersoll, Earl G., ed. *Conversations with Rita Dove*. UP of Mississippi, 2003.

Li, Stephanie. "Black Literary Writers and Post-Blackness." *The Trouble with Post-Blackness*. Ed. Houston A. Baker Jr. and K. Merinda Simmons. Columbia UP, 2015. 44–59.

Morrison, Toni. *Playing in the Dark: Whiteness and the Literary Imagination*. Vintage, 1993.

Rampersad, Arnold. "The Poems of Rita Dove." *Callaloo* 26 (Winter 1986): 52–60. doi: 10.2307/2931043.

Righelato, Pat. *Understanding Rita Dove*. U of South Carolina P, 2006.

Saunders, Raymond. *Black Is a Color*. 1967.

Steffen, Therese. *Crossing Color: Transcultural Space and Place in Rita Dove's Poetry, Fiction, and Drama*. Oxford UP, 2001.

Taylor, Paul C. "Post-Black, Old Black." *African American Review* 41.4 (Winter 2007): 625–40.

Thomas, M. Wynn. An Interview with Rita Dove. *The Swansea Review*, 1995, www.english.illinois.edu/maps/poets/a_f/dove/mwthomas.htm. Accessed January 1, 2016.

Touré. *Who's Afraid of Post-Blackness? What It Means to Be Black Now*. Free P, 2011.

Vendler, Helen. *The Given and the Made: Strategies of Poetic Redefinition*. Harvard UP, 1995.

INDEX

A

acculturation 116, 117
aesthetic contours 146
aesthetics
 Black 2, 3, 4, 10, 21, 98, 145, 151, 165, 181, 195, 196, 201
 literary 1, 21, 97
 music, of 17
affective 11, 35, 97, 107, 109, 110, 146, 152
affiliations
 cross-cultural 7
 postethnic 17, 32, 181, 197
anti-aesthetics 1
apotropaic 103
artifacts 17, 18, 29, 49, 51, 55, 61

B

Biblical
 genesis 20, 112
 imagery 20, 112
Black Arts Movement 13, 14, 16, 28, 38, 57, 64, 74, 141, 146, 148, 149, 150, 151, 188, 189, 198, 201
Black Nationalist protocols 4, 105, 150, 199

C

cadence 11, 21, 77, 79, 152
chronotope 169
Civil Rights 1, 2, 4, 13, 15, 18, 19, 73, 75, 84, 96, 146
code
 linguistic 5, 6, 27, 34, 177
 visual 5
color blindness 23, 154, 202
color-line 4, 8, 10, 11, 12, 21, 30, 31, 41, 49, 68, 72, 73, 74, 92, 98, 107, 146, 150, 151, 178, 197
connotations 3, 23, 30, 31, 32, 106, 107, 117, 125, 198
cosmopolitanism 4, 105

INDEX

crossroads 17, 33, 84, 87, 126, 160
cultural
   assimilation 130
   continuum 20
   markers 28
   symbols 34

D

demographic 18, 75
dialectics 15, 18, 29, 92, 93, 96, 98, 160
différance 160
discourse
   cultural 6, 19, 23, 35, 101, 202
   historical 103
   ontological 105
   social 103
distancing
   emotional 35, 36, 37, 41, 64, 74, 79, 88, 89, 141, 159
   temporal 37
double consciousness 8, 10, 73, 92, 146, 151
dystopian 112, 113

E

Edenic 20, 107, 111, 114, 115, 121
Emancipation 30, 42, 75, 83, 84, 147
embodiment 5, 117, 171, 173, 178, 189, 192, 197
enjambment 11, 16, 54, 95
Enlightenment 45, 63, 173, 176, 198
essentialism 3, 30, 31, 64, 86, 105, 147, 165
ethnocentrism 1, 27, 28, 29, 33, 92, 151
existential dilemma 56, 114
exoticism 23, 48, 109, 117, 118, 169, 171, 176

G

Great Migration, the 3, 18, 75, 77

H

Harlem Renaissance 73, 147, 148, 149
Hegelian 8, 12, 18, 22, 23, 59, 60, 61, 68, 70, 92, 93, 96, 98, 113, 153, 155, 191, 194, 196, 197, 200, 202
hegemonic 6, 9, 27, 29, 31, 45, 68, 69, 70, 71, 105, 148, 151, 173
heterotopia 17
historical progression 12, 18, 59, 89, 108
historicity 29, 32, 41, 73, 74
hybridity 32, 166

I

identities
   prescriptive 4, 59
   racial 93, 141
identity marker 3, 4, 5, 27, 28, 38, 68, 154, 165, 172, 179, 202
idyll 36, 127
idyllic 14, 110, 127, 141
imagery
   racialized 17, 75, 101
   signifying 7
   visual 2, 3
Imaginary 115, 116
incest 14

J

jouissance 12, 15, 23, 185, 194, 201

K

Kreutzer 22, 164, 165, 176, 200

L

labels 1, 2, 14, 15, 16, 27, 28, 181, 192, 196

Lady Freedom 19, 95, 192
liminal 8, 10, 17, 27, 29, 30, 32, 35, 36, 59, 64, 69, 73, 88, 138, 142, 151, 167, 180

M

margins 6, 8, 28, 72
metanarrative 3, 13, 16, 18, 29, 37, 44, 49, 51, 67, 69, 71, 74, 91, 102, 129, 137, 146, 160, 181, 198, 199, 201
miscegenation 14, 21, 29, 32, 33, 34, 40, 54, 61, 64, 71, 145, 146, 152, 153, 164, 181, 182, 186, 187, 199, 202
modernist binaries 3, 4, 7, 8, 13, 21, 27, 30, 32, 33, 68, 101, 106, 199
modernity 12, 32, 152
Montgomery Bus Boycott 19, 84
Monticello 186
mulatto 14, 22, 96, 105, 148, 150, 164, 169, 175, 179
myths
    biracial 105
    Greek 103, 104, 105, 106

N

narrative probability 11, 74, 156, 167
natal isolation 20, 44, 79, 86, 123
New Black Aesthetic 4, 6, 14, 21, 45, 49, 84, 148, 149, 201

O

ontological expansiveness 3, 12, 18, 21, 23, 89, 92, 93, 95, 96, 105, 153, 181, 187, 201
Orphic 93, 124
Otherness 28, 61, 89, 117, 151

P

panopticon 178
Paradise 22, 57, 125, 126, 153
poetic sublimity 155
postethnic 2, 3, 17, 21, 22, 27, 32, 48, 51, 62, 64, 69, 82, 84, 92, 98, 105, 139, 150, 15, 152, 164, 181, 196, 197, 201
post-historical 97, 142, 185, 196, 200
post-mythical 142
post-racial 3, 8, 23, 185, 197, 200, 202
power paradigms 30

R

racial identifier 82, 103, 119, 169
relational system 5, 6, 7, 102, 142
Rilkean sublime 112

S

segregation 19, 72, 84, 108, 109, 156, 159, 161
self-abjection 92, 117, 171, 172, 173, 178
self-actualization 164
self-realization 21, 152, 164
sightseer 185
signification 35, 51, 73, 102
signifiers
    racialization of 8
    racialized 19
    relational system of 5, 102, 142
    Saussurean 5
social learning 5, 34, 117
space
    created 8, 17
    cultural 15, 101
    dialectics of 29
    habitable 33
    liminal 17, 29, 30, 32, 69, 138, 167, 180

lived 5, 6, 8, 10, 12, 19, 29, 40, 41, 52, 67, 69, 76, 81, 83, 85, 88, 89, 90, 91, 152, 169, 178, 186, 190, 193, 198, 199
occupied 17, 29, 32, 33, 40, 53, 69, 75, 199
poetics of 14
racial 11, 32
trans- 9, 45, 46, 47, 186, 189, 194
transcultural 3, 9, 17, 27, 28, 29, 30, 34, 36, 40, 49, 50, 51, 59, 61, 69, 74, 101, 106, 181, 198
spatial revisioning 13
spatial specificity 40
Symbolic 20, 111, 115, 116, 124
synchronic immobility 101

T

teleology 19, 76, 160
tenor 21, 152, 164, 179, 180, 181, 200
tenor viol 179
threshold 7, 8, 17, 21, 29, 30, 33, 36, 64, 67, 69, 89, 141, 186, 188
trace 18, 160

transatlantic
    crossing 9, 14, 30, 33, 35, 38, 105, 151, 157, 158, 182
travels 30

U

un-naming 32, 166, 182
utopia 20, 23

V

visual arts 3, 6, 8, 12, 15, 17, 23, 146, 195, 197, 198

W

waste land 112, 113, 114, 131
Whiteness 2, 4, 6, 23, 28, 36, 37, 45, 72, 141, 142, 149, 178, 191, 198, 202
Womanist 150

Studies in Criticality

General Editor
Shirley R. Steinberg

Counterpoints publishes the most compelling and imaginative books being written in education today. Grounded on the theoretical advances in criticalism, feminism, and postmodernism in the last two decades of the twentieth century, Counterpoints engages the meaning of these innovations in various forms of educational expression. Committed to the proposition that theoretical literature should be accessible to a variety of audiences, the series insists that its authors avoid esoteric and jargonistic languages that transform educational scholarship into an elite discourse for the initiated. Scholarly work matters only to the degree it affects consciousness and practice at multiple sites. Counterpoints' editorial policy is based on these principles and the ability of scholars to break new ground, to open new conversations, to go where educators have never gone before.

For additional information about this series or for the submission of manuscripts, please contact:

> Shirley R. Steinberg, General Editor
> msgramsci@gmail.com

To order other books in this series, please contact our Customer Service Department:

> peterlang@presswarehouse.com (within the U.S.)
> orders@peterlang.com (outside the U.S.)

Or browse online by series:

> www.peterlang.com

www.ingramcontent.com/pod-product-compliance
Lightning Source LLC
Chambersburg PA
CBHW061713300426
44115CB00014B/2667